HOT
Springs
AND
HOT
Pools OF THE
SOUTHWEST

HOT Springs AND HOT Pools OF THE SOUTHWEST

Jayson Loam's Original Guide

Marjorie Gersh-Young

AQUA THERMAL ACCESS

Hot Springs and Hot Pools of the Southwest: Jayson Loam's Original Guide

Copyright 2007 by Marjorie Gersh-Young

Design, layout, and production
by Marjorie Gersh-Young

Front Cover - Tecopa Mud Baths, Southern California
        Photo by Debbie Johnson
Back Cover - Fifth Water, Utah
        Photo by Camilla Van Sickle and Bill Pennington

ISBN 10: 1-890880-07-8
ISBN 13: 978-1-890880-07-1

Manufactured in the United States

Published by: **Aqua Thermal Access**
        55 Azalea Lane
        Santa Cruz, CA 95060
        831 426-2956
        email:hotsprings@sbcglobal.net
        web page: www.hotpools.com

Please Note: It is not possible to include all of the dangers encountered in getting to and making use of the hot springs described in this book. It is up to you, the reader, to use common sense and learn as much as you can about the risks involved and the safety measures needed.

Grateful acknowledgements

All of the regional contributors who always went above and beyond their assignment to make this book interesting and accurate. All of you who have written in with updates and information. Staff members at state parks, national forests, national parks, and hot springs resorts for their cooperation and encouragement. Henry Young for his "eagle eye" and computer help. All of the wonderful people up at CDS who were so helpful and are always great to work with. A special thanks to Jane Leche, Public Affairs Specialist for the US Forest Service for her help with the Caring For the Outdoors section.

TABLE OF CONTENTS

Hunting for Hot Water / 7

Hot Springs Etiquette / 9

Using This Guide / 9
A Quick GPS Lesson / 10

Common Sense and Safety Tips / 11

Caring for the Outdoors / 12

Directory Section: Nevada / 14

Utah / 40

Colorado / 50

Texas / 78

New Mexico / 82

Arizona / 108

Northern California / 122

Central California / 144

Southern California / 190

Baja (Mexico) / 210

Hawaii / 227

For the Naturist
Palm Springs / 232
Club Directory / 234

Alphabetical Master Index / 235

We remember
Elon Yurwit
1949-2006
who
"positively changed the course of hot spring history"
(Camilla Van Sickle and Bill Pennington)

When I despair, I remember that all through history the ways of truth and love have always won. There have been tyrants, and murderers, and for a time the can seem invincible, but in the end they always fall. Think of it – always.

Elon's favorite quote by MAHATMA GHANDI

Elon and his wife, Wanda Fusilier, purchased Faywood Hot Springs when it was nothing but one pool on dry desolate land. Elon had a vision for this place. I first met him when he called Jayson Loam and asked to meet with him to explore with Jayson his ideas, the reasons he wanted to build a hot spring, and how to go about it. I was impressed with the blend of both his spiritual and his practical common sense. It seems he had explored in detail all the aspects he could think of. I remain in awe of the steady diligence with which he planned and worked on his vision, bringing it to fruition, adding and amending as the spirit moved him. In addition, he offered his knowledge to all who asked. His was a generosity of spirit as he shared what he had learned about the practical aspects of building and running a hot spring, dealing with the multiple city and state codes, what devoted hot springs soakers wanted to find when they got to a spring, and always honoring the multiplicity of differing needs. I will miss knowing he was there as a support as we all continue to do what we love, honoring the hot water of Mother Earth. (Marjorie Young)

Tributes to Elon by his many friends:

I have such good memories of all the help he was to me and to everyone in the hot springs community.

I found Elon to be an inspiring human being, a true one-of-a-kind man. I will never forget him and therefore he'll never leave me.

This sudden loss of Elon seems so strange since his presence has always been so dynamic. Elon had so many dreams for the hot springs and he went a long way toward fulfilling those dreams. The vision and energy he dedicated will remain a legacy to the community and hot spring lovers. We were constantly amazed by the breadth of his imagination, his many skills and his competence in achieving the vision you have both created. He was a lover of life, physical pleasures, hard work, a dedicated father and husband. Elon was a generous, kind and fun-loving person who will be missed greatly and remembered with fondness.

I remember Elon welcoming us here with open arms when we came to visit. I feel Elon in the silence and the stillness behind the trees and I know that love never dies. We will remember Elon fondly, and sitting in the springs, will always be expecting him to come through the gate with a friendly greeting. For those of us who have been coming to Faywood for so many years, Elon's presence will always be there.

Jayson Loam
1918-1994

I can never write a new edition of a hot springs book without dedicating it to Jayson. All of us who love hot springs have been influenced by his work. I believe that he would be proud of the fact that his books are still popular and the information he gathered has expanded onto multiple web sites. Without his initial research many of us would never have been introduced to the pleasure of hot water. He was truly "King of the Hot Springs."

It's hard for me to believe that I have been working on these hot springs books for over twenty-five years. I don't know if I am more surprised by the changes that have taken place (springs closing down, reopening, disappearing and reappearing in natural settings, etc.), or by the fact that many of my favorite places are still the same as they were when I first visited them. I still get excited when someone calls and describes a new spring that I can put in the book, and, hopefully, visit one day. Many of the Regional Contributors have been "hot springers" longer than I have and have been most generous in sharing their knowledge and the lore (and lure) of hot water. **MARJORIE YOUNG**

REGIONAL CONTRIBUTORS

PHIL WILCOX, also known as "The Solar Man", is mostly retired and lives comfortably in his solar home in Northern California. He loves to travel, usually in his solar equipped, 4x4, camper van, exploring his favorite hot springs and always looking for new ones. He may be spotted almost anywhere in the US but particularly loves the Northwest. He may be contacted at P.O. Box 1460, Lower Lake, California 95457.

CHRIS ANDREWS, who likes nothing better than to travel to new hot springs where he gathers accurate information and takes great photographs. He doesn't mind how far he has to hike to find a spring he hasn't visited.

SKIP HILL, former editor of the *Hot Springs Gazette* and still a giant part of the springster world. Known to many as the hot spring guru. Once famous and then renowned, but now just a legend. He has been more than kind in offering advice, directions, photos, and bits of information to make the entries in this book more accurate and allowing me to add some of his "finds."

CAMILLA VAN SICKLE AND BILL PENNINGTON, are inquisitive and tireless explorers who contribute greatly to both hot springs books, having traveled from Florida to Mexico, from Arizona to the Arctic Circle in Alaska and back to report on hot springs for your soaking pleasure. Presently they are developing Casa Blanca Hot Spring in Arizona for winter soaking and Wind Horse Mineral Spring at 7,600 feet in New Mexico for summer soaking. For information contact: CasaBlancaHotSpring@mindspring.com, or POB 10, Tonopah, Arizona, 85354.

SALLY JACKSON writes the definitive book on hot springs in New Zealand, her native country. She spends New Zealand winters here in the United States keeping warm by visiting as many hot springs as she can.

KARIN BURROUGHS AND BRIAN THOROMAN reside in Southern Oregon, and have been avid hot springs enthusiasts for over a decade. They love getting into the backcountry, so hot springs were a perfect fit. They put together www.soakersbible.com after years of traveling, as well as continual trips to all the nooks and crannies throughout the west.

A very special thanks to both of them for generously sharing their information and photos. (See p.239 for ad.)

DEBBIE JOHNSON always deserves special thanks not only for her hot springs contributions but for her editorial acumen and good general common-sense advise.

Many Thanks Also To:

Rob Williams—who lives and works at a Baja hot springs and took time to hit several state-side hot spots.

Wayne Estes, Steve Ehret who helped with new maps and directions in Baja.

And, to all the other "hot springers" who phoned, wrote, and emailed information and their experiences at many of the hot springs in the book.

My husband, **Henry,** who deals patiently with my computer glitches, and who is also a fine editor.

HUNTING FOR HOT WATER:
Where it Comes From

The cataclysmic folding and faulting of the earth's crust over millions of years, combined with just the right amount of underground water and earth core magma, has produced a hot surface geothermal flow that often goes on for centuries.

As volcanic activity dies down, igneous rocks which have solidified from hot liquids such as magma are formed in pockets deep in the earth below the remains of the volcano. The magma produces heat which is conducted through a layer of solid rock into the porous level where new water, or water which has never before been on the surface, is believed to be formed from available molecules. Fissures are formed in the solid rock layer above the porous layer and steam and hot water escape producing hot springs, geysers, and fumaroles. A hot spring is considered to be a natural flow of water from the ground at a single point. It is called a seep if it does not have enough flow to create a current. Springs may come up on dry land or in the beds of streams, ponds, and lakes.

Natural geothermal areas lie in the earthquake and volcano belts along the earth's crustal plates. In many areas, due to the earth shifting and moving, the hot magma has worked its way closer to the earth's surface. Surface water (water from rain, for instance) soaks into the earth through cracks and crevices down to the area where the hot magma again provides the heat source for the water. If there are no fissures or cracks for the water to use to come to the surface, wells can be drilled, for example. Each of the resorts in Desert Hot Springs, California has its own well.

Water temperatures vary greatly. When the water is at least fourteen degrees hotter than the average temperature of the air it is considered to be thermal water (or a hot springs). This definition means that there is a very wide range of what is considered thermal water as the air temperature in Iceland is certainly different from that of a California desert. The overall temperature of the water can range up to the boiling point. Geothermal resources in Italy, New Zealand, California, and Iceland have been used for a number of years to heat municipal and private buildings, and even whole towns. In Iceland, the early Norse carried hot water to their homes through wooden pipes.

As the water travels up through varying layers of the earth, it accumulates different properties. These are classified as alkaline, saline, chalybeate or iron, sulfurous, acidulous, and arsenical. At least as far back as the time of the Greeks and the Romans, medicinal cures were attributed to the different chemicals and certain springs were alleged to cure certain ailments from venereal diseases to stomach and urinary tract weaknesses. The waters were administered in a combination of drinking and soaking.

Of the thousands of hot springs found in the United States, most are found in the Western mountains.

A Bit of History

Long before the "white man" arrived to "discover" hot springs, the Native Americans believed that the Great Spirit resided in the center of the earth and that "Big Medicine" fountains were a special gift from The Creator. Later on during tribal battles over territory or stolen horses, it was customary for the sacred "smoking waters" to be a neutral zone where all could freely be healed. Back then, hot springs belonged to everyone, and understandably, we would like to believe that nothing has changed.

The Native American tradition of free access to hot springs was initially imitated by the pioneers. However, as soon as mineral water was perceived to have some commercial value, the new settlers' private property laws were invoked at most of the hot spring locations. Histories often include bloody battles with "white men" over hot spring ownership, and there are colorful legends about Indian curses that had dire effects for decades on a whole series of ill-fated owners. After many fierce legal battles, and a few gun battles, some ambitious settlers

The first bathhouse in Truth or Consequences, New Mexico, was built by the cowboys of the John Cross Cattle Company in the late 1880s. The Tumble Inn, an early tent lodging facility also had a bathhouse.

were able to establish clear legal titles to the properties. Then it was up to the new owners to figure out how to turn their geothermal flow into cash flow.

Pioneering settlers dismissed as superstition the Native Americans' spiritual explanation of the healing power of a hot spring. However, those settlers did know from experience that it was beneficial to soak their bodies in mineral water, even if they didn't know why or how it worked. Commercial exploitation began when the owner of a private hot spring started charging admission, ending centuries of free access.

The shift from outdoor soaks to indoor soaks began when proper Victorian customers demanded privacy. Then, affluent city dwellers, as they became accustomed to indoor plumbing and modern sanitation, were no longer willing to risk immersion in a muddy-edged, squishy-bottomed mineral spring, even if they believed that such bathing would be good for their health. Furthermore, they learned to like their urban comforts too much to trek to an outdoor spring in all kinds of weather. Instead, they wanted a civilized method of "taking the waters," and the great spas of Europe provided just the right model for American railroad tycoons and land barons to follow and to surpass.

Around the turn of the century, American hot spring resorts fully satisfied the combined demands of Victorian prudery, modern sanitation, and indoor comfort by offering separate men's and women's bathhouses with private individual porcelain tubs, marble shower rooms, and central heating. Scientific mineral analysis of the geothermal water was part of every resort's merchandising program, which included flamboyant claims of miraculous cures and glowing testimonials from medical doctors. Their promotional material also featured social amenities, such as luxurious suites, sumptuous restaurants, and grand ballrooms.

In previous decades, patronage of these resorts had declined, and many have closed down because the traditional medical claims were outlawed and modern medical plans refuse to reimburse anyone for a mineral water "treatment." There seems to be an upsurge as many resorts have added new facilities, particularly gorgeous, full-service spas, and other amenities such as golf courses, conference and exhibition spaces, and fitness

Two old bath houses, circa 1911 and 1915 were built near Geronimo Springs in what was then Hot Springs, New Mexico, and is now Truth or Consequences—The story goes that they were offered a sum of money by the quiz show to change their name. A fun area to visit and enjoy the waters.

centers. Even many of the smaller establishments offer some spa treatments and family-size soaking pools in private spaces for rent by the hour in response to customer demand. Some locations continue to offer separate men's and women's bathhouse facilities in addition to the new communal pools.

In addition to the privately owned hot spring facilities, there are many locations that are owned and operated by federal, state, county, or city agencies. States, counties, and cities usually staff and operate their own geothermal installations. Locations in US National Forests and National Parks are usually operated under contract by privately owned companies. The nature and quality of the facilities offered at these locations varies widely.

Although natural mineral water (from a spring or well) is required for a truly authentic traditional "therapeutic soak," there is a new generation of dedicated soakers who will not patronize a motel unless it has a hot pool. They know full well that the pool is filled with gas-heated tap water and treated with chlorine, but it is almost as good as the real thing and a lot more convenient. We chose also to include those locations that offer private-space hot tubs for rent by the hour.

According to California legend, the historic redwood tub was invented by a Santa Barbara group who often visited Big Caliente Hot Springs. One evening, a member of the group wished out loud that they could have their delicious outdoor communal soaks without having to endure the long dusty trips to and from the springs. Another member of the group suggested that a large redwood wine cask might be used as an alternate soaking pool in the city. It was worth a try, and it was a success. Over time, other refugees from the long Big Caliente drive began to build their own group soaking pools from wine casks, and the communal hot tub era was born.

HOT SPRINGS ETIQUETTE

A Word about Nudity

You had best start with the hard fact that any private property owner, county administration, park superintendent, or forest supervisor has the authority to prohibit "public nudity" in a specific area or in a whole park or forest. Whenever the authorities have to deal with repeated complaints about nude bathers at a specific hot spring, it is likely that the area will be posted with NO NUDITY ALLOWED signs, and you could get a citation without further warning.

The vast majority of natural hot springs on public property are not individually posted, but most jurisdictions have some form of general regulation prohibiting public nudity. However, there have been some recent court cases establishing that a person could not be found guilty of indecent exposure if he removed his clothes only after traveling to a remote area where there was no one to be offended.

In light of these court cases, one of the largest national forests has retained its general "nude bathing prohibited" regulation but modified its enforcement procedure to give a nude person an opportunity to put on a bathing suit before a complaint can be filed or a violation notice issued.

In practical terms, this means that a group at an unposted hot spring can mutually agree to be nude. As soon as anyone else arrives and requests that all present put on bathing suits, those who refuse that request risk a citation. If you are in the nude group, all you need from the newcomers is some tolerance. You may be pleasantly surprised at the number of people who are willing to agree to a policy of clothing optional if, in a friendly manner, you offer them an opportunity to say "Yes."

In a separate section titled "For the Naturist" we have included a special listing of landed clubs in those states where there are hot springs to give skinny-dippers alternatives to conventional motels/hotels/resorts. Most of the nudist/naturist resorts specifically prohibit bathing suits in their pools and have a policy of clothing optional elsewhere on the grounds. Most nudist/naturist resorts are not open to the public for drop-in visits, but the resorts listed in this book are often willing to offer a visitor's pass if you phone ahead and make arrangements.

Those resorts listed in the Palm Springs section are definitely open to the public. Just call for reservations.

USING THIS GUIDE

The primary tool in this guide is the KEY MAP, which is provided for each state or geographical subdivision. The KEY MAP INDEX on the outside back cover tells the page number where each of the KEY MAPS can be found. Each KEY MAP includes significant cities and highways, but please note that it is designed to be used with a standard highway map.

Within every KEY MAP, each location has been assigned a number that is printed next to the identifying circle or square. On the pages following the KEY MAP you will find descriptions of each location listed in numerical order.

The Master Alphabetical Index of Mineral Water Locations is printed at the end of the book and gives the page number on which each location description will be found. If you know the specific hot spring name, this alphabetical index is the place to start.

The following section describes the quick-read symbols that are used on the KEY MAPS and in the location descriptions.

● **Natural Locations with Minor Improvements**

On the key maps and in each hot spring listing, a solid round dot is used to indicate a natural hot spring, or hot well, where no fee (or minimal fee) is required and pools are generally created by the rearranging of rocks or by using other materials, such as cement, to create a place to soak (bathtubs and stock tanks qualify). At a few remote locations, you may be asked for a donation to help maintain the spring, or to pay a parking fee.

■ **Commercial Mineral Water Establishments**

On the key maps in this book and in the hot springs listings, a solid square is used to indicate a mineral water commercial location. A phone number and address are provided for the purpose of obtaining rates, additional information, and reservations.

❑ **Tubs Using Gas-heated Tap Water or Well Water**

Listings of rent-a-tub locations, indicated by a white square, begin with an overall impression of the premises and with the general location, usually within a city area. Premises are described. Nearly all locations require reservations, especially during the busy evening and weekend hours.

Common Sense and Safety Tips

Respect is the key word when considering using a wilderness hot spring—respect for both the water and the area surrounding it, and for the people using it. Safety is also a key issue. The following guidelines will help make your soak safe and enjoyable.

It's Hot: Always, always check the temperature of the water before entering. Even if you have been to a spring several times, conditions affecting water flow and temperature change constantly.

It's Smelly or Not: Structures built over hot springs often prevent natural gasses from escaping. These can often build up and cause you to become dizzy and pass out. Be extremely cautious about staying within structures for any length of time.

Heads Up: Because many forms of bacteria and other organisms live in hot water, it is recommended by many that you do not put your head in the water.

Check it Out: If there is a ranger station in the area it is a good idea to talk to someone in the office to check for back country weather conditions, to see if any permits are needed, get maps, and make sure you have appropriate and sufficient supplies for your hike.

Over the River: The roads to many of the hot springs are often very primitive, cross deep washes, and are heavily rutted; stay on the roadway. Make sure your vehicle can make the trip. It is also often necessary for you to walk across running rivers to get to a springs. Cross at a wide, shallow spot that isn't above rapids or falls in case you get pulled downstream. Test rocks and logs before putting your weight on them. Face upstream while crossing and unbuckle the waiststraps of your backpack. Use a stick to increase stability.

The Gang's All Here: This is where consideration for other soakers comes in. If you arrive at a full pool, ask how long they plan on staying; or ask if you may join them. If you're the first person there, invite others to join you. You'd be amazed at the interesting people you meet. If people are waiting for you to get out before they get in, determine a reasonable length of time, and leave when agreed upon. Take a walk, watch the sky, read a book, and return later.

Cry of the Wild: Dogs go with their owners, and kids go along with their parents. It is up to the adults in this situation to take care of their children and their pets. Dogs do not belong in the pools, and loud barking is intrusive on an otherwise quiet time. As most of us know, when going to the bathroom in the wilderness, it is necessary to go off the trail 200 feet and away from the rivers and springs. This also holds true for your animals. Clean up after your pet. Bring a leash and use it if necessary; some areas require that you do.

It's a wonderful thing to introduce children to wilderness activities. However, as with any outdoor activity, particularly ones involving water, and often very hot water, close supervision is necessary. This is a great opportunity to teach children to respect nature and others.

No Noo: Sex No! Glass No!

Everything in Moderation: Alcohol (follow posted signs and local ordinances, use common sense).

Rub-a-dub-dub: While some springs actually use a bathtub as a soaking pool, they are not the place to wash yourself, your clothes, or your cooking utensils. Soap, shampoo, detergent, and toothpaste really mess up the water.

It's Mine: Some of the hot springs in the book are on private property, and sometimes it is necessary to cross private land to get to a spring. Be particularly courteous when encountering these situations if you want to be able to continue to use these lands. Close all gates you need to open, stay on marked trails and roads, leave it cleaner than when you found it, and, if stated, ask permission before entering the area or the springs. Behave responsibly so that the springs will remain open.

CAUTION

NATURAL HOT SPRINGS

- Water temperatures vary by site, ranging from warm to very hot . . . 180°F.

- Prolonged immersion may be hazardous to your health and result in hyperthermia (high body temperature).

- Footing around hot springs is often poor. Watch out for broken glass. Don't go barefoot and don't go alone. Please don't litter.

- Elderly persons and those with a history of heart disease, diabetes, high or low blood pressure, or who are pregnant should consult their physician prior to use.

- Never enter hot springs while under the influence of: alcohol, anti-coagulants, antihistamines, vasodilators, hypnotics, narcotics, stimulants, tranquilizers, vasoconstrictors, anti-ulcer or anti-Parkinsonian medicines. Undesirable side effects such as extreme drowsiness may occur.

- Hot springs are naturally occurring phenomena and as such are neither improved nor maintained by the Forest Service.

CARING FOR THE OUTDOORS

This is an enthusiastic testimonial and an invitation to join in supporting the work of the US Forest Service, the National Park Service, and the several State Park Services. At all of their offices and ranger stations we have always received prompt, courteous service, even when the staff was busy handling many other daily tasks.

Nearly all usable primitive hot springs are in national forests, and many commercial hot spring resorts are surrounded by a national forest. Even if you will not be camping in one of their excellent campgrounds, we recommend that you obtain official Forest Service maps for all of the areas through which you will be traveling. Maps may be purchased from the Forest Service regional offices listed below. To order by mail, phone or write for an order form:

web site: www.fs.fed.us
The web site also lists the individual forest offices in each region.

Rocky Mountain Region 303 275-5350
(Eastern Wyoming, Colorado)
740 Simms St., Lakewood, CO 80401

Intermountain Region 801 625-5306
(Southern Idaho, Utah,
Nevada, and Western Wyoming)
324 25th St., Ogden, UT 84401

Southwestern Region 505 842-3292
(Arizona, New Mexico)
333 Broadway SE, Albuquerque, NM 87102

Pacific Southwest Region 707 562-8737
(California, Hawaii)
1323 Club Dr., Vallejo, CA 94592

When you arrive at a national forest, head for the nearest ranger station and let them know what you would like to do in addition to putting your body in hot mineral water. If you plan to stay in a wilderness area overnight, request information about wilderness permits and camping permits. Discuss your understanding of the dangers of water pollution, including giardia (back country dysentery) with the Forest Service staff. They are good friends as well as competent public servants.

Leave No Trace

Plan ahead: Whenever you travel into the wilderness areas be sure to leave word with friends as to your exact destination. Read the signs at the trailhead for any new information and where they have a registration book, use it. In case you do get lost, search and rescue teams will have a start in locating you. Know the regulations for the area you are entering.

Take a good orienteering class and know basic first aid. Carry a compass and purchase a topo map for the area.

Watch the weather: Always check with the local authorities before you start out.

High elevations: Acclimate yourself before you hike. Drink plenty of water. If you experience any symptoms such as dizziness, severe headaches, etc., head back down.

Don't cut switchbacks: A little less time to your destination is not worth ruining fragile vegetation. In areas with no trails, try to walk on firm surfaces and avoid cutting a new trail.

Respect: archeological, historical, or natural items. It's against Federal law to remove them. Don't go into old mining structures as they are unstable and dangerous.

Camping: Select a previously used campsite. Camp away from the trails and at least 200 feet from lakes and streams. Keep campsites small and focus on areas without vegetation. Avoid places where impacts are just beginning.

Clean up: Set up camp, wash dishes, and bathe at least 200 feet from water (this is especially necessary near hot springs). Use biodegradable soap or no soap; soil and pine needles or dry sand make great scouring pads for dishes. Separate leftover food and bag it to take back. Scatter gray water away from water sources and camp sites. Don't bury trash (animals dig it up).

Campfires: Try to avoid building campfires in high-use areas where wood is scarce. If you do build a fire, use existing fire rings and make sure to burn all remaining pieces of wood and charcoal down to white ashes. Soak with water and crush any remnants. Or better yet, bring a small gas stove.

Bury human waste: Dig six-inch-deep holes at least 200 feet from camp, trails, and water. Carry out toilet paper in doubled plastic bags (wild animals will dig up buried paper).

Sally Jackson

Pack it in, pack it out: Avoid burning trash. To do so takes an intense fire, almost always leaving bits and pieces that will not burn. Don't bury trash. Animals, time, and erosion will unearth it.

Leave the area cleaner than when you found it.

Leave No Trace is a non-profit organization dedicated to inspiring responsible outdoor recreation by teaching and promoting minimum impact practices. They offer for sale items relating to this philosophy to help you maintain and protect our open spaces and wildlands. I encourage you to get their brochures for the specific area (e.g., Rocky Mountains, Sierra Nevada) you will be hiking in before you go. Their web site is www.LNT.org, and their phone is 800 332-4100.

THE SEVEN PRINCIPLES OF LEAVE NO TRACE

Plan Ahead and Prepare
Travel and Camp on Durable Surfaces
Dispose of Waste Properly
Leave What You Find
Minimize Campfire Impacts
Respect Wildlife
Be Considerate of Other Visitors

Whether camping in the desert or the mountains, or sharing a hot spring where some are clothed and some are not, respect for the environment and for each other is the key to a successful time in the wilderness which you can repeat over and over.

Camilla Van Slickle and Bill Pennington

Welcome back to *Pah Tempe* in Utah. For more information see entry on page 239.

NEVADA

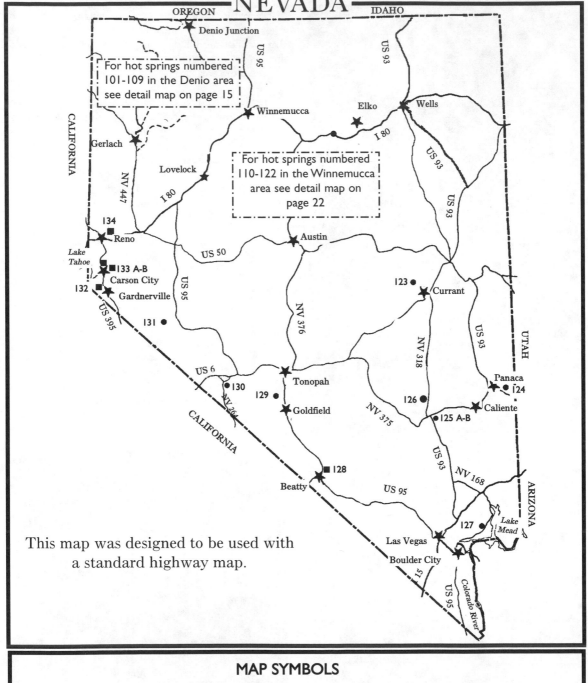

For hot springs numbered 101-109 in the Denio area see detail map on page 15

For hot springs numbered 110-122 in the Winnemucca area see detail map on page 22

OREGON · IDAHO · CALIFORNIA · UTAH · ARIZONA

Denio Junction

Winnemucca · Elko · Wells

Gerlach

Lovelock

134 Reno

Lake Tahoe

133 A-B Carson City

132 · Gardnerville

131

Austin

123 · Currant

130 · 129 · Tonopah

Goldfield

126

125 A-B · Caliente

Panaca · 124

128

Beatty

127 · Lake Mead

Las Vegas

Boulder City

Colorado River

US 95 · US 93 · I 80 · NV 447 · US 50 · US 95 · NV 376 · US 6 · NV 264 · NV 375 · NV 318 · US 93 · NV 168 · I 15 · US 95

This map was designed to be used with a standard highway map.

MAP SYMBOLS

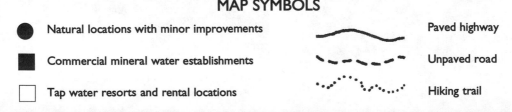

● Natural locations with minor improvements

■ Commercial mineral water establishments

□ Tap water resorts and rental locations

〰 Paved highway

- - - Unpaved road

· · · Hiking trail

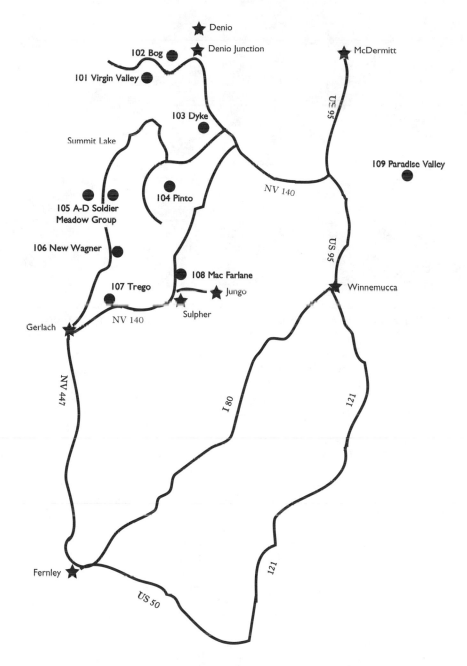

HOT SPRINGS OUT OF DENIO
AND THE GERLACH AREA

Chris Andrews

Chris Andrews

101 VIRGIN VALLEY WARM SPRING

● **In the Sheldon Wildlife Refuge**

A charming, gravel-bottomed, warm pond adjacent to a small campground in the high desert foothills near the Nevada-Oregon border. Elevation 5,100 feet. Open all year, subject to snow blocking the road. Small fee for soaking.

Natural mineral water emerges from the pond bottom (and is piped from other nearby springs) at 89°. The rate of flow maintains pond temperature at approximately 85°, depending on air temperature and wind speed. A cement pad and ladder into the pond have been installed and the bank between the pond and the bathhouse has been reinforced. No chemical treatment of the water is necessary. Bathing suits are required. The pool and facilities are handicap accessible with assistance.

Natural hot water continually flows through two indoor showers and to an outside pump for washing. The campground is equipped with chemical toilets. Free camping is available. Services are twenty-seven miles away in Denio.

Directions: On NV 140, 25.4 miles west of Denio Junction and 10 miles east of the Cedarville Road Junction, watch for a road sign to Virgin Valley, Royal Peacock Mine. Go south on the gravel road 2.4 miles to campground.

GPS: N 41 5.75 W 119 00.103

102 BOG HOT SPRINGS

● **Near the town of Denio**

A large, sandy-bottom ditch carrying hot mineral water to an irrigation pond. Located on brush-covered, flat land just below the Nevada-Oregon border. Elevation 4,300 feet. Open all year.

Natural mineral water flows out of several springs at 122°, is gathered into a single man-made channel, and gradually cools as it travels toward the reservoir. A dam with spillway pipe has been built at the point where the temperature is approximately 105°, depending on air temperature and wind speed. Water flows profusely through the pipe as it fills the two-foot deep soaking pond. Around the dam, brush has been cleared away for easy access and nearby parking, but it is possible to soak in the ditch farther upstream if a warmer water temperature is desired. Clothing optional is probably the custom at this remote location.

There are no services available, but there is an abundance of level space on which overnight parking is not prohibited. It is almost fourteen miles to a restaurant, store, service station, motel, and RV hookups in Denio Junction.

Directions: From Denio Junction, go west on NV 140 9.2 miles, turn right and drive north 3.9 miles on gravel road to a pond on the left. At 0.3 miles past the pond turn left and drive 100 yards to ditch and turn around area.

GPS: N 41 55.07 W 118 48.054

Skip Hill

104 PINTO HOT SPRINGS (EAST)

● **South of Denio Junction**

A geothermal heaven with many hot springs bubbling and flowing through trenches and troughs in the travertine rock. Located in the remote north end of the Black Rock desert region, named after the wild horses found there. Elevation 4,095 feet. Accessible only seasonally. Not a good trip for children and animals as very hot water flows all over the ground and you can easily get scalded.

Natural mineral water flows up through the bottom of a fifteen by twenty-foot pool found on the south end of a geothermal mound. The water temperature is around 109°, but may be hotter so check very carefully before going in. Carrying a thermometer to check all desert pools is a good idea. Clothing optional.

There are no facilities, and while you can camp on the open land it is very hot and there is no shade. Bring all supplies and extras with you. There is sometimes gas, a small cafe and several motel rooms at Denio Junction, thirty miles away. It is 107 miles to Winnemucca for all other services.

Directions: Go west on Leonard Creek Road, south of Denio Junction off SR140 and 0.4 miles south of mile marker 36. Continue 5.5 miles to the intersection of Jackson Creek Ranch Road. Stay right for another 14 miles going through the Leonard Creek Ranch. Drive slowly through here. Stay on the the main road 4.5 miles going through the Clark Field Ranch. Continue another 8 miles through the Battle Creek Ranch. Proceed 2.2 miles and turn left (east) on a very primitive dirt road heading into the desert. Go 4.5 miles to the top of a hill. Pass Pinto West (no springs to soak in) to Pinto East.

(Note: Only high clearance vehicles should attempt this trip, and then only when the road is dry, often not until late summer. Small washes, huge mud holes and large ruts are frequently found on the road.

Source map: USGS *Pinto Mountain* ,7.5 minute
GPS: N 41 21.736 W 118 47.385

Chris Andrews

103 DYKE HOT SPRING

● **South of Denio Junction**

Old porcelain bathtub set in a ravine against the hills on the western side of the Quinn River valley with hills to the west and broad vistas across the valley to the east. Elevation 4,000 feet. Open all year.

A small natural mineral water stream with a slight sulfur smell flows out of the hills at 150° and is carried by a plastic pipe into the old bathtub. To control the temperature in the tub, remove the hot water pipe and allow the water to cool down. If tub water is dirty, empty tub and refill. Clothing is optional even though the tub is near the road. Traffic is seldom a problem.

Overnight camping is not restricted. All services are thirty-nine miles away in Denio Junction.

Directions: From Denio Junction, drive south on Hwy 140 about 26 miles. Just past mile post 41, turn right onto Big Creek Rd. Go 6.9 miles to "T" and turn left onto Woodward Rd. Pass ranch on left (1.7 miles) and take first left (another 2 miles) and to 0.1 mile to spring. Tub is hidden in the ravine.

GPS: N 41 34.024 W 118 33.974

Sally Jackson

105 A   SOLDIER MEADOWS WARM POND

● **North of the town of Gerlach**

Delightful, deep pond located in the middle of a large meadow with a beautiful view of the surrounding desert and nearby Calico Mountains. Near High Rock Lake in the Black Rock Desert of northwest Nevada. Elevation 4,500 feet. Open all year; may be difficult to reach during winter storms. Spring and fall are best times.

Mineral water seeps up through the bottom of this natural, two-foot deep, sand and stone pond. A wooden ladder leads into the pond from a small wooden deck. Water temperatures range from 90-102°, depending on air and wind conditions. A second, small squishy-bottom pond at about 100° is about half a mile away, surrounded by alkali desert. The apparent local custom is clothing optional.

The hot springs are located on the private property of Soldier Meadows Guest Ranch and Lodge, a private working ranch and bed and breakfast. (For reservations: PO Box 67, Likely, CA 96116, 530 279-4881. www.soldiermeadows.com.) There is a $10 fee to camp and use the springs. There are no services available, but the owners do not mind anyone using the springs if you ask first at the ranch house. Please close all gates and camp outside the ranch fence and posted areas. It is sixty-two miles to a service station and mini-mart in Gerlach. It is recommended that you get gas in Gerlach.

There is also a landing strip if you want to fly in.

Directions: There is a no trespassing sign at the turnoff to the springs. However, if you turn into the large white gate and go up to the ranch house and ask for permission and directions, the owners seem happy to see you. They ask that you drop by and ask first as a courtesy so they are aware of who is on their property.

Note: There are numerous other hot springs on the road to High Rock Lake, but a four-wheel drive vehicle is recommended since the road is rough.

GPS: N 41 22.793 W 119.10.884

Soakers Bible

105 B   BATHTUB SPRING
(SOLDIER MEADOWS)

● **North of the town of Gerlach**

Check in first at the Ranch. Then head back out on the main road and turn left for 0.25 miles. Cross a cattle guard, then turn right following the fence line that is on your right. This road bends to the left after 0.5 miles and then forks. Take the left fork for a few hundred yards. The pools will be on the right.

105 C   SOLDIER MEADOWS HOT CREEK

● **North of the town of Gerlach**

Rock dams built in a hot creek to form a series of wonderful soaking opportunities in a remote desert location. Elevation 4,450 feet. Open all year; may be difficult to reach after rain. Spring and fall are the best times.

Clear odorless water flows down a small gully. The three pools nearest the campsite range from a toasty 112 to 106° and the water continues to cool as it heads downstream. A rare snail lives in these springs and the BLM requests visitors to be particularly careful about not washing off soap, sunscreen or insect repellent, etc. into the creek. Unfortunately orange mites sometimes frequent these pools—they run across the surface of the water and their bite can come up like a mosquito bite (some people seem more sensitive to them than others).

The springs are located on BLM land. The adjacent campground is free (tents only—trailers not permitted). There are fire-pits and a vault toilet. It is sixty-four miles to a service station and mini-mart in Gerlach.

Directions: Driving north from Gerlach on Soldier Meadows Road turn left (west) 1 mile south of Soldier Meadows Ranch towards High Rock Lake (signposted). Drive 1.2 miles to a gate. Continue 0.3 mile and turn right at the junction that has an information board that shows the location of the springs (there's a small cabin nearby on the right side of the road). Proceed 1.8 miles on a rough road that will require high clearance and perhaps even a 4WD (a toilet block will now be visible on the left). Veer left for 0 .2 miles to the BLM campground. The springs are on the right (west) down a rock-lined path.

GPS: N 41 21.531 W 119.13.502

105 D   CHUKAR GULCH
(SOLDIER MEADOWS)

● **North of the town of Gerlach**

The water from several springs flow down a small trench directly into a large twenty-foot round pool that averages three-feet deep. The crystal clear water is about 104°. The sandy bottom does not silt up which makes for a great soak. There is even a table built into the center of the pool so you can set your drink down.

Follow directions to Soldier Meadows Hot Creek, and at the last right fork go left instead. The left fork will take you over three yellow cattle guards. Then hang a right at the next fork and follow it up and over a small incline and then down the back side to the springs. The pool is about 1 mile from the place where you took the left fork.

Photos by Soakers Bible

● **North of the town of Gerlach**

A bathtub in a small grove of cottonwoods and Russian olives. A pleasant view including the Black Rock volcanic outcrop, makes up for the tepid temperature. Elevation 4,000 feet. Open all year. Not currently posted.

A pipe supplies 87° water to a single bathtub.

Directions: From Gerlach, take highway 34 north and east for 12.2 miles. Turn right on Soldier Meadows Road for 21 miles then take a right at a small sign 'Wagner Spring' and proceed .1 mile to a gate. The springs are 50 feet past the gate amongst a small grove of trees.

For those heading south from Solder Meadows this turnoff is 0.2 mile past Gardner Blvd.

GPS: N 41 08.194 W 119 08.292

Chris Andrews

107   **TREGO HOT DITCH**

● **Northeast of the town of Gerlach**

A hot ditch next to Western Pacific railroad tracks. Located on the Eastern side of the Black Rock Desert with a backdrop of the Pahsupp Mountains. Elevation 4,000 feet. Open all year.

Natural mineral water bubbles up out of the ground by the railroad tracks at 185° and cools gradually as it flows through the ditch. Water temperature varies greatly depending on air and wind conditions. Clothing is optional, but ditch can be seen from the tracks, and trains pass frequently.

No services are available, but overnight parking is not prohibited. It is twenty miles to a service station and mini-mart in Gerlach.

Directions: From Gerlach, go 3.3 miles south on Route 447. Turn left on gravel County Road 48 (sign to Winnemucca, 96 miles). Continue north 17 miles and turn left toward railroad tracks and a communications antenna. Continue 1 mile and turn right at the first fork, left at the second, and right at the third (antenna on left). Take the next left toward the railroad track (ditch not visible) and continue on a one-lane, sandy, dirt road for 0.3 miles up a gradual slope. Bear left across clearing with campfire rings, toward railroad tracks. Ditch is on the right.

GPS: N 40 46.272 W 119 06.990

● **East of the town of Gerlach**

An on-again, off-again spring on the east border of the Black Rock Desert. Different seasons offer varying water levels, depending on rain. Cattle often drink from the pools and trample the edges. Bring a shovel! Elevation 4,079 feet. Late spring or early summer, before the springs dry up, may be the best time to come. If roads are wet, do not attempt it.

Hot mineral water between 140-170° emerges from several springs and is carried by channels carved into stone by the water creating several small pools near the base of a hill. There is one man-made pool, about ten feet around and six inches deep, dug out and made of wooden slats. The bottom is heavily silted and could use some hard work to make the soak enjoyable. The only way to cool down the water is to divert the flow. Clothing optional.

Camping is allowed near the spring. There is a large parking area at the south end of the pool. The nearest supplies are fifty-six miles away in Gerlach. The nearest large town is Winnemucca.

Directions; From Gerlach go south on SR 447 2.7 miles. Turn east onto a gravel road signed "Winnemucca 96 miles." Continue 40 miles to what is left of the town of Sulphur and turn north crossing the railroad track and continue on a very poor road for another 12.5 miles to the spring.

From Winnemucca: At the corner of Melarky St, and Jungo Rd, take Jungo Rd. west for 54.4 miles. Turn right at the fork and follow the main track another 3.2 miles to another right fork. Follow this dirt road north for 13 miles to Jackson Mountain. The road runs right into it, impossible to miss. If you are coming from Trego Hot Springs, go past the turnoff for Trego and continue to a left turn in 25.2 miles signed SR140. Cross the railroad tracks and continue 12.5 miles north to the the spring.

GPS: N 41 03.036 W 118 43.146　　Skip Hill

Chris Andrews

You are welcome to use this spring which is located on private property. However, please do not camp on the property. BLM land is very close to the springs and you can camp there.

109　PARADISE VALLEY HOT SPRINGS

● **North of the town of Winnemucca**

Perched above the Little Humboldt River this desert hot spring is well worth the trip. Open all year; accessible only during the dry season.

Natural mineral water boils up through a small caldera and is piped from the source to a galvanized soaking tub. Clothing optional. The tub is handicap accessible with assistance.

There are no services available at this spring which is on private property. No camping at the springs. You can camp on the nearby BLM land. Minimal supplies can be found in the town of Paradise Valley, an old, unique farming village worth the visit in itself. All other services are about thirty-five miles away in Winnemucca.

Directions: Head 22 miles north on US 95 from Winnemucca and follow the signs east on NV 290 to Paradise Valley, about 18 miles. At the north end of town turn right towards Chimney Reservoir. Consider this point 0. At 2.9 miles bear right. At 10.4 miles bear left. At 11.2 miles turn right and go through the gate. The springs are 250 yards past the gate. Make sure you close the gate after entering from the main road, otherwise you may wind up sharing your soak with a herd of cattle.

GPS: N 41 25.322 W 117 23.231

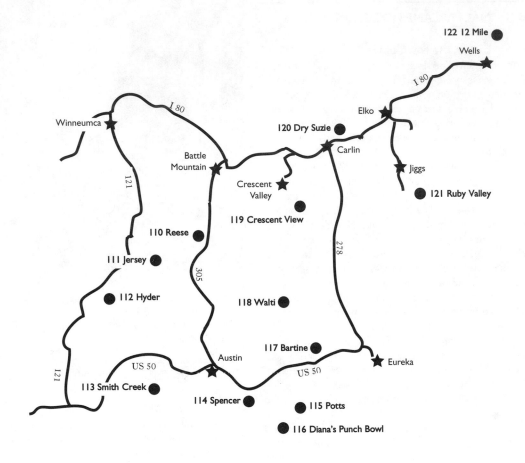

122 12 Mile
Wells
I 80
Elko
120 Dry Suzie
Carlin
Jiggs
121 Ruby Valley
Winneumca
I 80
121
Battle
Mountain
Crescent
Valley
119 Crescent View
278
110 Reese
111 Jersey
305
112 Hyder
118 Walti
117 Bartine
Eureka
Austin
US 50
US 50
121
113 Smith Creek
114 Spencer
115 Potts
116 Diana's Punch Bowl

HOT SPRINGS EAST OF WINNEMUCA
AND OUT OF AUSTIN

110 REESE RIVER HOT SPRINGS (VALLEY OF THE MOON)

● North of Austin, South of Battle Mountain

A nice stone pool fed with clear hot spring water, tucked away near the Reese River on a private ranch. Elevation 4,805 feet. Open all year.

Clear, odorless mineral water forms a hot stream that runs down a small hill and into a wetland through a series of pipes into the pool. Adjacent to the source, a twelve-by twenty-foot, three-foot deep stone pool has been carefully constructed. Hot water is gravity fed into the side of the pool keeping it constantly full. Water temperature stays about 105°, and with a well-balanced pH level, the water is just about perfect. Clothing optional.

There are no services available at the spring, except for a picnic table, so bring your lunch. Camping is definitely restricted. The owner does not want anyone camping on the ranch. All services can be found fifty-four miles back in Austin.

This is the northern most of three hot springs also know as Valley of the Moon Hot Springs. This has the largest flow of the three and the best soaking possibilities.

Directions: Take I 80 to Battle Mountain, then take NV 305 south. From the BLM office on the way out of town, continue 34.8 miles to a right turn onto a dirt road that leads to an abandoned farmhouse. Follow the dirt road for 0.8 miles, through a gate and right at the fork leading uphill to the pool. You'll see the drainage area first, and just ahead is the in-ground pool surrounded by cow proof fencing.

From Austin: Directions: 0.3 miles north of MM 84 on SR 305 and 54 miles north of the intersection of 305 and Hwy 50 (2 miles west of Austin) turn west on gravel road for and another 0.2 miles and go through the gate and into the springs.

Source map: USGS *The Cedars Nevada*, 15 minutes

111   JERSEY VALLEY (HOME STATION RANCH) HOT SPRINGS

● **South of Winnemucca**

A single nice pool in a very remote desert area offers a relaxing hot bath after a long dusty drive. Views of the Fish Creek and the Tobin Mountain Ranges. Elevation 4,498. Open all year; use extreme caution during wet weather.

Hot sulfur springs emerge from a large pool at 120° and flow down a channel and right past a lovely rock-and-mortar soaking pool. Measuring ten by eight by three-feet deep, this comfortable pool has room for several friends. PVC tubes set into the hot stream carry water into the tub after passing through a small footbath. A tennis ball is used as a plug. Bring an extra just in case. The tub fills quickly but you will probably need to wait for it to cool. Remember to drain the water before you leave, this helps deter cows and algae growth.

There are no services at the spring. Come fully prepared. No restrictions on camping in the area. Clothing optional. Handicap accessible with assistance.

Soakers Bible

Skip Hill

Directions from Winnemucca: From the intersection of US50 and SR121 head north on paved road for 27 miles where the road turns to gravel. Continue another 42 miles to microwave tower. Turn right (east) and go approximately another nine miles to the pool on the left (north).

Directions from Lovelock: Take Interstate 80 to exit 112 north of Lovelock, signed to Coal Canyon Road. Take this exit and head east for 13.6 miles to a left turn signed for Dixie Valley. Follow this paved road for 32.5 miles and turn right. Continue for 7 miles and turn left at an unsigned 'Y' intersection. Follow this for 2.6 miles and turn left at a 'T' intersection near some power lines. After 2.2 miles continue straight, and in another 5.4 miles turn left at the fork, and left again in 2.9 miles. Follow this road about 50 yards to the first source spring which you'll smell before you see. Park and walk down the road about 50 yards further to the tub on the right.

GPS Coordinates: N 40 10.652 W 117 29.807

Skip Hill

112   HYDER HOT SPRINGS

●   **South of Winnemucca**

Several seeps and hot springs scattered on a barren desert hillside offer several possible soaking options. Some are too hot to enter, so be sure to test the water before jumping in. Elevation 4,497 feet. Open all year, weather permitting.

Several source pools on the hillside range in temperature from 95 up to 150° at the source. The water flows through a ditch into a pool situated on the west slope of a large tufa mound. This is the most useable spot. The pool is about twelve by twelve and very shallow. It is also quite hot. Rocks could be used to divert the flow, allowing the pool to cool down. Other pools were dug but dry, some PVC piping could probably solve the problem.

There are no services on the premises and it is eighty-two miles from Hyder back to Winnemucca. Come fully prepared for all possibilities.

Directions: From the microwave tower as described in Home Station Ranch Hot Spring, go east about 1 mile, turn right (south) for 2 miles to the old abandoned McCoy Ranch. Continue through the ranch still heading south for 2.5 miles to the first intersection. Turn right (west) heading for the lower Jenkins Ranch. Go through the ranch, continue going west another 7 miles to the turnoff to Hyder. Park at the turnout and follow the track a short distance to several springs up on the hill. Walk down the backside of the hill to the left and follow the fence line down to an opening, where you will find the best spot to soak.

Note: If road is wet from McCoy Ranch to Hyder, do not attempt even with a 4WD.

GPS Coordinates: N 40 00.192 W 117 43.134

Betty Prange

113   SMITH CREEK (RAINBOW) HOT SPRINGS

●   **Southwest of the town of Austin**

Located in the Smith Creek Valley. While this spot has a trough to soak in, there are many other springs bubbling up close by in this desert landscape. Open all year; weather dependent.

Natural mineral water from one of many springs measuring a 197° is piped down to a large round cattle trough. Can be cooled down by blocking pipe to reduce the water flow. Clothing optional.

No signs prohibit overnight parking. All services about forty miles back in Austin.

Directions: From Austin go 2.7 miles west on US 50, turn south (left) on SR722 and head into Smith Creek Valley over Railroad Pass a distance of approximately 20 miles. At MM LA (for Lander County) 6 bear right on gravel Old Overland Road heading west. Go over the third cattle guard to a primitive dirt road on the right; if there has been rain, this track may be impassable. Go north 0.3 miles toward the dry lake bed.

Note: Another eight-foot metal stock tank with water piped in at 110° is reported to be located 0.9 miles off Smith Creek Ranch Rd.

Rainbow is a hundred yards farther north on the same track. There are small springs and seeps all over the place.

GPS: N 39 18.940 W 117 32.950. Smith Creek Hot Spring

Chris Andrews

114   SPENCER HOT SPRINGS

● **Southeast of the town of Austin**

A group of volunteer-built soaking pools on a knoll with a view of barren hills and snow-capped mountains. Elevation 5,700 feet. Open all year.

Natural mineral water flows out of several springs at 128°, then through a shallow channel down the slope of the knoll. Volunteers have dug a small, three-foot deep, sand-bottom soaking pool next to this channel. A gate valve controls the temperature of the tub which varies between approximately 101-104°. A wooden slat deck has been built near the soaking pool. Volunteers have also installed a large metal stock tank downhill for soaking in 107° water. A second stock tank has been installed about one-quarter of a mile to the north where the water is about 112°. Water temperature to the tanks is controlled by the gate valve or by removing the pipe or hoses carrying the hot water. Handicap accessible with assistance. Clothing optional.

There are no services available, but there is a limited amount of level space on which overnight parking is not prohibited. A steel fire pit has been built near the metal soaking tank, and there are several large bins for trash collection. Please do your part to keep this location clean.

Directions: From the intersection of US 50 (12 miles east of Austin) and NV 376, go 400 yards south on NV 376 and turn left onto FS road 001 with a sign saying Monitor Valley. Continue on a gravel road about 5.5 miles southeast and take the first left after the power lines. Follow this road 1.1 miles to the springs which are on the west face of the knoll.

GPS: N 39 19.824 W 116 51.288

A favorite with all of the regional contributors to this book. It was difficult to choose which pictures to use—and there were quite a few.

Photo above by Phil Wilcox
Photo below by Betty Prange

26

It's no smoking and no camping at *Pott's Ranch Hot Spring.*

---

115   POTT'S RANCH HOT SPRING

● **Southeast of Austin**

A watering tank large enough for four set into the hillside with views of the high desert of the Monitor Valley, surrounded on both sides by the Toiyabe National Forest. Elevation 6,700 feet. Open all year.

Natural mineral water comes out of the source spring at 113° flows down a ditch and is piped to an eight-foot round cattle tank and bathtub. Water temperature is adjusted by diverting the hot water pipes. Local volunteers have built a small wood deck and bench and help keep the area quite clean. Handicap accessible with assistance. Clothing optional.

There are no facilities out here so be prepared with everything you need as the nearest supplies are forty-three miles away in Austin or ninety miles away in Tonopah. The Toquima Campground is thirteen and one-half miles away. Local ranchers have closed the area before due to trash and overnight campers, and will do so again if area becomes a nuisance. Sheriff will cite anyone camping or building a fire.

Directions: See directions to Diana's Punch Bowl (number 116). The directions are the same until you come to the fork at the 28 mile odometer reading. To get to Pott's bear left at 28 miles and stay straight onto Rte. 25 at the cattle guard. At 30.4 pass an old ranch house on the left. At 30.8 bear right and the spring is at 31.3.

GPS: N 39 04.788 W 116 38.400

116   DIANA'S PUNCH BOWL

● **Southeast of Austin—**

Volcanic crater filled with very hot water whose overflow forms a wide body of water for soaking. Elevation 6,700 feet. Open all year.

Natural mineral water at 183° runs down from Diana's Punch Bowl forming a hot creek about five miles wide, allowing the water temperature to cool down to the low 100s at the far end of the creek. Several dams have been built along the waterway providing areas to soak, many at least waist-high. Very difficult handicap access. Clothing optional.

There are no services on the premises, but there is a lot of flat, unposted area to camp overnight. Toquima Campground is sixteen miles away. All other services are forty-six miles away in Austin.

Directions: From the intersection of US 50 and NV 376 go 0.25 miles south on 376. Bear left on a gravel road. Consider this point 0 on your odometer. This is FS Road 001. At 14.4 miles pass the road to your left, and at 17.8 miles pass Toquima Campground. At 24.2 miles bear right at a major fork in the road. At 24.5 you'll pass through a ranch yard, bear left. Bear right at the fork at 28 miles. At 32.7 miles turn left on a small dirt road toward a large conical butte a couple of miles away. This butte is Diana's Punch Bowl. It is worth a hike up to the top to see the spring inside. A road goes around to the right to the springs (about 0.5 miles).

GPS: N 39 01.824 W 116 40.002

Hot water overflows from a volcanic crater and forms a hot creek. Bring a shovel, choose the temperature you like and dig your own pool.

Phil Wilcox

Evie Litton

117   BARTINE HOT SPRINGS

● **West of the town of Eureka**

Soaking pool located on a tufa mound in the middle of the high desert. Elevation 6,100 feet. Views of snow-capped peaks, along with a large tufa mound add to the natural wonders of this area. Open all year; weather dependent. (The spring is on-again, off-again, depending on the water table.)

Natural mineral water enters a concrete box about four feet square by two feet deep filled with 105° clear, clean water via a well casing set in the middle and is piped to a four-foot by eight-foot oval soaking pool that is often in need of repair. No cold water is available so temperature can only be controlled by diverting the pipe that goes into the pool. Handicap accessible with assistance. Clothing optional.

Unofficial camping at or near the springs. All services are twenty-seven miles away in Eureka.

Directions: 0.6 miles east of mile marker EU 12 on US 50 turn north on Three Bars Rd. Travel 2.1 miles then turn right onto a bumpy power line road. Travel another 1.4 miles, then bear left 0.1 mile to the spring on the tufa mound.

Source map: *USGS Bartine Ranch* (15 minute).
GPS: N 39 33.474 W 116 21.630

118   WALTI HOT SPRINGS

● **North of Austin**

Another of the desert hot springs. Shaded by cottonwood trees, this one is located on the Gund Ranch which is owned and operated by the University of Nevada, Reno and open to the public. Open all year. Check at the ranch before using the springs.

Several sources of natural mineral water flow out of the banks at 160° and flow into a large pond at least a couple of hundred feet long, forty- to fifty-feet wide and deep enough to dive into. The water temperature in the pond varies from one end to the other making it easy to find just the right temperature. A bench and deck are all the amenities provided. (The deck is metal and can get quite hot when the sun is out.)

No camping permitted.

Directions: From US 50, east of Austin and between Austin Summit and Bob Scott Summit, take the Grass Valley Rd. heading north. It starts out paved but after about 4 miles, turns to a good gravel road. Continue north, following the signs to Gund Ranch for almost 38 miles until you see the ranch on your left. Be sure and check in before proceeding to the springs.

GPS: N 39 54.240 W 116 35.280

Several reports have come in that Crescent View may be completely closed, others say it is open. Check before going down there with the local BLM office.

Often trashed, tubs a mess and water coming in at a trickle. You also need to watch out for the masses of crickets that fly around and then land in the tubs. Never great, but often soakable.

119   CRESCENT VIEW HOT SPRINGS

● **Southeast of the town of Crescent Valley**

A variety of stock tanks and bathtubs on a remote sagebrush-covered hillside overlooking the Crescent Valley. Elevation 5,300 feet. Open all year; cars may have problems if roads are wet.

Natural mineral water from a hillside spring is piped and channeled through troughs to an eight-foot stock tank, several bath tubs, and one tub in an old aluminum trailer. The source temperature is 185°. Water temperature is controlled by diverting the piped hot water. Clothing optional.

There is unofficial camping at or near the springs which is on BLM land. Limited services are fifteen miles away in Crescent Valley.

Directions: At the north end of the town of Crescent Valley turn east on McDaniel St. Consider this point 0. At 0.6 miles the pavement ends. At 4.0 miles bear right towards an A-frame house and hot pool. Pass the house and continue to the "T" at 11.8 miles. Turn left towards the ranch and at 13.1 miles turn right (just before the ranch) and drive 1.1 miles to the spring.

Source map: *USGS Frenchie Creek* (15 minute).
GPS: N 40 18.966 W 116 26.052

120   DRY SUZIE (HOT SULPHUR) HOT SPRINGS

● **Northeast of the town of Carlin**

A shovel and a new tub would make this spring which comes out of a hillside in the rolling hills of the high desert a great place to soak. Elevation 5,000 feet. Open all year; high-clearance vehicles recommended.

Natural mineral water flows out of a hillside at 145° and is piped to a small plastic pool. There is also a stock tank that may be used with a tarp, as vandals have shot numerous holes in the tank. With a little work you could also create a hot shower. The only way to cool the water in the tubs is to divert the incoming hose. Clothing optional.

Unofficial camping at or near the springs is allowed. All other services are nine miles away in Carlin.

Directions: Get off I-80 at exit 282 and consider this point 0. Travel north on a good gravel road. At 1.6 miles bear right, then turn right onto a dirt road heading up a hill. At 1.8 miles you'll cross a creek washout. Continue up a steep hill, go down the other side and up another hill. At 3.2 miles there is a cross road, continue straight. From here you may see some darker green vegetation a mile ahead and to the left. This is the thermal area. At 4.1 miles the road skirts around the fenced thermal area and the gate to the springs is at 4.7 miles.

Source map: *USGS Huntsman Ranch* (7.5 minute)
GPS: N 40 45.954 W 116 02.550

Skip Hill

Camilla Van Sickle and Bill Pennington

121   RUBY VALLEY (LAKES) HOT SPRINGS

● **South of the town of Elko**

Series of natural hot spring pools located in the spectacular high desert near Ruby Lake National Wildlife Refuge on the east side of the Ruby Mountains with views of Humboldt National Forest. Elevation approximately 7,000 feet. Open all year; may be impassable during heavy rains.

Hot, 122° water emerges up through the ground at various spots on a grassy knoll just outside the border fence of the Wildlife Refuge into several pools where water temperatures range from 106-122°. The area around the springs is a marshy bog, and even with several wooden planks which have been set down as walkways, you still sink into the marsh. Clothing optional.

There are no facilities and no shade, but plenty of flat areas (BLM land) away from the marshy hot springs where you can park overnight. The nearest town is Jiggs (thirty-six miles away) where you can purchase gas, and food.

Directions: Ruby Valley can be reached from US 93 (drive west), from I-80 east of Elko (drive south) or from I-50 (drive north). Follow signs along these highways to Ruby Valley National Wildlife refuge. From Elko, drive south on excellent paved NV 228 for 36 miles to Jiggs. Continue until the pavement ends and the road becomes unpaved Harrison Pass Rd. which crosses Humboldt National Forest at Harrison Pass (elevation 7,248 feet). The road is not maintained in winter. On the east side of the mountain, Harrison Pass Rd. ends at a wide gravel road. Turn left for 0.3 miles, then right onto a one-lane dirt road. At 3.5 miles bear right at the fork and follow the fence around the wildlife refuge. At 0.3 miles go right when the road forks. The hot springs are on a knoll surrounded by dark green bulrushes which are visible from the refuge.

GPS: N 40 15.120 W 115 24.450

122   TWELVE MILE HOT SPRINGS

● **North of the town of Wells**

Very large soaking pool formed by a rock and concrete wall at the base of a large hill. Located in a small canyon near Bishop Creek. Elevation 5,000 feet. Open all year; roads may not be passable and fording Bishop Creek may be dangerous in wet weather or times of high water.

Natural mineral water flows out of the rocks directly into a large, clean, gravel-bottom pool about twelve feet wide, ninety-feet long and approximately three-feet deep, making it one of the biggest hot soaking pools at 104° that we've ever found. While the apparent local custom is clothing optional, keep a suit handy on the weekends.

All services, except level ground for overnight camping, are back in Wells.

Directions: Consider the intersection of 6th St. and Lake Ave. in downtown Wells as point 0. Turn northeast on Lake Ave. Cross the railroad tracks and turn left on 8th St. Continue across Wells Ave on what is now a dirt road. One mile further the road is again paved. Continue north. At 9.7 miles and just past 2 farmhouses the road curves sharply west. Turn onto the dirt road that comes off to the right and continue straight on this road to the main pool at 11.7 miles. (There is a large steel and wood bridge approximately 0.1 mile before the spring.) The road in is very rough and a very high clearance vehicle is suggested.

Note: There are hot water seeps along the banks lining Bishop Creek where other pools could be built.

GPS: N 41 14.570 W 114 56.890

Two large ditches leading away from this popular soaking pond serve as a watering trough for cattle on this open range land.

123 DUCKWATER POND

● **North of Currant**

Large spring-fed pond located in a generally flat desert landscape. Used by locals as a swimming hole and by ranchers as a water source. Elevation 5,600 feet. Open all year.

Natural mineral water flows in the pond from a large hole in the bottom at around 90°, filling the five-foot deep pond with a huge flow of crystal clear water. Ten iron steps lead down into the water. Handicap accessible with assistance. Clothing optional, depending on desire of those present.

Overnight parking is not prohibited. It is about forty miles to Black Rock Station on Hwy 6, 20 miles west of Currant for all other services.

Directions: From the intersection of Hwys 6 and 379 in Currant, drive north on Hwy 379 for 20 miles where the pavement ends. Turn left also immediately on first dirt road and drive 0.1 mile to pond.

124 PANACA WARM SPRINGS

● **North of Panaca**

A large, warm swimming hole maintained by the town of Panaca, located on BLM land surrounded by low mountains and ranch land in the high desert of eastern Nevada near the Utah border. Elevation 4,742 feet. Open all year.

Natural warm springs flow out of the hillside and through a marsh into a large dammed pond which is as deep as ten feet near the dam, and varies in temperature from 78-86°. A five-step ladder leads into the pond. Once a year the pond is drained and cleaned by the town. Algae is cleaned off the bottom the beginning of every summer. Handicap accessible with assistance. There are no clothing requirements; however, the spring is right along a heavily traveled road, the area is mainly Mormon, and citations may be issued. Used as a swimming hole by the locals who strongly object to nudity.

Overnight parking is not prohibited. Gas, a store, and a mini-mart are available in Panaca and auto service and a restaurant are five miles away at the Highway 93 junction.

Directions: In Panaca turn north off Main St. to Fifth St. Follow the straight dirt road for about 1 mile to the spring.

GPS: N 37 48.420 W 114 22.800

Photos by Phil Wilcox

125 A   ASH SPRINGS

● **North of the town of Alamo**

Natural warm-water swimming holes formed in channels under the shade of ash and cottonwood trees, in the barren desert foothills. Elevation 4,000 feet. Open all year.

Hundreds of gallons per minute of natural mineral water flows out of several springs on Bureau of Land Management (BLM) property where it maintains approximately 92° temperature as it runs into a soaking pool, fifteen- to twenty-feet across and, depending on water flow ranges from shallow to slightly deeper water. A separate spring feeds an adjacent rock, brick, and cement pool where water temperature measures 98°. Handicap accessible with assistance. Bathing suits required.

Facilities include pit toilets, a picnic area, firepits, trash collection, and level BLM land for parking with a two hour limit. No alcohol or glass allowed. Sheriff will cite violators. No overnight camping. "R Place," a service station, restaurant, well-stocked store, campground, and RV park, is open across the highway twenty-four hours a day Do not enter any marked, private land.

Directions: From Las Vegas, drive 90 miles north on US 93 to Alamo. Continue 7 miles on US 93. Continue north beyond the end of the private resort property fence and immediately turn right on a narrow dirt road for 100 yards to the soaking pools.

GPS: N 37 27.780 W 117 37.920

Crystal Springs was used as a watering place and campsite and was the principal stopover on the Mormon Trail alternate route.

125 B   CRYSTAL SPRINGS

● **Near Ash Springs**

A real oasis has been created by warm water pouring through a wide irrigation spout into an overgrown pool just off "Extraterrestrial Highway" near Nellis Air Force Base. Elevation 4,000 feet. Open all year.

Spray rises from the profuse flow of 81° water as it is funneled through the irrigation spout into a broad pool where it seeps into the shrubbery along the banks. The spring and pool are located behind a barbed wire fence with paths leading to the running water. Although it is near the highway, the water is not visible to the few motorists who pass by, so bathing suits are optional.

There are no services or facilities. Level areas along the highway may be used for overnight parking. Most services can be found approximately seven miles away at "R Place," across from Ash Springs.

Directions: From "R Place" across from Ash Springs, drive north on US 93 for about 5 miles. Turn left (west) onto Hwy 318. Continue about 0.5 miles where Hwy 318 goes off to the right. Stay on US 375 and look for Crystal Springs sign on left about 100 yards past the "Y" Park and walk 20 yards south to the spring.

GPS: N 37 31.920 W 115 13.980

Soakers Bible

126 HOT CREEK SPRINGS AND MARSH AREA

● **North of Ash Springs and Hiko**

A large, crystal clear hot spring fed swimming hole at the base of Hot Creek Butte in the White River Valley. Elevation 5,201 feet. Open year round.

Crystal clear spring water feeds a great swimming hole with 85° mineral water. The pool is forty feet across and up to five feet deep. Iron stairs lead down into the warm water. The water has a beautiful bluish color, and the huge flow rate keeps even the sandy bottom totally clean. Clothing optional. Handicap accessible with assistance.

No services at the spring, but there are pit toilets at the campground. Free camping at several campgrounds nearby. Dave Deacon Campground offers free camping with an eight day limit.

Directions: From Hiko head north on NV318 and take the first left heading into Kirch Wildlife Management Area. Follow this bumpy road 4.5 miles to a four-way intersection with an information board. Continue straight ahead through a fence and over the dyke that spans the south end of Adams McGill Reservoir. At 2.4 miles past the cattle guard the right fork takes you to Dave Deacon Campground. Continue on the left fork for 1.1 miles to the springs.

GPS: N 38 22.46 W 115 09.06

ENDANGERED FISH SANCTUARY
THIS SPRING IS INHABITED BY THE RARE WHITE RIVER SPRINGFISH, ONE OF THE FEW NATIVE FISHES OF THIS AREA. THIS SANCTUARY WILL HELP TO INSURE ITS CONTINUED UNMOLESTED EXISTENCE. UNLAWFUL TO REMOVE ANY FISH FROM THIS WATER OR TO INTRODUCE ANY SPECIES...
NEVADA DEPT. OF WILDLIFE ...

Phil Wilcox

Truly a desert oasis, complete with a warm watering hole and palm trees.

127 ROGERS WARM SPRING

● **Near the town of Overton**

A refreshing warm pond and shady picnic oasis, complete with palm trees, on the barren north shore of Lake Mead in the Lake Mead National Recreation Area. Elevation 2,000 feet. Open all year.

Natural mineral water at approximately 90° flows directly up through a gravel bottom into a 100-foot-diameter pool at a sufficient rate to maintain the entire three-foot deep pool at approximately 85°. Hundreds of gallons per minute flow over a cement and rock spillway in a series of small waterfalls. With assistance, wheelchairs could enter the pond. Bathing suits would be advisable at this location. Signs suggest keeping your head out of the water.

There are restrooms and three shaded picnic benches. Overnight parking (after 10 PM) is prohibited. It is eight and one-half miles to a store, restaurant, and service station in Overton, and five miles to a very nice campground at Valley of Fire State Park.

Directions: From the intersection of US 93 and NV 147 in the city of Henderson, go northeast on Lake Mead Dr. At the intersection with Northshore Rd. (NV 169), follow Northshore Rd. northeast toward Overton. Rogers Warm Spring is 4 miles beyond the Echo Bay Marina turnoff.

Alternate Directions: When approaching from the north, take the I-15 exit Logandale/Overton. Turn east on NV 169 to Lake Mead National Recreation Area and continue south for 27 miles to the Rogers Spring sign.

GPS: N 36 22.680 W 114 26.580

128 BAILEY'S HOT SPRINGS
Box 387 775 553-2395
■ Beatty, NV 89003

An older hot spring, rich in railroad history, now primarily an RV park with three large indoor, hot mineral water soaking pools. Located in the high desert country just east of Death Valley National Monument. Elevation 3,500 feet. Open all year.

Natural, crystal clear, odorless mineral water emerges from the ground at 110° and bubbles up through the gravel bottoms of three indoor soaking pools that used to be railroad water reservoirs. Flow rates are controlled to maintain different temperatures in the three pools, approximately 98-101°, 103-105°, and 105-108°. The rate of flow-through is sufficient to eliminate the need for chemical treatment of the water. Bathing suits are optional in the private-space pools. Pool use is included in the overnight RV fee, and pools are available on a day-use basis to tent campers and the general public for a small fee.

Facilities include fourteen tree-shaded, RV spaces with water and electric, a picnic area and barbeque pits, showers, restroom, and a lawn for tent camping. No credit cards accepted. It is five miles to a store, cafe, and service station.

Directions: From the only traffic signal in Beatty, go 5.5 miles north on US 95. Watch for the large sign on the east side of the road.

Phil Wilcox

Phil Wilcox

129 ALKALI (SILVER PEAK) HOT SPRING

● North of the town of Goldfield

Two remote, brick-lined soaking pools at the edge of a salt flat in the remains of an abandoned turn-of-the-century hot springs resort with stunning views of the high Sierra to the west. Elevation 5,000 feet, Open all year.

Natural mineral water flows out of the ground through a flow pipe at 115°. On one edge of the source spring, volunteers have used bricks to build two large (four-six person) soaking pools in which the temperature is controlled by diverting or admitting hot water as desired. Outside temperatures of 105° contributed to the top pool being 114° and the bottom pool 106° with thick brown algae. Wooden steps lead to the pools, and pieces of old carpet are around for sitting or sunning. Trash cans are available to collect the party trash. Handicap accessible with assistance. Clothing optional.

There are no services on the premises, but there is plenty of level ground on which overnight parking is not prohibited. It is eleven miles to a store, service station, and motel in Goldfield.

Directions: From the town of Goldfield (27 miles south of Tonopah) drive north on US 95 for 4 miles and look for a sign to "Alkali/Silver Peak" on the west side of the highway. Turn west and drive 6.8 miles on a paved road to a power substation. A large abandoned swimming pool is near the road, just past the power station. Follow the channel 50 feet up the hill toward the station to the soaking pools. The hot springs is on the south side of the road. This area can be very muddy after rain or snow so stay on the pavement.

GPS: N 37 45.660 W 117 37.920

Photos by Phil Wilcox

130   FISH LAKE HOT WELL

● **Near the town of Dyer**

A cement-lined soaking pool on the edge of a barren desert wash in Fish Lake Valley, approximately half way between Reno and Las Vegas. Winter is most beautiful, with snow-capped peaks encircling the valley. Elevation 4,800 feet. Open all year.

Natural mineral water emerges from a well casing at 105° and at a rate of more than fifty gallons per minute. The well was discovered in the 1880s when ranchers were drilling for oil. The well casing is surrounded by a six-foot by six-foot cement sump that maintains a water depth of four feet above a gravel bottom. From there it flows into a large, 102° (often warmer) cement soaking pool that can easily hold ten to twelve people. A three-foot wide cement walk surrounds the pool, with cinder block and wooden benches on three sides. Overflow goes into a large man-made swimming hole stocked with a variety of large goldfish where water temperature measures 95°. Then the water flows into a second pond at 85° and into a third cooler pool. The pool is handicap accessible with assistance. As of this writing, the posted

signs saying no nude bathing were missing, but the custom seems to be clothing optional at your own discretion, depending on the people present.

There is an abundance of level space for overnight parking. Facilities include a fenced-off area around the tub and pools, metal barbeque stands, campfire rings, and trash receptacles. Signs about not trashing or vandalizing the area reflect the feeling that this is now a heavily used party and camping site. Please help keep it clean.

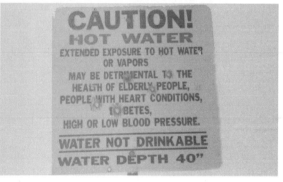

The county is doing its best to keep *Fish Lake* open—please do your best to help. Of interest is the fact that the sign prohibiting nudity has gone missing.

Directions: From the junction of NV 264 and NV 773, go 5.7 miles south on NV 264 to a gravel road on the east side of the highway. Follow this for 7 miles to a fork, then bear left for 0.1 mile to the springs. The gravel road is subject to flash-flood damage and should not be attempted at night.

Source maps: USGS *Davis Mountain* and *Rhyolite Ridge* (well not shown on map).

GPS: N 37 51.600 W 117 59.022

131   WALKER WARM SPRINGS

● **Southwest of the town of Hawthorne**

Cottonwood trees line the river and tall grasses hide a beautifully constructed rock tub up against a hillside in the Nevada desert about 150 yards from the East Walker River. Remote, in the wilds of Western Nevada, right on the California border and below Lake Tahoe. Elevation 4,375 feet. Open all year to high-clearance vehicles only.

Natural mineral water flows directly into a spotless rock and concrete soaking pool, five-feet by eight-feet, two-feet deep, and capable of holding five or six close friends. There is an attached foot washing pool with a plumbed drain. The water at the source comes in at between 110-120°. Check water first before getting in. The only way to cool off the hot water is to haul buckets of cold water from the river (or bring a tennis ball to stop up the valve). Clothing optional.

Unofficial camping at the springs. Good fishing. Bring everything you need with you. All services are thirty-six miles away in Hawthorne.

Directions: From Hawthorne, Nevada, go south on SR 359 for 3.9 miles. Turn right (southwest) on the sometimes-one-lane dirt road called Lucky Boy Pass, not at all recommended for RV's since the road is very crooked and extremely steep. Proceed 18.5 miles to East Walker Rd. and turn right (north). Go 8 miles and turn left (west). At this point the road narrows and becomes much rougher. Go 2 miles and turn right (north) on a rock

A rock bench runs along one side of the pool. The builders used nice flat stones for this pool and the backrest slopes slightly, providing a comfortable rest.

strewn road. Continue 0.5 miles and bear left (the right fork heads into a wash) heading up to the top of the canyon. If you plan to hike in, you should park here and follow the road down into the canyon, passing the remains of a gold mine and an old school bus. Continue walking down the wash to the river. Turn left (upriver) and go 0.4 miles. The spring is on the left opposite the river.

From Bridgeport, CA: Take Hwy 182 towards Yerington, NV (Becomes Hwy 328 at the Nevada state line. 15.1 miles from the 182 turnoff at Bridgeport, turn right on Sweetwater Rd. (Sign indicates that Hawthorne is 38 unpaved miles ahead.) At 30.0 , turn left of E. Walker Rd. At 38.0 miles, turn left. At 39.8 miles turn right, and at 40.3 miles turn left. At 42.6 miles is the old mine operation. At 43.6 miles turn left (right turn is a dead end). At 44.0 miles is the spring.

Warning: High clearance, 4WD required, especially when there are rains and flash floods in the region, Walker River Rd. and Lucky Boy Pass can be closed. Steep, narrow grade with loose gravel and a sandy wash.

Source maps: *NV Gazetteer, Aurora* 15 min.
GPS: N 38 29.460 W 118 58.782

132 WALLEY'S HOT SPRINGS RESORT SPA
PO Box 158   775 782-8155
2001 Foothill Rd.
■ Genoa, NV 89411
www.davidwalleys.com

Tastefully restored 1862 spa and luxury hotel located twelve miles east of Lake Tahoe at the foot of the Sierra Nevada. Elevation 4,700 feet. Open all year.

Natural mineral water flows from several wells at temperatures up to 160° and is then piped to the bathhouse and to six outdoor cement pools (two with jets) where the temperatures are maintained from 96-104°. The cement swimming pool uses bromine-treated creek water and averages 85°. Bathing suits required in the outdoor pools. Handicap accessible.

Overnight accommodations are available. The main building is a two-story health club with separate men's and women's sections, each containing a sauna, steambath and weight training equipment. Massage is also available in each section. Facilities include dining rooms and bars. Major credit cards accepted. Phone for rates and reservations.

Photos by Jayson Loam

In refurbishing *Walley's* the new owners carried on the tradition of relaxed elegance that was the signature of the original resort built in 1862.

Phil Wilcox

133 A   BOWERS MANSION
■   4005 US 395 North   702 849-0644
Carson City, NV 89704

A Washoe County Park with extensive picnic, playground, and parking facilities, in addition to a large swimming pool. Elevation 5,100 feet. Park open all year; pools open every day, noon to five, from early June to late August. Call to verify. There is a charge for using the facilities.

Natural mineral water, pumped from wells at 116°, is combined with cold well water as needed. The swimming pool and children's wading pool are maintained at 83°. Both pools are treated with bromine. Bathing suits are required. Pool and picnic facilities are A.D.A. handicapped accessible.

There are no services available on the premises. Tours of the mansion are conducted from Mother's Day to the end of October. It is four miles to restaurants, motels, service stations, and RV hookups in Carson City.

Directions: Go 10 miles north of Carson City on US 395. Watch for signs and turn west on side road, 1.5 miles to location.

Phil Wilcox

133 B   CARSON HOT SPRINGS
■   1500 Hot Springs Rd.   775 885-8844
Carson City, NV 89706   888 917-3711
www.carsonhotspringsresort.com

Completely remodeled older hot springs, in operation since 1849, with swimming pool and ten large private rooms, each containing a sunken tub comfortable enough for six people. Located in the northeast outskirts of Carson City. Elevation 4,300 feet. Open all year.

Natural mineral water flows out of the ground at 121°. Air spray and evaporative cooling are used to lower the water temperature when pools are drained and refilled each day. No chemicals or city water is added. The outdoor swimming pool temperature is maintained at 98° in the summer and 102° in the winter. Pool temperatures in the newly-refurbished individual rooms can be controlled as desired, from 95-110°. Bathing suits are required in the swimming pool, and are optional in the private rooms.

A complete restaurant and bar with banquet facilities, limited number of motel rooms and a bed and breakfast in a refurbished 1860s home are available on the premises. Dancing on the weekends. RV park under construction. Massage by appointment. Credit cards accepted. It is one mile to a store and service station.

Directions: From US 395 at the north end of Carson City, go east on Hot Springs Rd. 1 mile to springs.

Left: If there are too many kids in the outside pool you can rent an individual room at *Carson Hot Springs* for a bit more privacy.

Photos courtesy of Steamboat Hot Springs

134 STEAMBOAT VILLA HOT SPRINGS SPA
16010 S. Virginia St.   775 853-6600
■ Reno, NV 89511
www.steamboatsprings.org

Historic spa location designated a state historical site. Completely renovated, the lobby looks like a Mexican mansion. Copious amounts of steam billow up from what looks like a mountain, but is actually a tufa mound more than 500 feet high. Elevation 4,500 feet. Open all year. Call for open hours.

Natural mineral water reaches the surface of a hot well across the street at temperatures above 204°, is cooled in holding tanks and fills seven indoor tiled tubs where you can adjust the water temperature to your liking. Each room has a shower and is cleaned after each use. Each private room has a stained glass window. There is also an outside tub open to all guests located behind the building overlooking Steamboat Creek. A rainbow of colors are reflected over the water in the evening. There is also a geothermal steam room. Bathing suits are required in all public areas.

Several modalities of therapeutic massage, and body wraps with a mud formula are offered. T'ai chi, yoga, and aerobics classes are available. Gift shop. Membership plans available. No children under fourteen.

Location: On Hwy 395, 2 miles south of the Mt. Rose intersection at Rhodes Rd. Eleven miles south of Reno.

UTAH

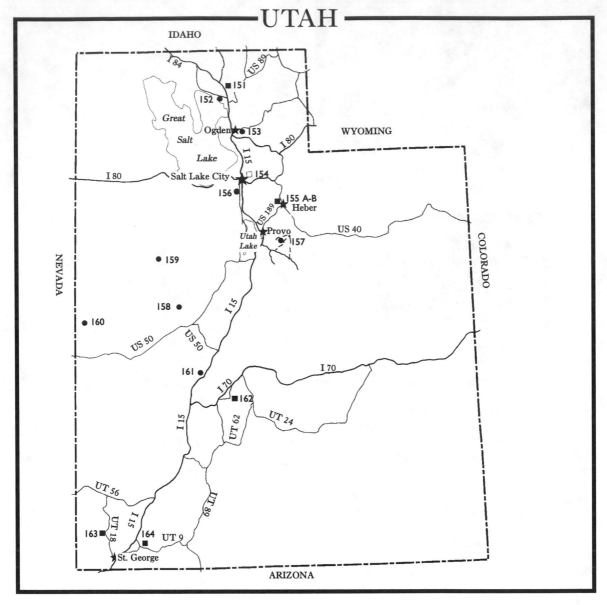

This map was designed to be used with a standard highway map.

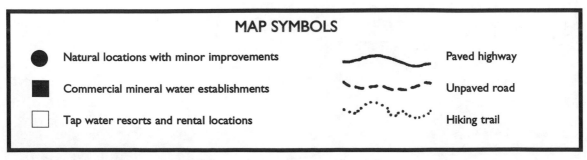

MAP SYMBOLS

● Natural locations with minor improvements

■ Commercial mineral water establishments

□ Tap water resorts and rental locations

⎯⎯ Paved highway

− − − Unpaved road

······· Hiking trail

Chris Andrews

Phil Wilcox

Crystal Hot Springs has been a commercial venture since 1901. The Native Americans, Chinese and Japanese who helped build the nearby railroad certainly didn't have the opportunity to choose among the five different pools with varying temperatures, and water slides were undreamed of.

151   CRYSTAL HOT SPRINGS

8215 North Hwy 38	801 547-0777
Honeyville, UT 84314	435 279-8104

www.crystalhotsprings.net

Small, historical resort featuring one of the world's largest side-by-side hot and cold springs. The property includes spacious, tree-shaded lawns for picnics and camping. Elevation 4,200 feet. Open all year; summer and winter hours.

Natural mineral water flowing out of a hot spring at 120-132° and a cold spring at 52° is piped to an Olympic-size swimming pool, a "soaker pool" large enough to swim in, three outdoor hydrojet pools, the mineral pool, a lap pool and the catch pool for the two waterslides. The pools are filled on a flow-through basis requiring a minimum of chlorine treatment. Various pools on the premises range from temperatures of 85-105°. Lap pool and slide pool are heated during the winter. Facility is handicap accessible with assistance. Bathing suits required.

Group picnic sites are available for parties, the lodge can be reserved for dances, reunions, classes, etc. Locker rooms, sand volleyball court, large camping area and RV hookups are available on the premises. It is two miles to a store and fifteen miles to a motel. Major credit cards accepted.

Directions: From I-15, take the Honeyville exit #372. Go one mile east on UT 240 to UT 38, then 1.7 miles north to the resort on the west side of the highway.

152   INDIAN SPRINGS (STINKY SPRINGS)

● **West of the town of Brigham City**

The latest structure is an architectural delight compared to the previous long history of hastily erected tents. Located alongside a highway in the flat country north of the Great Salt Lake. A sign posted at the spring advises that you use this spring without the owner's or the Utah Department of Health's permission and you should use extreme caution. Elevation 4,000 feet. Open all year.

Natural mineral water flows out of a spring at 118°, through a culvert under the highway, and into three cement soaking pits. Temperature within each pool is controlled by diverting the hot water flow. Volunteers try to keep the party trash to a minimum, but the water does have a sulfur dioxide smell and is often bright green due to algae growth. Be sure to keep the flaps open to provide sufficient air circulation. Clothing optional within the structure.

There are no services available on the premises.

Directions: From I-15, take exit 368 and travel 2.4 miles west to the town of Corinne. Bear left at the fork and travel a little over 6 miles to the springs. The springs are on the south side of the road shortly before you reach Little Mountain, a rocky hill on the north side of the road.

GPS: N 41 34.566 W 112 14.022   Phil Wilcox

Phil Wilcox

153 OGDEN HOT SPRINGS

● **East of the city of Ogden**

Small, primitive hot springs at the river's edge, located in a beautiful river gorge in Ogden Canyon. Elevation 4,800 feet. Open all year, subject to annual flooding.

Natural mineral water flows out of a spring at 130° and through a pipe and hoses to a volunteer-built, rock and mud pool at 107°. The water continues flowing into a rock and cement-bottomed pool at 101°. The sides have been built up to prevent the entrance of river water. The temperature is controlled by diverting the hoses when desired. Another small tub has been built downstream. The apparent local custom is clothing optional, even though the highway is visible.

There are no services available on the premises.

Directions: Exit I-15 in Ogden at SR 39 (12th St.) and go east 4.9 miles to the mouth of Ogden Canyon. Park on either side of the road just after passing under suspended water pipe. Short trail downstream to spring starts at mile 9 green marker. (If pulling a trailer, go 1 mile farther upstream to a turnaround and come back to park.)

GPS: N 41 14.154 W 111 55.452

154 WASATCH SPAS
3955 S. State St.   801 264-TUBS
Salt Lake City, UT 84107

Private hot tub rentals, plus spa sales and service, on a main street in Salt Lake City.

Four indoor rooms and one out-of-doors area enclosed by a beautiful redwood gazebo are for rent to the public by the hour. Temperatures are set at 102° and tubs are treated with bromine. Major credit cards are accepted. Phone or email (hottubs@aros.net) for rates, reservations, and directions.

155A MOUNTAIN SPAA RESORT
800 N. Mountain Spaa Lane   435 654-0807
■   Midway, UT 84049   435 654-0721

Historic, rustic resort located in beautiful Heber Valley, one mile from Wasatch Mountain State Park. Elevation 5,700 feet. Open from Memorial Day to Labor Day on Thursday, Friday, and Saturday.

Natural mineral water flows from cone-shaped tufa craters at 120° and is piped to two pools. The outdoor swimming pool, with kiddie slide and large deck area, is maintained at 86-98°. The indoor swimming pool, built inside a large crater, maintains a temperature of 87-103°. Both pools are drained twice weekly, disinfected, and refilled.

Guest house, cabins, soda fountain, snack bar, game room, locker rooms, lawn and picnic area, overnight camping, and RV hookups are available on the premises. Banquet room and pavilion facilities available for large groups. Credit cards accepted.

Directions: From Heber City on US 189, go west on UT 113 to the town of Midway. Turn north on River Rd., go 0.7 miles to 600 North in Midway, and follow signs to the resort.

Chris Andrews

Courtesy of The Homestead

155 B THE HOMESTEAD

◼ 700 N. Homestead Dr.   435 654-1102
Midway, UT 84049   800 327-7220
www.homesteadresort.com

Tucked up against Utah's Wasatch Mountains, the resort offers a spectacular setting and a wide array of activities, amenities, conference space and accommodations for both groups and vacationers. Open all year.

The Homestead Crater is a 55-foot high rock dome that contains a mineral-rich hot spring. A 110-foot tunnel was hollowed out at the north side of the crater in 1996, which provided access to the hot springs inner depths. The crater maintains a year-round temperature of approximately 95° and serves as a world-famous swimming, snorkeling and scuba diving facility. The Crater is open to the public.

Crater mineral water is piped to one small outdoor mineral bath that averages 100° and is non-chemically treated. The large outdoor swimming pool is maintained at 85°, the indoor hydro jet pool at 102°, and the indoor pool at 85°. There is also a dry sauna available. Pool use is available to registered guests and pool members.

The Homestead Resort's 18-hole championship golf course has the distinction of being the only course in Utah located on the premises of a conference resort. The course has a putting green, chipping green, driving range, equipment and cart rental and an award-winning golf shop.

The Homestead is a four-season, full-service resort with a variety of activities that will excite you and at the same time provide relaxation.

Available on the premises are hotel rooms, suites and condominiums. A full service resort spa is available as well as dining rooms and a pub. In the summer, golf; and Corporate Wellness Teambuilding, such as Orienteering, Pioneering Skills and Geo-Caching are available. Horseback riding; mountain biking; wagon and buggy rides; tennis, and lawn games are favorites also. During the winter enjoy snowmobile tours, cross-country skiing, sleigh rides, Alpine skiing; and snowshoeing. Go to the Homestead website, www.homesteadresort.com, to review current packages.

Homestead is located approximately two miles from stores, service stations and RV hookups. Major credit cards accepted.

Directions: From Heber City on U.S. 189, go west on UT 113 to the town of Midway and follow the green directional signs to the resort.

● **South of Salt Lake City**

Sulfur-free hot water fills a newly built soaking pool, located at the southern end of the Salt Lake Valley near the Jordan River. Elevation 4,480 feet. Open all year.

Natural mineral water is piped out of Crystal Springs where it collects in a hot pond near the Jordan River. A new soaking pool has just been completed, using the water flow from this pond as its source. The concrete and mortar pool has been built with a hot water supply pipe and faucet, and also includes a drainage pipe for easy cleaning. Once the pool is filled you must turn off the faucet and allow the water to cool as it comes in at 150°. It will cool to soaking temperatures in about an hour. Be sure to unplug the drain after soaking so that algae have no chance to develop. The pool is four-feet deep at one end, with built-in seats, steps and a handrail. The pool is located in an area of thick foliage, so it remains secluded among the olive trees and grasses.

There is no camping on the premises due to the urban location. All services can be found just a short distance away.

Directions: There are two ways to reach the soaking pool.

The Short Way: Approach from the south. Take Exit 293 (Bangerter Highway) from I-15. Travel west for 1.6 miles. Park in a dirt turnout on the north side of Bangerter Highway where the highway crosses the Jordan River. Walk around the locked gate and fence and go to the paved Jordan River Parkway jogging/bike path. (Don't worry; the locked gate is to keep vehicles from entering the area.) Travel north on the Parkway Path for 0.75 miles. About 20 yards before you reach the hot pond of water, look for a dirt path that goes down toward the river. This path will lead you to the soaking pool that is nestled down in the privacy of the trees below the hot pond and above the Jordan River.

Soakers Bible

The Long Way: Approach from the north. Take Exit 294 (12300 South) from I-15. Travel 1.4 miles west on 12300 South to where 12300 South crosses the Jordan River, and park at the parking lot. Take the paved jogging/bike path for 2 miles where you will crest the top of a hill. Below you will see a hot pond of water that is 100 yards long. The soaking pool is located in the trees below the pond, but above the river. To find the path that leads to the soaking pool, continue south down the paved jogging/bike path. At 20 yards past the pond look for a dirt path that goes toward the river. This path leads you to a wonderful soak.

Sally Jackson

157 FIFTH WATER CANYON HOT SPRINGS
(also known as Diamond Fork)

● Near Spanish Fork (South of Provo)

Three delightful sections of rock pools in a beautiful canyon at the end of an easy hike, with a flowing creek and a large waterfall. Elevation 5,800 feet. Open all year.

The upper set consists of three ingeniously crafted rock and cement pools, all nicely shaded by tall trees, with stone steps, shelves. The lowest one is about 150 feet downstream from the upper pair. Continue downstream to find the breathtakingly beautiful, unshaded waterfall area. Thousands of gallons of hot water of varying temperatures flow out of the canyon walls on both sides of the stream and up out of the stream bed (in some cases making small gushers) into at least three different soaking pools, mostly all hotter than the uppermost set of pools with the exception of the waterfall pool, which ranges from cool in the middle under the waterfall to scalding on either side, depending on stream flow. The waterfall itself ranges from freezing cold to tepid, varying with the season and stream flow. Walk a few more yards downstream to find yet another set of unshaded rock and cement pools, a couple of which are very skillfully built against the edge of a small cliff and fed by a plastic hot water pipe which can be moved aside. All pools in all areas can be temperature controlled to some extent by letting in less or more cold creek water or moving the hot water inflow. Discretion is needed when skinny dipping as authorities have been know to issue citations.

There are no services on the premises, but overnight camping is not prohibited at the trailhead and at the many pullout spots along the creek. Bring water and supplies with you.

Directions: At Spanish Fork, south of Provo, Utah, on I-15 northbound, take exit 260 east; if southbound, take exit 261 east. Go east on US Rt 6 for 10.7 miles, passing Diamond Fork Road on the left. Go east on US 6 for 11 miles until you reach the Diamond CG turnoff on the left.

Phil Wilcox

Fifth Water Canyon Hot Springs is indeed the jewel in Utah's crown. The best hot spring in the state offers three hot soaking pools and a spectacular waterfall.

Take this road for 9.4 miles to the "Three Forks" trailhead (this forest service sign is not easily seen from the road). There is limited parking in very small turnouts. From here ford the stream, pass the toilet block and head 2.4 miles upstream. Cross the stream and start up the trail. Stay straight and do not turn right at the second bridge. After 1 mile cross the large foot bridge and follow the well-defined trail 1.5 miles. This paved road climbs steeply and has many sharp curves, but is okay for large vehicles. At 13.2 miles from US 6, park at the Fifth Water trailhead. Close any gates that you need to open to pass through. Don't worry if there are many cows about; just walk through them and they will move aside. Hike downstream for one hour, descending 750 feet. Unless you're in great shape, plan on at least 1.5 hours for the hike out. Some people ride in on horseback or mountain bikes and as far as we could tell, trail motorcycle access is allowed. When a slight sulphur odor can be smelled, look for steep trails down to the left leading to the pools. Watch your children carefully as there are rattlesnakes in the area!

GPS: N 40 04.962 W 111 19.080

Phil Wilcox

Soakers Bible

While this can be a great place to soak, it is also quite the party place. Help keep it clean by packing out more than you carried in.

158   BAKER HOT SPRINGS

● **Northwest of Delta**

Concrete soaking pools and a great place to relax are all that remain of an old resort located in the high desert in western Utah. Elevation 4,600 feet. Open all year although roads are not maintained.

Natural mineral water flows out of a spring at 135° into an earthen channel which directly feeds the three five-foot by eight-foot soaking pools. Each pool has a set of stairs leading down into the two-foot deep tubs. Cold spring water runs through a parallel channel and can be piped to each tub to cool the water to a comfortable temperature. The water in the tubs was measured at 128°, 100° and 91°. Handicap accessible with minimal assistance. Clothing optional.

There are no facilities available on the premises but there is plenty of open land which can be used for camping. North of the pools there are many seeps which could fill a dug-out soaking pool away from the main area. Bring a shovel. All services are twenty-seven miles away in Delta.

Directions: From the junction of US 6 and UT 174 (10 miles northeast of Delta) drive west on 174 for 19.3 miles. Turn right on a good gravel road and drive 7.1 miles. Turn right into springs parking area.

Note: If you have a good atlas you can drive dirt roads to Baker, then to Wilson and then on to Gandy. The roads are fairly well marked and easily traveled.

GPS: N 39 36.630 W 112 43.824

159   WILSON HEALTH SPRINGS

● **Northwest of Delta**

Located on the salt flats near a very large hot source pool in the high Utah desert at the south edge of the Wendover Bombing and Gunnery Range. Elevation 4,500 feet. Open all year although roads are not maintained.

Natural mineral water at 120° flows through two channels dug out of the clay directly into tubs set into the ground. There is no way to control the hot water except by letting it cool as it heads away from the source, so be careful. A smaller, very shallow, cooler pool was dug downstream. Clothing optional.

There are no facilities on the premises but lots of places for unofficial camping nearby. (Camping at Baker or Gandy is more appealing.) All services are located ninety-five miles away in Delta or 120 miles away in Wendover.

Directions: from intersection of gravel road to Baker Hot Springs and CR 174, travel west (174 ends and becomes Rte. 1958) to end of pavement. Continue straight on gravel road for 14.8 miles to a "T." Turn left and almost immediately enter the Fish Springs National "Wildlife Refuge. Drive 4.9 miles past the ranger station and turn right on a gravel road by an old burned out bus. Drive about 0.4 miles (don't go any further or you could wind up in a bog). Walk about 100 yards past the second abandoned bus to a slight reddish-colored rise where the first very hot spring hole can be found. Proceed very carefully to the second hole as the roads and paths are often a muddy quagmire during any season.

Source map: USGS *Fish Springs NW* (spring not on map).

GPS: N 39 54.390 W 113 25.813

Don't forget to bring a water-proof flashlight to explore the forty-foot long cave beneath the waterfall.

160   GANDY WARM SPRINGS

● **Northwest of Delta**

Refreshing warm waterfalls, caves and a large pond to soak in makes this a must on a warm day. At the base of a large volcano-shaped butte in the high Utah desert, not far from the Utah-Nevada border. Elevation 5,300 feet. Open all year although roads are not maintained.

Natural mineral water flows from a spring at over 4,400 gallons per minute at a temperature of 82°. The warm water flows through a large creek to fill the sandy-bottom swimming hole which is two- to four-feet deep. Temperatures range between 78-82° depending on winds and air temperature. Handicap accessible with assistance. While the local custom seems to be clothing optional, it is a good idea to have a suit handy.

There are no facilities available on the premises but there is plenty of open land which can be used for camping and at least two good RV spaces. Basic services are available in Baker, NV forty-two miles away. All services can be found in Delta, UT 114 miles away.

Directions: From north (Wilson Health Springs) follow main dirt road toward Gandy sign on east side of road, only visible if traveling north. Just north of this sign are 2 pump houses on east side or road. Take dirt road on west side and stay on this main road for about 2.7 miles. Bear right near end of road heading yourself towards the volcano-shaped butte. If coming north from US 50, turn north on gravel road just east of Border RV park and store and drive about 28 miles to Gandy sign and then west where 2 pump houses are on east side of road.

GPS: N 39 27.594 W 114 02.226

161   MEADOW HOT SPRINGS

● **South of Provo, near Meadow**

Two large pools, formed from travertine or mineral deposits, with ample sitting room on underwater stone ledges. Located in the pasture lands of Utah with unobstructed views of the Pahvant Mountain Range. Elevation 5,200 feet. Open all year.

Natural mineral water flows up through the bottom from an undeveloped cave to fill a beautifully clear, room-size pool, more than twenty-feet deep, at 100°. Heavy ropes pulled through a PVC pipe are anchored across the pool, allowing you to remain on the surface while viewing the clear, deeper portions of the pool. There is a distinct foot track through the grasss leading to a cooler second pool located about 200 yards south of the first pool. Handicap accessible with assistance. Owner-posted sign: "No Nudity. People caught with their pants down will be prosecuted and persecuted."

There are no facilities on the premises, but overnight parking is not prohibited. Overnighters should park away from the gate to avoid being disturbed. It is six miles to a store in Meadow.

Directions: From I-15 (south of Provo) take exit 158 at Meadow. From Meadow on the east side of I-15, go south on Hwy 133 for 1.6 miles, turning right (west) on the gravel road 0.5 miles south of mile marker 6. Head straight west for 5 miles to the end of the road. Spring is about 200 yards south. A chainlink fence with walk-through gate has been installed at the parking lot.

GPS: N 38 51.876 W 112 30.198   Photos by Phil Wilcox

The pipe strung across the pool allows you to hold on to something as you gently bob around in this very deep pool.

Photos by Phil Wilcox

162 MYSTIC HOT SPRINGS OF MONROE

475 East 100 North   435 527-3286
Monroe, UT 84754
www.mystichotsprings.com

One hundred thirty-three acres, adjoining a national forest, allows for sightings of bald eagles and visits to Indian ruins, and overlooks the Sevier Valley with spectacular mountain views. Elevation 5,200 feet. Open all year.

Natural mineral water flows at 200 gallons per minute out of a spring at 168°, cooling as it flows across the mountains into two soaking pools where the temperature ranges from 92-102°. A huge travertine mound engulfs seven bathtubs offering a soak for one or two people. The water then flows on to the natural tropical fish ponds. Bathing suits required.

Biking and hiking trails, picnic area, camping, full RV hookups, pioneer cabins, tepees, and a sweat lodge are available on the premises. Showers, toilets etc. are available at the RV park. An ongoing concert program is presented for your enjoyment. Check the web site for current schedule. It is a short walk to the large and colorful Red Hill Spring. A service station is within four blocks. Soaking is available for day use or free with overnight stay. No alcohol. Credit cards accepted.

Directions: From the intersection of Main St. and 100 N in the town of Monroe (Mystic sign on pole at intersection) proceed east on 100 N to the very end of the road where springs and registration office are located (office at RV park which you will pass first is not staffed).

701   GROVER HOT SPRINGS
        Box 188   530 694-2248
■   Markleeville, CA 96120

Swimming pool and soaking pool next to a major state campground and picnic area, located in a wooded mountain valley. Elevation 6,000 feet. Open all year.

Natural mineral water flows out of several springs at 147° and into a holding pond from which it is piped to the pool area. The soaking pool, using natural mineral water treated with bromine, is maintained at approximately 103°. The swimming pool, using domestic water treated with chlorine, is maintained at 70-80°. Domestic water is used to cool down the hot mineral water. Admission is on a first-come, first-served basis, and the official capacity limit of fifty persons in the hot pool and twenty-five in the cold pool is reached early every day during the summer. Bathing suits are required. For handicap accessibility there is a ramp to the pool, although there is not a ramp into the pool. Bathrooms and parking spaces are provided.

Campground spaces are available by prior reservation, as with all other California state parks. Cross-country skiers are encouraged to camp in the picnic area during the winter and to ski in to use the soaking pool. The road is also plowed during the winter making for easy access. It is four miles to the nearest restaurant, motel, and service station in Markleeville.

Location: On Alpine County Road E4, 4.5 miles west of Markleeville. Follow the signs.

Photos by Mark Gillespie

In summer, as big as this hot soaking pool is, it fills up very quickly. In winter, skiing or driving in lets you soak almost by yourself.

Wonderful hot springs with beautiful mountain views are to be found along the banks of the East Fork of the Carson River in Toiyabe National Forest. The springs are accessible during the rafting season, approximately May through July, depending on water flow. Elevation 5,000 feet.

There are no services available at any of the hot spring sites, although the BLM has installed out-houses at the major springs. While the apparent local custom at the pools is clothing optional, please be respectful of those people already there. These springs are not shown on any Forest Service or USGS map but are well known to raft trip guides.

While you can navigate this river yourself if you are an experienced kayaker, for a real treat, one-day and two-day raft trips (Class 2 rapids) are available through commercial outfitters.

Note: It is possible to access this spring by car from Gardnerville, however, according to all reports, it is at the end of "seven of the most miserable miles a 4 WD can handle." It also takes you across a working ranch; during the months of April to November they really do not want you on the property. During the other months you must stay out of the fields and travel only on the road. The field hands will chase you out of the area. An extremely steep trail requiring the 4 WD vehicle puts you down at the river's edge where there is a campground and outhouse on BLM land. **River Run** is located directly across the river and in plain sight. During low water time in the summer you can walk or drive very carefully across the river. The spring is totally inaccessible during high spring runoff except by raft.

GPS: N 38 46.049 W 119 43.310

Marjorie Young

702 A   RIVERSIDE HOT SPRING

● **Near the town of Markleeville**

Approximately eight miles downstream from where you put into the water three small pools are visible from the river on your right (east). Natural mineral water flows into the upper pool at approximately 92° and then continues flowing into the lower pools. The lower tub has been lined with a tarp by some volunteers. During high water these pools are often underwater and need to be rebuilt annually.

Camping is possible near the springs.

702 B   HILLSIDE HOT SPRINGS

● **Near the town of Markleeville**

Just before you round the bend to get to River Run a small pool has been built of rock and cement that will hold four to six people comfortably. The water was 104° but varies with the ambient temperature.

Mark Gillespie

You can also get to this pool by hiking around the bend from *River Run Hot Springs*.

Debbie Johnson

Saturday nights find trucks crossing the river to get to *River Run* often making this pool "the party spot"—rather noisy and very crowded. Early in the morning it was lovely to find the pool almost empty.

702 C   RIVER RUN HOT SPRINGS

● **Near the town of Markleeville**

Natural mineral water emerges from several springs on the hillside at 110° or hotter and cools as it flows toward the river. The temperature of the water drops to approximately 100° by the time it reaches the large cement and river stone pool on the edge of an eight-foot cliff above the river. The large pool is equipped with fill spout and drain and is about four feet deep. The small upper pools are quite hot and should be approached with caution.

There is a large open area available for camping, but there are no facilities except an outhouse near the springs.

702 D   HOT SHOWERBATH

● **Near the town of Markleeville**

One mile downstream from River Run Hot Springs, a small pullout is visible on the left (west). Due to earthquakes and other natural phenomena the water only trickles over the embankment and the pool is barely ankle deep.

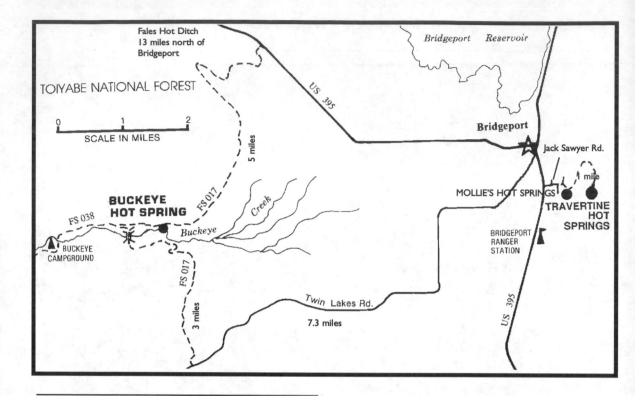

703   FALES HOT DITCH

● **North of the town of Bridgeport**

A primitive pool on Hot Springs Creek in the sage-brush foothills of the Eastern Sierra. Elevation 7,200 feet. Open all year.

Natural mineral water emerges at 140° from a spring on the property of an old resort, now closed, and flows down Hot Springs Creek, gradually cooling as it goes. Volunteers have dammed the creek to form a thigh-deep, rock and sand pool, ten-feet by twelve-feet and four-feet deep on the east side of the highway 0.3 miles past the old resort (which is on the west side of the highway). Although the soaking pool is twenty feet below the highway and out of sight of passing vehicles, it is advisable to wear a bathing suit or have it close at hand.

There are no services on the premises. It is seven miles to a Forest Service campground and thirteen miles to all other services in Bridgeport.

Directions: From Bridgeport, drive north on US 395 for 13 miles to a boarded-up, fenced, brown wooden structure that used to be Fales Hot Springs Resort (on the west side of US 395). The gated property just north of the old resort is private and posted "no trespassing." However, from the old resort, drive 0.3 miles north and park along the shoulder of US 395 on the east side of the road. The pullout is right before mile marker 90. The creek and soaking pool are 20 feet below the highway (not visible until you park and look over the small cliff).

GPS: N 38.21.152 W 119 24.290

Marjorie Young

Jayson Loam

Along with these soaking pools by the river, there is a small cave (to the left under the overhang) where the water drips off the roof forming a soaking area.

---

704   BUCKEYE HOT SPRING

(see map on page 148)

●   **Near the town of Bridgeport**

Delightful hot spring in a superb natural setting on the north bank of Buckeye Creek in Toiyabe National Forest. One of the best. Elevation 6,900 feet. Open all year; not accessible by road in winter.

Natural mineral water flows out of the ground at 135°, runs over a large cliff built up by mineral deposits, and drops into the creek. Volunteers have built loosely constructed rock pools along the edge of the creek below the hot waterfall. The pool temperature is controlled by admitting more or less cold water from the creek. A new dam and drain has been added to the upper pool.

There is another small outflow of hot geothermal water on the bluff near the parking area. Volunteers have dug a new, larager soaking pool that maintains a temperature of approximately 100°. It is near the foot of the only pine located in the upstream direction from the parking area. The apparent local custom at both pools is clothing optional, however during the day there are usually clothed families there with young children.

Three hundred yards upstream from the parking area are several acres of unmarked open space on which overnight parking is not prohibited. It is one mile to a Forest Service campground and nine miles to all services in Bridgeport. Twin Lakes, a bit closer, also provides gas, food, and a campground. There is a parking turnout on the south side of the road on the bluff above the springs.

Directions: (This is the easier route.) At the north end of Bridgeport, take Twin Lakes Rd. west for 7.3 miles to Doc & Al's Resort. Turn right (north) onto FS 017, a two-lane, graded, washboard road, for 3 miles to the second bridge over the creek, where the road intersects with FS 038 toward Buckeye Campground to the left. Branch off to the right for a few hundred yards up a short hill on the north branch of FS 017 to a large flat parking clearing on a big knoll. The upper pool is a few steps away (slightly downhill and to the right) under a tree, at the crest of the knoll overlooking Buckeye Creek. Several unofficial paths lead down the slope to the pools located along the creek at the foot of a large mound covered over by the mineral deposits.

Source maps: *Toiyabe National Forest*, USGS *Matterhorn Peak*.

GPS: N 38 14.384 W 119 19.568

Debbie Johnson

This pool on the hillside has recently been enlarged so that it will now hold at least four people.

Sally Jackson

Soakers Bible

Travertine Hot Springs is named after the mineral which has built up here to form this tufa mound. The area around the pools is carefully maintained so please stay on the trails to help conserve the fragile vegetation.

705 A   TRAVERTINE HOT SPRINGS
(see map on page 148)
● **Southeast of the town of Bridgeport**

An unusual group of volunteer-built soaking pools on large travertine ridges with commanding views of the High Sierra. Located two miles from the center of Bridgeport. Elevation 6,700 feet. Open all year; wet weather can turn road into a slippery slide.

The flow of natural mineral water (115-156°) out of several geothermal fissures can be interrupted or shifted to a new outlet by underground movement resulting from local earthquakes. The scalding water is channeled to a series of volunteer-built soaking pools in which the individual pool temperatures are controlled by temporarily diverting the hot water inflow as needed. The upper pool is handicap accessible with assistance. Clothing optional, but determined by who is there first.

At the upper ten- by five- by two-foot deep pool, scalding water issues out from a small hole and is directed through a stepped channel with a "bear claw" configuration at pool's edge. The source is diverted to control pool temperature. There is a plug for draining and cleaning the pool, which is done fastidiously by volunteers. Overflow goes into a small adjoining foot bath for rinsing off before entering the pool. Since you can drive right up to this pool it is handicap accessible with assistance.

Four lower wood, rock-and-cement pools, one-hundred yards below, are at the foot of a large travertine ridge the water is channeled along the top of the ridge into the pools at about 100°. A primitive 80° rock and mud pool nearby is fed by a separate underground source. The first and hottest small pool was built in the early 1900s for dipping sheep and original boards still exist.

There are no services and overnight camping is not permitted. Other primitive amenities include a large deck around the pools covered with old carpets for sunbathing, a picnic table, and "butt cans." There is no trash collection, so please pack it out. All other services are in Bridgeport.

Directions: From the ranger station 0.5 miles south of Bridgeport, drive north on Hwy 395 for 0.2 miles. Turn right on Jack Sawyer Rd., the first paved road on your right. At 0.4 miles the paved road makes a 90-degree turn to the right. Do not bear right. Continue straight ahead on the unpaved, ungraded road for approximately 1 mile to the pools. On the way you will pass a sign on your left to Bridgeport Barrow Pit; continue straight to the forest service sign on your left. If you continue straight, the second turnoff just ahead on the right leads to the lower pools. Or continue uphill to where the road curves around to the right to reach the upper cement pool.

GPS: N 38 14.729 W 119 12.323

Pictures top and right by Camilla Van Sickle and Bill Pennington

705 B   MOLLIE'S HOT SPRINGS

(see map on page 148)
● Southeast of the town of Bridgeport

Carefully built to use all the available flow, this hot springs in built on public land by special people and offers great views in all directions.

Natural mineral water flows into a three- to four-person tub carefully built out of rock and with a squishy bottom. A wood bench offers a place to enjoy the view. Clothing optional.

Directions: From the lower pools at Travertine Hot Springs, walk due west toward US 395, angling slightly left toward the high travertine wall that also runs approximately west. After 100 yards, cross over that wall where it has crumbled nearly down to grade, heading approximately southwest. In a short time, a primitive road becomes visible, along with a tall pole due south of the road which runs approximately east to west. With the pole straight ahead, the pool is just on the south side of the primitive road, almost invisible in the surrounding white stones, mostly travertine. The large white board beam of a bench, nearly the same color as the rocks, may be easy to spot because its shape stands out from the rocks.

Two of the regional contributors to this book, Petty Prange and Bill Pennington, enjoying a soak.

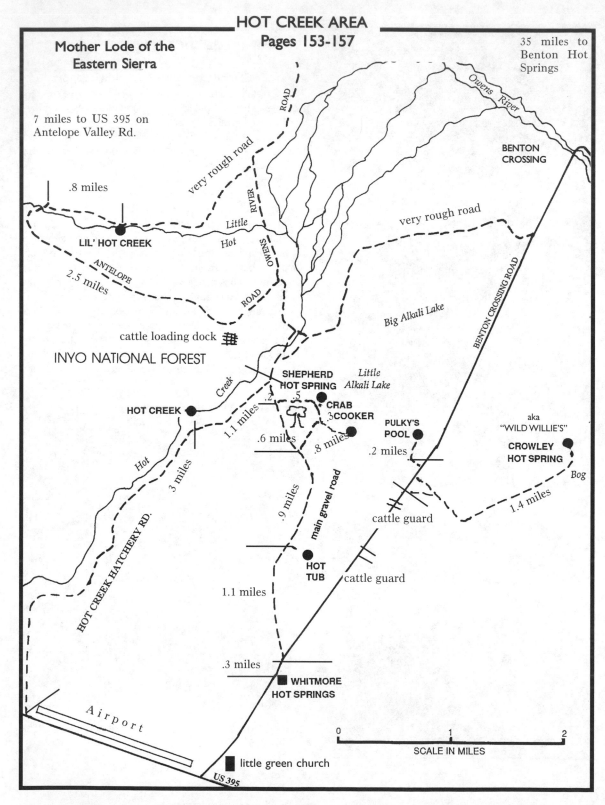

**Mother Lode of the
Eastern Sierra**

35 miles to
Benton Hot
Springs

7 miles to US 395 on
Antelope Valley Rd.

Owens River

**BENTON
CROSSING**

very rough road

very rough road

.8 miles

ROAD

RIVER

Little

LIL' HOT CREEK

Hot

OWENS

ANTELOPE

2.5 miles

ROAD

Big Alkali Lake

BENTON CROSSING ROAD

cattle loading dock

INYO NATIONAL FOREST

Creek

**SHEPHERD
HOT SPRING**

*Little
Alkali Lake*

.2   .5

**CRAB
COOKER**

HOT CREEK

1.1 miles

.3

**PULKY'S
POOL**

aka
"WILD WILLIE'S"

.6 miles

.8 miles

.2 miles

**CROWLEY
HOT SPRING**

Hot

3 miles

.9 miles

Bog

HOT CREEK HATCHERY RD.

main gravel road

cattle guard

1.4 miles

**HOT
TUB**

cattle guard

1.1 miles

.3 miles

**WHITMORE
HOT SPRINGS**

Airport

■ little green church

0	1	2

SCALE IN MILES

US 395

At the time of this printing, Hot Creek is closed for soaking. No final decision has been made as to whether or not it will be reopened for public use.

Photos by Phil Wilcox

706 A   HOT CREEK

(see map on page 152)

● **East of the town of Mammoth Lakes**

Primarily a geologic observation and interpretive site with some limited use by bathers. Open daylight hours only.

Natural mineral water with a slight sulfur smell emerges from many fissures as steam or boiling water, and several danger areas have been fenced off for safety. Substantial amounts of boiling, geothermal water also flow up from the bottom of the creek. A bend in the creek provides a natural eddy in which the mixing of hot and cold water stays within a range of 50° to 110°. Those who venture into this confluence experience vivid thermal skin effects, but they must be careful to avoid the geothermal vents because of the danger of scalding. The trail from the main pool goes upstream 400-500 feet where cold water is diverted around other hot spots in the river. Bathing suits required.

In the past, night use of this location has resulted in many injuries and some fatalities, so the area may be used only from sunrise to sunset. Citations are issued by the Forest Service to anyone found there after sunset or before sunrise. During the winter, when snow blocks the access road, skiers and hikers may still enter the area during daylight hours.

Facilities include men's and women's changing rooms, pit toilets, and an asphalt parking area with a paved, fenced pathway down to the creek, making the area handicap accessible with assistance. Overnight parking is prohibited. It is ten miles to all services in the town of Mammoth Lakes.

Directions: From US 395, 3 miles south of the Mammoth Lakes turnoff, turn east on Hot Creek Hatchery Rd./Airport. At 0.5 miles, turn right at the sign to "Hot Creek Geothermal Area." From this sign, it is 3 miles to the parking area for Hot Creek. Only the first 1.2 miles are paved. Or, from Benton Crossing Rd., take 3S50, the main gravel road, for 2.8 miles. Turn left for 0.3 miles to the Hot Creek gate and another 0.8 mile to the parking area.

Source maps: *Inyo National Forest*, USGS *Mt. Morrison*.

GPS: N 37 39.629 W 118 49.700

Bill Franks

Dave Bybee

706 B   LIL' HOT CREEK

(see map on page 152)

● **East of the town of Mammoth Lakes**

A very hot flowing creek fed by a 180° geothermal spring. The name Lil' Hot Creek has been given to a large, squishy-bottom soaking pool, six feet across, located just below where the flow from several cold springs cools the hot stream to approximately 107°. The thigh-deep cement and rock pool, three feet deep, has tiered seats used as steps, so you can soak at different depths. Pool temperature can be controlled by opening or capping a four-inch plastic pipe that brings the water in from the nearby creek. There's a plug for draining and cleaning the pool. Spillover goes through a tiny channel back to the creek. As you leave, please shut the inflow of hot water so the next ones in will not be scalded–water can get up to 120-125°.

Wood benches and a boardwalk edge one side of the cement pool. Plenty of level ground, as well as hideaway spots among the pine trees in the nearby national forest, are available where overnight parking is not prohibited. The apparent local custom is clothing optional.

Directions: There are four routes, depending on your starting point.

1. (This is the best.) From the main gravel road (3S50, Benton Crossing Rd.), drive a total of 3.3 miles to the sign for Owens River Rd. (This is 0.7 miles past the turnoff to Shepherd.) You'll pass a cattle loading dock on the left just before Owens River Rd. Turn left for 0.7 miles to Little Antelope Rd. Turn left onto Antelope Rd. for 2.5 miles across a flat open area. At 2.5 miles, at the beginning of the pine forest, is a cattle guard. Make a sharp right just past the cattle guard and follow this very rough, ungraded

Hot water from the tub is recycled back into the hot stream. Water temperature varies greatly, often up to 120 degrees, so be careful! Nearby brooms and scrub brushes are evidence that volunteers continually maintain the pools.

dirt road for 0.8 miles to the springs on your right. Whenever the road forks, keep bearing right, following the fence until you come to a flat open area for parking. You'll see steam rising from the creek to your right as you follow the fence. At the parking area, look for a small wooden portion in the wire fence and a cattle-proof entrance. Go through the gate and over log planks across the creek to reach the hot soaking pool.

2. Take Hot Creek Hatchery Rd. from US 395 for 3 miles to the Hot Creek asphalt parking area. Continue past the parking area for another 1.1 miles to a fork in the unpaved road. Do not bear right, but continue straight ahead for another 0.1 mile to where the road ends at a wide gravel road. This is 3S50, the main gravel road. Turn left, and on your left you'll see the cattle loading dock mentioned above. Follow directions above.

3. A very beautiful but much longer drive begins at US 395. At the turnoff to Mammoth Lake, instead of heading west toward the lakes, turn east and follow the sign to Little Antelope Valley (not Chalk Hills). At 6.3 miles you will be at the cattle guard at the edge of the pine forest. Turn left onto the ungraded dirt road and follow the fence as described above to reach the soaking pool.

4. For those with 4WD vehicles, or at least with good clearance, continue past the turnoff to Antelope Rd. another 1.3 miles and turn left. Follow the washboard road 2 miles to the springs, which are now on the left.

GPS: N 37 53.416 W 118 50.555

Camilla Van Sickle and Bill Pennington

At present, there is no water in *Crab Cooker*. However, several people have offered to go in and replace the valve and piping to make it useable again.

Betty Prange

Crab Cooker overlooks a boggy meadow with mountains forming a stunning backdrop.

706 C   SHEPHERD HOT SPRING
(see map on page 152)

● **East of the town of Mammoth Lakes**

Natural mineral water flows out of a spring and through a plastic pipe to a twenty by twenty-four inch deep rock and cement tub. There are benches in the pool, which is large enough for three or four people. Pool temperature is controlled by diverting the hot water flow from the nearby source pool which can often be as hot as 130°. The white plastic inflow pipe has a ball valve to control the flow and if allowed to run the temperature in the pool can be very, very hot—be careful. There is a plug for draining the pool, capped with a tennis ball. However, local volunteers prefer emptying the pool with a bucket before scrubbing. A scrub brush is on site.

There are no facilities except a primitive campfire ring. A posted sign prohibits overnight parking. The apparent local custom is clothing optional.

Directions: From Benton Crossing Rd., turn north on 3S50 (the main gravel road) 0.3 miles past the Whitmore public swimming pool. Drive 2.6 miles to a dirt road on your right. Follow this across an open bog for 0.5 miles to the pool on your left.

From Crab Cooker, follow the dirt road back the way you came in for 0.5 miles to a four-way, dirt-road intersection. To reach Shepherd, turn right at this intersection and go 0.2 miles to the small clearing where the pool is located.

GPS: N 37 40.014 W 118 48.213

706 D   CRAB COOKER
(see map on page 152)

● **East of the town of Mammoth Lakes**

Natural mineral water flows out of a spring at over 120° and through a cement casing across the road to a rock-and-cement soaking pool. The pool temperature can be controlled by turning off a valve just outside the pool when the desired soaking temperature is reached. (Please turn off this valve when leaving so as not to scald the next soakers.) Do not tamper with the pipes in the nearby well, as special plumbing equipment is required to fix them.

There are no facilities on the premises. The apparent local custom is clothing optional.

Directions: Follow the main gravel road for 2 miles from Benton Crossing Rd. (0.9 miles past the turnoff to Hot Tub). Watch for a lone juniper tree on the right side of the road. The road to Crab Cooker is on the right just before this tree. Two separate roads appear to head off to the right, but they merge after a short oval and continue as a rocky, one-lane dirt road for 0.1 mile to a large white mound of rocks. Follow the road around the left side of these rocks for another 0.2 miles to a four-way dirt-road intersection. Continue straight for another 0.5 miles across cow pastures to where the road ends at a flat open area where you will see the pool.

GPS: N 37 39.775 W 118 48.507

706 E   DAVE'S WARM TUB

● **East of the town of Mammoth Lakes**

As of 1995, there was no longer a tub here and the existing water is only 80° in a shallow seep.

Debbie Johnson

706 F   PULKY'S POOL (HILLTOP)
(see map on page 152)

● **East of the town of Mammoth Lakes**

Natural mineral water flows out of a spring at 131° and through a PVC pipe to a free-form, rock and cement pool up on the plateau. This pool, with a temperature of about 107° features a very clear water and a plug in the bottom to facilitate easy cleaning. The hot water pipe (green) has a gate valve and a second pipe (red) admits cold water allowing for temperature control.

Primitive facilities include a small carpeted deck for undressing and sunbathing, and a cement bench. The area is posted for day use only; no overnight parking is permitted. The apparent local custom is clothing optional.

Directions: From US 395, drive 2 miles past Whitmore Pool over one cattle guard to the second cattle guard. The turnoff to Crowley, 706-G, is just past the second cattle guard on the right (south). For Pulky's, continue on Benton Crossing Rd. for another 0.4 miles to an unpaved road on the left (north). Follow this road as it curves around a large alkali field for 0.4 miles to a flat parking area and park by fence. The pool is up on the plateau. Caution: Do not attempt to drive to the plateau, stay on the road; even 4WD vehicles have become stuck in the soft ground. Road is very rough.

GPS: N 37 39.838 W 118 47.359

Marjorie Young

706 G   CROWLEY HOT SPRING
(ALSO KNOWN AS WILD WILLIE'S)
(see map on page 152)

● **East of the town of Mammoth Lakes**

Natural mineral water flows out of a spring and down a small creek channel at 110°, then into a cement and rock pool large enough for thirty people. Surface cooling keeps the pool temperature about 104° most of the year.

Fifty feet away, at the foot of a large rock outcropping, is a squishy, mud-bottom pool at approximately 100°. Natural mineral water flows from a separate source near the rock into this knee-deep pool. The pool is large enough for a half-dozen people. Clothing optional.

There are no facilities on the premises, but overnight parking is not prohibited in the large parking area.

Directions: From Benton Crossing Rd., drive 2 miles past Whitmore Pool. Immediately past the second cattle guard, two rough dirt roads cut off to the right. Take either one (they join up) and drive 1.1 miles to a large rock. Follow the road to the right side of the rock and take an immediate left at the fork. Drive 0.3 miles to a large level parking area bordered by logs. Do not attempt to drive any farther. To reach the pools, follow the walkway from the end of the parking area for approximately 250 yards to where it joins a trail from the opposite direction and a path leading down a small hill to the left. The primitive pool is under some trees near the big rock ahead on your left; the pool with the deck is ahead on the right.

Caution: Do not attempt to drive across the bog to the pool area. Even 4WDs have been trapped. A new wooden and gravel walkway has been constructed from the parking lot to the pools—please use it!

GPS: N 37 39.550 W 118 46.270

706 H   HOT TUB

(see map on page 152)

● **East of the town of Mammoth Lakes**

Natural mineral water flows out of a spring at 110° and through a black PVC pipe to a three-foot deep rock and cement pool. The pool temperature is controlled by diverting the hot water inflow whenever the desired soaking temperature has been reached. There is a plug for draining, and the pool is kept clean by a group of local volunteers. The thigh-deep pool can hold about six people comfortably.

There are no facilities, but there is plenty of level area surrounding the pool, and overnight parking is not prohibited. Campers, please be considerate of others. Park away from the tubs, and keep the noise level down. The apparent local custom is clothing optional.

Directions: From Benton Crossing Rd., drive 1.1 miles on 3S50 (the main gravel road) to the second one-lane dirt road on the right. Turn right and go for 0.1 mile to a clearing, then bear left for another 0.1 mile to the pool.

706 I   WHITMORE HOT SPRINGS

(see map on page 152)
904 Benton Crossing Rd.   760 935-4222
■ **Mammoth Lakes, CA 93546**

Large, conventional public swimming pool jointly operated by Mono County and the town of Mammoth Lakes on land leased from the Los Angeles Department of Water and Power. Open during the day, Monday through Saturday, approximately mid-June to Labor Day.

Natural mineral water is pumped from a well, propane boosted, and piped to the swimming pool where it is treated with chlorine. Depending on air temperature and wind conditions, the pool water temperature averages 82°. An adjoining shallow wading pool averages 92°. Bathing suits are required. Bathrooms, showers, and slide-gate entrance are handicap accessible.

A small access fee includes showers (campers take note) and a barbeque area. A full aquatic schedule is available on the premises. Parking is permitted only during hours of operation. No credit cards are accepted.

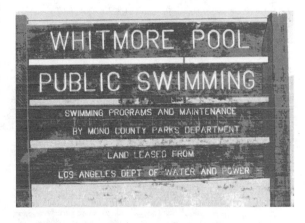

Photos by Phil Wilcox

707 THE OLD HOUSE AT BENTON HOT SPRINGS

55045 Hwy 120   (tubs) 760 933-2507
■ Benton, CA 93512   (inn) 760 933-2628
www.395/oldhouse.com

Two facilities next to door to each other: one houses the antique store and rents out the hot tubs in back by the day or hour; the other is the B&B that includes the use of the private tubs on that property with the room rental. Tubs are located in an oasis-type setting under cottonwood, Russian olive, tamarisk, and locust trees in high desert and sagebrush-type country along the eastern border of California near the Nevada state line, with views of Montgomery and Boundary Peaks (highest points in Nevada). Elevation: 5,500 feet. Open all year.

Natural, soft, silky mineral water flows out of a spring at 135° and supplies water to the entire town of Benton Hot Springs. A cooling/evaporation tank at The Old House provides the only cool water in town. There is no chemical treatment of the water in the tubs. A group of redwood tubs were cut from an old redwood pipeline that used to go to the generating plant. The four tubs, located under the trees, are drained and scrubbed after each use. Each tub has a hot and cold faucet to adjust water temperature. The five-foot diameter tubs are about three feet deep, have seats inside, and are large enough for four to six people. Bathing suits are optional in the tubs, except for one which is not screened. Owners operate on a body-tolerant basis.

Snacks and beverages are sold on the premises and there are also camping spaces. A small store in the town of Benton sells the basics, and a cafe offers meals.

Directions: From Bishop, take US 6 north for 36 miles to the tiny town of Benton. Turn west on CA 120 and drive 4 miles until you see the old green and white house on the north side of the street. Or, from US 395 in Lee Vining (Tioga Pass from Yosemite), take CA 120 east for 46 miles to Benton Hot Springs. If you are coming from the series of natural springs outside Mammoth, take Benton Crossing Rd. south of the Mammoth Airport for 36 miles to where it ends at CA 120. Take 120 east for 3 miles to Benton Hot Springs.

Each of the tubs at the two locations offer beautiful views and privacy. You can also adjust the temperature to your liking.

Top photo: Courtesy of Benton Hot Springs
Middle photo: Debbie Johnson
Bottom photo: Camilla Van Sickle and Bill Pennington

Steve Heerema

Scott Harwood

708 A   RED'S MEADOW HOT SPRINGS

● **In Red's Meadow Campground near Devil's Postpile National Monument**

Tin-roof shed with six cement shower-over bath tubs in six small private rooms, on the edge of a mountain meadow campground. Elevation 7,000 feet. Road open approximately Memorial Day to September 20. No charge is made for the use of the tubs, which are available on a first-come, first-served basis. Donations accepted.

Natural mineral water flows out of the ground at 114°, into a storage tank, and then by pipe into the bathhouse. Depending on the use, water temperature out of the shower heads will vary from 90-100°.

In summer, all water from the spring is diverted into the bathhouse. During the winter, the cement hot water storage tank is used for soaking and can only be reached by snowmobilers and cross-country skiers.

A Forest Service campground, open during the summer, adjoins the hot springs. It is four miles to a cafe, general store, rustic cabins, and pack station at Red's Meadow Resort, and twelve miles to an RV park and other services in Mammoth Lakes.

Directions: From the town of Mammoth Lakes, take CA 203 west to the end, then follow signs through Minaret Pass to Devil's Postpile National Monument and to Red's Meadow Campground. Note: During the day in summer, private vehicles are prohibited beyond Minaret Pass. A frequent shuttle bus service originates at Mammoth Mountain Inn.

Source map: *Inyo National Forest;* USGS *Devil's Postpile.*

GPS: N 37 37.080 W 119 04.440

708 B   IVA BELL (FISH CREEK) HOT SPRINGS

● **South of Devil's Postpile National Monument**

A delightful cluster of volunteer-built soaking pools, some with spectacular views of the wilderness. Elevation 7,400 feet. Open all year.

The pools adjoin the Iva Bell camp area that includes numerous camping sites separated by meadows and stands of pines. A 102° bottom-fed pool may be reached by following a path thirty yards across a meadow.

From the first pool, a path leads due east for fifty yards to a cozy campsite. From this site, a steep one-hundred-yard path leads up to four more pools, ranging in temperature from 101° to 110°. Two pools are carved into the face of the hillside with spring water cascading into them, and two more rock and log pools are on top of the hill near the 124° source. The nicest pool has a sandy bottom and is nestled on the back side of this ledge, where a 106° trickle flows out of a fissure slowly enough to maintain a 101° temperature in the summertime.

Note: In summer you must pay to enter Reds Meadow and take a shuttle to the area. You must also obtain a backcountry permit and a mandatory bear canister from the ranger station. Empty your car of anything that might entice a bear into boxes provided at the parking area.

Directions: Take the trail to Rainbow Falls and continue towards Fish Creek for 8 miles eventually dropping into Fish Creek Valley. Cross the bridge and continue upstream 4 more miles and turn left at the turn marked Fish Valley. The unmarked camping area and springs are just past this turn. Also check with the Mammoth Ranger District of Inyo National Forest, 760 873-2408.

Source map: *USGS Devil's Postpile.*

GPS: N 37 31.920 W 119 01.500

709   LEWIS CREEK WARM SPRINGS

● **North of the town of Oakhurst**

Spectacular scenery and a hot pool filled by warm water flowing out of the cracks in the rocks at the top of gorgeous Corlieu Falls. Situated in a heavily-wooded river valley surrounded by pine and madrone in the Sierra National Forest.

Natural mineral water fills a small two-person pool that has a temperature of around 85° and is located on the far side of Lewis Creek. Clothing optional. There is also a nice swimming hole you can access directly from the hot spring.

Large campsite nearby. All other services back in Oakhurst.

Directions: From the town of Oakhurst go north about 7 miles to the marked midpoint of the Lewis Creek trail. You will go about 0.25 miles on the trail and then down a few hundred feet to the river where you will see the campsite. Be careful and don't take the trail to the base of the waterfall as the spring is located at the top of the waterfall across from the campsite.

Map source: USGS *Poleta Canyon* Quad
GPS: N 37 16.000 W 118 16.340

While I don't have a picture of *Lewis Creek Warm Springs*, this is the type of habitat to be found in that area and would certainly make for a beautiful hike.

710 A   MONO HOT SPRINGS

■

●

(Summer) 7200 Hwy 168		559 325-1710
Mono Hot Springs, CA 93642		
(Winter) PO Box 215		559 683-5857
Lake Shore, CA 93634		
Northeast of Fresno		
www.monohotsprings.com		

A vacation resort offering fishing, hiking, and camping in addition to mineral baths with access across the river to several natural springs. Located on the south fork of the San Joaquin River near Edison Lake, Florence Lake, and Bear Dam in the Sierra National Forest. Elevation 6,500 feet. Open May to October for summer season;.call for winter snow packages.

Natural mineral water flows from a spring at 107° and is piped to a bathhouse containing four two-person soaking tubs in private rooms. Tubs have geothermal water only, measuring 100-105°. Tubs are drained and refilled after each use, so no chemical treatment of the water is necessary. An outdoor hydrojet pool is maintained at 103-105° and is treated with chlorine. Bathing suits are required except in private rooms. Facilities are available on a day-use basis, as well as to registered guests, and are handicap accessible with assistance.

On the south side of the river directly across from the resort is a series of springs and soaking pools that are open all year, but only to cross-country skiers and snowmobilers in winter. Water from one spring feeds into a holding tank. From there it is piped across the river to the resort. Nearby is a cement soaking tub called "The Coffin" due to its size and shape. Above the riverbank are several cement soaking tubs that remain from an historic bathhouse. A rock and mud pool is near the cement tubs and another primitive pool, called "The Rock," is next to a large boulder ten feet up the hill from the cement tubs. Pool temperatures are approximately 101°. Bathing suits are advisable in the daytime.

Facilities include a restaurant, store, service station, tent cabins and cabins. A forest service campground is on the edge of the property. Massage is available on the premises. Credit cards accepted.

Directions to the resort: From the city of Fresno on CA 99, go 80 miles northeast on CA 168 to the ranger station at the northeast side of Huntington Lake. Inquire here about road conditions before attempting to drive in. The one-lane road is very narrow and winding. Allow at least one hour for this 15-mile stretch.

At 15 miles, you come to the High Sierra Ranger Station. Stop here for info and campfire permits, needed even for cooking in your van. One mile past this station the road forks. Bear left to Mono Hot Springs. At 1 mile, you will cross a small bridge. Continue downhill to a second green bridge. Mono is less than 0.25 miles past the bridge on your left.

To reach the soaking pools on the south side of the river, use the wooden bridge that starts at the forest service campground. "The Rock" is up a small hill to your left, the cement pools a few feet ahead uphill from the river.

Phil Wilcox

The cement pools are the remains of an old bathhouse located across the river from the resort. The pool below is only one of several in the area.

Scott Harwood

710 B   LITTLE EDEN
ROSE GARDEN

● **Northeast of Fresno**

A primitive, squishy-bottom, thigh-deep pool surrounded by grass and large enough for a dozen people, with a gorgeous view of the surrounding mountains and a real feeling that you are out in nature. Elevation 6,500 feet. Open all year; accessible only to cross-country skiers and snowmobilers in the winter.

Natural mineral water bubbles up through the sandy pool bottom at around 100°. Because of its large size, pool temperatures measure only in the nineties. The apparent local custom is clothing optional.

There are no facilities on the premises. Services are less than a mile away at Mono Hot Springs Resort.

Directions: Follow directions given for Mono Hot Springs to the High Sierra ranger station. 2.1 miles past the station, and 1.1 miles down the left fork at the "Y" is a steel bridge. Park at turnout on right just before bridge or on left just past the bridge. A steep, unofficial trail to the pool begins on the left (north), approximately 50 feet before the bridge, and goes around a large rock outcropping, through some marshy spots, and down to the pool at the base of the rocks. From the other direction, Little Eden is below the green bridge that is just past the spring that fills the Rose Garden and then flows over the road

GPS: N 37 19.313 W 119 11.172.

Note: A mushy bottomed dirt pool has recently been dug out located just across the road from the trail down to Little Eden. Called the Rose Garden for the obvious reason.

Scott Harwood

711 A   MUIR TRAIL RANCH

Lakeshore CA 93634
www.muirtrailranch.com

Located in a beautiful valley in the high mountains of central California east of Fresno, surrounded by soaring granite peaks and the John Muir Wilderness of the the Sierra National Forest. Near the John Muir Trail. Elevation 7,600 feet.

For information, write the owner, Adeline Smith, Box 176, Lakeshore, CA 93634 from mid-June to October, or Box 700, Ahwance, CA 93601 from November through May. For more details check out their web site.

Over a thousand gallons per hour of fresh, hot water gushes out of a crack in the bedrock, flows along a streambed, then pours into a large pool that is surrounded by flowers and a beautiful enclosure. The pool is eight by ten feet and about two-and one-half feet deep. The 107° water flows through the pool sixteen times a day. This pool offers a magnificent view of granite peaks over the meadow. There is a place to wash up before entering the pool. They supply the soap and shampoo.

If that pool is too hot, there is a second one only a few feet away. It is enclosed too and has cooler water, about body temperature, coming in from a spring up the hill. There is a place to wash up here, also.

Muir Trail Ranch offers rustic log cabin comfort to organized groups on a bring-your-own-food basis, or hire a caterer from a list of cooks who have worked there in the past. There are three options if you want to visit the Ranch: Get a group of fifteen to twenty-plus people together and rent the whole place; stay a full week by joining another group; or stay for one night or more during our Short Stay periods in June and September. Horseback trips are available and range from half-day, full-day, or a several day pack packing trip. They encourage catch-and-release fishing and only fly fishing on the ranch. If you want to use lures or bait, fish anywhere off the ranch property. Only keep what your immediate family will eat. Get license before you come.

Directions: From the boat landing follow the yellow bricks to the sign board marking the trail. Be careful not to end up on the trail going back around the lake. Follow the trail to the Muir Trail Ranch and then either veer right at the private property sign through the ranch following the signs and fence to the springs or take the bypass and just after the first switchback take the trail to the right to the back country campsite. Cross the San Joaquin at the "No Camping Here" sign and follow the short trail to the spring and lake.

The eleven-mile trail from the road's end has an elevation gain of 500 feet and requires fording the South Fork of the San Joaquin River. In the summer it is possible to avoid five miles of walking by renting one of the boats to take you across the lake. From this part of the John Muir Trail it is only a hike of five miles down the Florence Lake Trail to reach the springs.

With all the hiking and physical activity on and around the ranch, soaking in one of the pools (cooler one on the top) would certainly feel good.

Photos by Bill Ralph

711 B BLAYNEY HOT SPRINGS

● **Southeast of Florence Lake**

A combination hot springs and a mudbath in a grassy High Sierra meadow, nine- and one-half miles from the road's end at Florence Lake. Elevation 7,600 feet. Open all year.

While several springs flow across the meadow, hot mineral water oozes up through the squishy bottom of this large pool, surrounded my meadow grass, maintaining a temperature of approximately 102°. This pool is located across the river from the tent cabins at Muir Trail Ranch. While this pool is open to the public, it is not over-used. Be sure to check the water temperature at any of the other hot water sources as they can be quite hot. The apparent custom is clothing optional.

Near the natural springs across the river is Warm Lake, more like a large pond that is fed by both hot and cold springs. If you float on top, the water is warm, if you dangle your feet you can feel the chill. The lake is accessible in mid-to-late season when the river flow diminishes a bit and it's easier to get across. You will probably be sharing it with some fish.

There are no services at this location except nearby backpacker campgrounds. It is ten miles to a store and any supplies.

Source map: USGS *Blackcap Mountain.*
GPS: N 37 14.040 W 118 52.860

Scott Harwood

Phil Wilcox

Stephaine Turlow

712 A   KEOUGH HOT SPRINGS

800 Keough Hot Spring Rd. 760 872-4670
Bishop, CA 93514
www.keoughshotsprings.com

The Sierra foothills is home to this historical site where the original pool was built in 1919. Elevation 4,200 feet. Open all year.

Natural mineral water flows out of the ground at 128° and through an aerator at the end of the enclosed one-hundred- by forty-foot swimming pool (86-92°) and the twenty-four- by forty-foot wading pool (102-104°), using flow-through mineral water so that only minimal amounts of chlorine need to be added. Full-time lifeguard on duty. Bathing suits are required.

An RV campground with water and electric, tent sites, gift shop and snack bar are available on the premises. On-call massage is available. Credit cards accepted. It is seven miles to the nearest restaurant, motel, service station, and store. Call for schedule and rates.

Directions: Go 7 miles south of Bishop on US 395, then follow signs west from US 395.

712 B   KEOUGH HOT DITCH

● **Near Keough Hot Springs**

Runoff from Keough Hot Springs cools as it flows through a series of volunteer-built rock pools in a treeless foothill gully. Elevation 4,100 feet. Open all year.

Natural mineral water flows out of the ground at 128° on the property of Keough Hot Springs, then meanders northeast for about a mile. (When the aerator is turned off at 7 pm at the swimming pool, the water that flows from the resort through the culvert jumps from 85 to 105°.) Volunteer-built rock dams create several primitive soaking pools and swimming holes on both sides of the road, each one cooler than the preceding one upstream. The apparent local custom is clothing optional.

No services are available on the premises. The land is posted for day-use only, no overnight parking, but reports are that parking for one night is not a problem as long as you leave nothing but tire tracks. Please do not bring any glass objects to the area, since broken glass is the biggest problem at Keough. It is one mile to an RV park and eight miles to a restaurant, store, and service station in Bishop.

Directions: Seven miles south of Bishop on US 395, turn west on Keough Hot Springs Rd. at approximately 0.6 miles. At the only intersection with a paved road (old US 395), turn north 200 yards to where a cold stream crosses under the road. (Note: There is an abundance of level parking space on the north side of the cold stream, but the stream must be forded with care.) Walk an additional 50 yards north to Keough Ditch. Either stream may be followed to where they form a series of warm pools.

GPS: N 37 15.340 W 118 22.440

713   "THREE DISH" WARM SPRINGS

● **East of the town of Big Pine**

This warm pond makes for an ideal soak on hot desert summer days. Open all year; spring and fall the best seasons.

Natural mineral water flows out of the vegetation-covered hillside at 85°. The high flow rate is able to maintain the pool at nearly the same temperature all year. Clothing optional.

There are no facilities on the premises other than a small fire ring and trash barrel. There is a small level place where overnight parking is not prohibited. The closest place for supplies is Big Pine, about nine miles away.

Directions: At the intersection of Hwy 395 and Hwy 168, just north of Big Pine, reset your odometer to 0. Head east on Hwy 168 for 1.9 miles to the remains of Zurich Station. Turn left on Leighton Lane heading for the huge "celestial" observation dishes. At 5.2 miles turn right at the "Caltech Owens Valley Radio Observatory" sign. Another sign read "Owens River 3." Proceed straight ahead 5.4 miles and veer left at 6 miles. The road becomes rather difficult, rutted, and hard to see towards the end. The spring is at 8.9 miles.

GPS: N 37 39.660 W 118 46.071

714   SALINE VALLEY HOT SPRINGS

● **Northeast of the town of Olancha**

A sometimes crowded, spring-fed oasis located on a barren slope of land in a remote desert valley that was recently annexed to Death Valley National Park. Elevation 1,500 feet. Open all year, but access roads may become impassable at any time of the year due to heavy rainstorms or snow. Be sure to bring extra supplies of water and car repair tools.

Natural mineral water flows out of the main source springs at 107°, or hotter. Volunteers have installed pipes to carry this water to two cement and rock soaking pools.

Lower Warm: According to latest reports, the water is flowing again and the lower pool is filled all the time.

Palm Spring: Two pools are fed from this source.

Wizard Pool: With temperatures ranging from 105°-112°, this one's the hottest in Saline Valley. Built nearly thirty years ago by a determined group who took exquisite care to make this one a great soak. This hexagonal shaped rock and concrete pool is sunk into the ground with seating all the way around. The deepest spot is about three and one-half feet deep, and more than twenty people could squeeze in for an occasion although usually fewer folks makes it more enjoyable. Offers one of the best mountain views in the area.

Volcano Pool: Traditionally this is the kiddy pool due to its cooler temperature. An above ground tub fashioned from rock and cement, with a bench across one side. The pool is about fifteen feet by eight feet and three-feet deep and comfortably seats ten. Temperatures range from 98°-104°, warmer after a recent cleaning.

Upper Warm: Small squishy-bottom pool at about 102°, and cool pond. This spring is enclosed by a fence, installed to exclude predators when pupfish were transplanted from Death Valley in the 1970s. (The pupfish did not survive.)

All pools have valves and drains for controlling water flow and cleaning, except the natural upper warm spring. Most of the pools and facilities are handicap accessible with assistance. The area is currently designated as clothing optional by the Park Service.

Vault toilets have been installed by the Park Service. There is level space on which overnight parking is permitted, with a limit of up to thirty days per calendar year for the entire park. It is more than fifty-five miles, mostly unpaved, to a store or service station in Big Pine, and more than eighty-five miles to Olancha and Lone Pine. Everyone hauls out their own trash, as well as ashes from campfires, which are permitted in the existing firepans.

Temperatures regularly soar over the 110° mark in the summer, so this desert location with very little natural shade is preferred in the fall and spring. It becomes very crowded on major holidays and three-day weekends. The peace and quiet of the desert can best be enjoyed during the week.

Directions: The southern route via Olancha is shown on the map. The unpaved portion of the Saline Valley Road is county maintained. An alternate route starts just north of Big Pine on US 395. Drive northeast on CA 168 for 2.5 miles and turn right (southeast) on Death Valley Road. Drive approximately 15 miles and turn right on Waucoba-Saline Rd. Drive 32 miles south to a triangular intersection on the left (east) side of the road. Turn left (east) for 7 miles to the first group of springs. From US 395 it is at least a 3-hour drive via either route. All roads in are quite rough and a high clearance vehicle is recommended. The 2.2-mile road from the lower springs to the far upper springs is particularly rough. Either entrance route may be temporarily washed out by infrequent but severe flash floods, or blocked by snow. Inquire about road conditions before making the trip.

Source maps: So. CA Auto Club *Death Valley*, USGS *Waucoba Wash and New York Butte*.

GPS: N 36 48.346 W 117 46.404

Chris Andrews

Note: All visitors are expected to pay a park entrance fee, but no pay stations are available along either route into the Valley. Before entering, please purchase a $10 entrance permit, or an annual Park Pass, in Death Valley National Park, or at a designated Federal facility.

Photos by Skip Hill

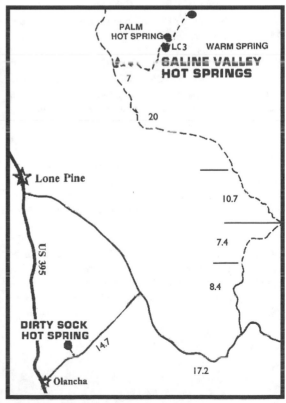

Miners from the now extinct silver mine of Cerro Gordo used to come down out of the surrounding hills to bathe here. The water is actually effervescent.

715   DIRTY SOCK HOT SPRING

● **Near the town of Olancha**

Large, shallow pool in an open desert area. Elevation 3,600 feet. Open all year.

Natural mineral water flows up through a large vertical pipe into the bottom of a circular, algae encrusted, cement-lined pool at 90° and flows out about a foot below water level at various temperatures, depending on wind and air temperature. Several sets of steps lead down to the somewhat slippery pool bottom. Word has it that it gets so scummy in the summer the fire department comes and sucks out the scum. Clothing optional.

No services are available on the premises, and there are no remaining buildings. There are many acres of unmarked level space on which overnight parking is not prohibited. It is five miles to the nearest restaurant, motel, service station, and store.

Directions: From the intersection of US 395 and CA 190, go five miles northeast on CA 190. There are no signs on the highway, so look for a narrow, paved road on the northwest side and follow it 300 yards to the spring.

GPS: N 36 19.750 W 117 56.900

716   KERN HOT SPRING

● **On the upper Kern River**

A small concrete soaking pool offering a truly spectacular view in return for a very strenuous three-day hike from the nearest road. Elevation 6,900 feet. Open all year.

Natural water flows out of the ground at 115° directly into a shallow soaking pool built at the edge of the Kern River. Water temperature is controlled by adding buckets of cold river water as needed. Bathing suit policy is determined by the mutual consent of those present.

There are no services available except a backpacker campground 100 yards away. The spring is 31.5 miles west of Whitney Portal and 37 miles east of Crescent Meadow. Situated in the mile-deep canyon of the upper Kern River, this spring has magnificent views in all directions. Detailed directions to such a remote location are beyond the scope of this book. We recommend that you purchase *Sierra South*, published by Wilderness Press, and also consult the Tule Ranger District of the Sequoia National Forest, 32588 Highway 190, Springville, CA 93265. 209 539-2607.

Source map: USGS *Kern Peak*.
GPS: N 36 28.680 W 118 24.280

Gateway to the Giant Sequoia National Monument.

717   JORDAN HOT SPRING

● Northwest of the town of Little Lake

Hot water flows on Ninemile Creek have been formed into pools in the southernmost part of the Golden Trout Wilderness. Many buildings including a sawmill remain to be explored in the recently abandoned pack station. Elevation 6,500 feet. Open all year.

Natural mineral water flows out of a spring at approximately 120° down to the river where it may be mixed with cold creek water to form casual pools. Permanent pools are not legally permitted, however, someone packed in concrete and built a nice two-foot deep, three person tub, with a murky rock pool be low. Leave the plug out so the iron and algae don't accumulate in the upper pool. A clever system of dams allow you to control the temperature of the lower pool while the upper pool remains a toasty 109°. Clothing optional.

Directions: The trail starts at Blackrock Station where there is a pack station and small campground (no water). Follow the trail until it opens into a large meadow, then cross the creek and veer left heading down, down, down till you get to the springs at an abandoned pack station. The trail has an elevation change of 3,000 feet.

It is six miles to the nearest paved road at Sequoia National Forest Road 21S03, reached via County Road J41 from south of Little Lake on US 395.

Consult with the Mt. Whitney Ranger District of Inyo National Forest, Lone Pine, CA 93545. 760 873-2408.

GPS: N 36 13.740 W 118 18.120

718   CALIFORNIA HOT SPRINGS
42177 Hot Springs Dr.   661 548-6582
■   California Hot Springs, CA 93207

Historic resort that has been restored and expanded to offer family fun. Located in rolling foothills at the edge of Giant Sequoia National Monument. Elevation 3,100 feet. Open all year except Thanksgiving, the week before Christmas, and New Year's day.

Odorless natural mineral water flows out of several artesian wells at a temperature of 125° and is piped to the pool area where there are two large, tiled hydrojet spas maintained at 100° and 104°. A flow-through system eliminates the need for chemical treatment of the water. There is one large swimming pool containing filtered and chlorinated spring water that is maintained at 85° in the summer and 94° in the winter. Handicap access is at west end of pool. Bathing suits are required.

The restored main building houses the office, delicatessen, ice cream parlor, grocery store, gift shop, and dressing room facilities. With advance notice, meals can be arranged for groups. Massage is available on the premises by appointment only. Full-hookup RV spaces are adjacent to the resort area. Credit cards accepted.

Directions: From CA 99 between Fresno and Bakersfield, take the J 22 exit at Earlimart and go east 38 miles to the resort.

719   KERNVILLE WARM SPRINGS

● ☐   **Near the town of Kernville**

Another warm spring known only to the locals, offers a warm bath next to a cold plunge in the scenic Kern River. Elevation 3,512 feet. Summer is best after spring runoff as river must be low in order for the springs to emerge.

Warm springs flow out of the rocky banks on the far side of the Kern River where the water is channeled into a river rock pool. The springs are easy to spot due to the deep red residue on all the nearby rocks. Pools are reconstructed every season so the shape and size is always changing. During the last visit the pool measured 86° and had room for four adults. The valley gets so hot during summer that the river is practically overrun by swimmers, inner tubers and fishermen. You won't have the place to yourself, but you may be the only one interested in the warm water instead of the river.

Camp across the river at any of the nearby campgrounds or turnouts. There are many places to park where you can tote your tent and cooler down to the beach and sleep next to the river for free. McNally's Restaurant is open for dinner and cocktails; the burger bar serves up lunch. The hotel there has about a dozen rooms.

Directions: From Kernville go north on Sierra Way to McNally's on the left. Park here and follow the trail behind the motel, crossing the suspension bridge over the river. Head upstream along the bank for about 200 yards to the reddish orange rocks.

GPS: N 35 46.638 W 118 26.340

Photos by Soakers Bible

720   REMINGTON HOT SPRINGS

● **Near the town of Lake Isabella**

A delightful, two-person cement tub, an adjoining river-level tub and a one-person tub higher up on a hillside in an unspoiled, primitive, riverside setting of rocks and trees. Located in the Kern River Canyon down a steep trail from old Highway 178. Elevation 2,500 feet. Open all year, except during high water in the river.

Natural mineral water at 104° emerges from the ground at 3.5 gallons per minute. This flow comes directly up through the bottom of a volunteer-built, cement, two-person tub and provides a form of hydrojet action, maintaining the pool temperature at 105°. There is a second, larger tub adjacent to the first and further out into the river. An enlarged and deeper riverside tub, with steps leading to the river, is filled by a pipe and drained by pulling the plugs so it can be cleaned. A new cement and rock pool is filled with the overflow from the first pool along with a valve-controlled pipe and is around 98°. Twenty yards uphill is a drainable, one-person rock and cement pool that is fed by a smaller flow of 96° water, and has a valve for draining. The apparent local custom is clothing optional. However, don't be surprised by clothed people floating down river in rafts, inner tubes, or canoes.

There are no services available on the premises. It is six miles to a motel, restaurant, and service station and two miles to a Forest Service campground.

Directions: From Bodfish (by Lake Isabella) drive west on Kern Canyon Rd. (old CA 178, now CA 214) to Hobo Forest Service Campground. Continue west 1.5 miles to a large turnout on the right with a telephone pole in the middle. (This is the second turnout with a telephone pole.) Flat areas for camping can be found near the parking areas. From the parking area, two trails head

The ecosystem in this area is very fragile. Do not attempt to bring vehicles down to the river and please walk on already defined trails to help preserve the vegetation which in turn prevents erosion.

down toward the river, 300 yards below. A steep, narrow dirt trail on the left leads to a flat area along the river where camping is permitted. To reach the tubs, hike down the very steep trail to the right to the rock foundation of an old building. Do not attempt to bring a vehicle down this road as it is often muddy and vehicles can get stuck. Also, it is very destructive to the hillside area. Just before this foundation on your left is a footpath with some natural rock steps leading down toward the river. Under a tree on your left, a spur path leads to the shallow rock and cement pool. Follow the main path to the cement pools by the river. This is not a good area for children, please be careful. Help keep this special place beautiful by packing out all trash.

GPS: N 35 34.540 W 118 33.120

MIRACLE HOT SPRINGS

● **Near the town of Lake Isabella**

The pools have all been torn out and at this time there is no legal place to soak.

Soakers Bible

Phil Wilcox

721   PYRAMID HOT SPRING

● **At the lower end of Kern River Canyon**

A delightful but hard to find, natural pool beneath a giant boulder at the edge of the Kern River. Open all year but not accessible during the high water of spring runoff. Elevation 1,900 feet.

Natural mineral water flows out of the ground at 109°, under a giant boulder, and into a sandy-bottom soaking pool large enough for two people, where it maintains a temperature of 103°. The apparent local custom is clothing optional, but the site is visible to vehicles on CA 178.

There are no services available at the location. It is one and one-third miles east to a Forest Service day-use campground (Live Oak) and fifteen miles to all other services in Bakersfield.

Directions: From Bakersfield, go east on CA 178 to the beginning of the Kern River Canyon. Continue 2.5 miles east beyond dam and power plant to a paved turnout on the left with a 6-foot high pyramid-shaped boulder at its east end. Look across the river slightly westward to locate a large, cube-shaped boulder on the opposite bank. The pool is under that boulder. To reach it, follow the trail from the east end of the turnout to the large downstream boulder where you can hop across the river. Then follow a faint unmarked path upstream to the pool. Stay next to the river and beware of poison oak.

GPS: N 35 28.640 W 118 45.111

722 A   SESPE HOT SPRINGS

● **Near the Sespe Condor Sanctuary**

Note: An adventure pass is required to park at any trailhead leading into this area. You can pick one up at the Los Padres National Forest ranger station in Ojai (1190 E. Ojai Ave., 805 646-4348). A forest service fire permit is also required. Horses and mules are also allowed on the trails. Be sure to inquire at the Los Padres National Forest office about fire season closures, flood warnings, and the adequacy of your preparations for packing in and packing out. Make sure to get a map!

A remote, pristine hot spring river located in the rugged, desert mountains of a designated wilderness area. Elevation 2,700 feet. Open all year, subject to flash flooding and Forest Service closures.

Hot water streams down a hillside at near boiling temperatures, and cools as it flows down rocky channels and into seasonal rock pools. The mineral water is clear and clean, and offers a variety of soaking temperatures as it mixes with cool creek water. All pools are built by volunteers, and probably become washed out every year. Large boulders in the rocky streambed line the main soaking area, which must be scooped out every season. There are many seeps up and down the creek bed which aren't as hot as the main springs. Depending on the level of the cold creek water mixing with the hot and warm, many pools of different temperatures can be found. Be sure to explore the whole area. There's a hot waterfall and even a rock sauna near the source, but be careful, the water is very hot! Clothing optional.

There are no services on the premises. You can get everything back in Ojai. Pack in everything you will need, and remember to camp a little ways away from the springs. There are several flat areas in the canyon near the hot springs, including a group of huge palm trees which shade a great camp spot.

Directions to Sespe: From Ojai take Highway 33 north for 14.3 miles to a right turn signed for Rose Valley. Follow this paved road for 3.1 miles and pass by the Rose Valley Work Camp. In another 1.4 miles you'll reach the end of the road where there's no place to camp, just the Piedra Blanca Trailhead parking area and pit toilets.

The Hike: Follow the directions into Willett's Hot Springs, which is a great place to camp for the first night out. From the cabin at Willet's follow the path across the first side stream and then cross Sespe Creek to the south bank. Follow the trail east for about 3/4 of a mile to the next crossing. This one can be swift during spring runoff so scout out the best route, probably just a little upstream. Follow the established trail past Hartman Camp to the next crossing. This one can be skirted by staying on the north bank. You'll have to clamber through some brush but it's not bad and won't take as long as changing into sandals for the crossing. Within a few hundred yards the trail becomes reestablished on the north side of the creek. After some smooth hiking you'll reach a big sandy beach and a beautiful, deep swimming hole. This is great during summer, but another deep crossing during spring. Probably waist deep in April, but at least this one has no swift current. There are some underwater ledges that aren't that deep, so again, scout out your route to avoid surprises. From here the trail goes up a hill and down to the last crossing back to the north bank.

Once on the north side you'll hike up an arroyo and through lots of scratchy brush on the narrow trail that leads up a long hill. Once on top you'll have a nice view of Coltrell Flat (watch for ticks throughout this section). The trail can be hard to follow through the flat meadow, but it basically skirts around the larger bushes and heads up to the left to go up the next hill where you can see the trail from a distance. The trail is still overgrown, and will lead up to another viewpoint; there's a sign up there with old trail numbers that points toward the east. The main path curves north and begins up Hot Springs Canyon. You will be in and out of the creek for the next mile as the trail meanders up the canyon—about 5 crossings, most of which you can hop rocks to cross. After the last crossing watch for the sign to Mutau Flat, there's a second trail that leads off to the right, under the Mutau Flat trail. Take the lower trail about 0.25 miles to the wide rocky canyon where you'll find palm trees and hot springs. Explore the whole area to find many soaking pools, a hot waterfall and rock sauna!

GPS: N 34 35.680 W 118 59.870

Soakers Bible

722 B   WILLETT'S HOT SPRINGS

● **Near the Sespe Condor Sanctuary**

> Note: An adventure pass is required to park at any trailhead leading into this area. You can pick one up at the Los Padres National Forest ranger station in Ojai (1190 E. Ojai Ave., 805 646-4348). A forest service fire permit is also required. Horses and mules are also allowed on the trails. Be sure to inquire at the Los Padres National Forest office about fire season closures, flood warnings, and the adequacy of your preparations for packing in and packing out. Make sure to get a map!

A remote and rarely visited hot spring located at the top of a side canyon above Sespe Creek, in the Los Padres National Forest above the remnants of an abandoned ranch. Elevation 3,000 feet. The best times to visit are summer and fall as there are many fords which are much easier after the creek level goes down. There are many long uphill climbs, so hot summer weather could be something to avoid.

Sulphur springs emerge at 108° and flow down steep waterfalls where PVC pipe has been installed to divert the water into a huge soaking tank. The tank is about 8-feet wide and neck deep when sitting back and enjoying the scenery. It's perched at the very top of a side canyon well away from Sespe Creek, and the only water you'll hear flowing is that from the hot waterfalls cascading over the steep cliffs above. There is a drainpipe installed in the tub to drain off the top, but it's sometimes removed and soakers just plug the hole at the bottom—either way it only takes about fifteen minutes to fill the big tub. Because the sulphur water develops algae easily, leave the tub empty when you leave. Clothing optional.

There are no services on the premises. However, a pack group still maintains a drinking water spring, corral and barbecue area. While some of the cabins are in ruins, one is still available for use with four bunks, running water and an outdoor kitchen. Water has a sulphur taste. The outfitters often leave their tents up.

Directions: Follow driving directions to Sespe Hot Springs, from Ojai to the Piedra Blanca Trailhead up Hwy 33. From the trailhead the path leads downhill and almost immediately starts crossing Trout Creek. You will have to cross it 4 times within the first 30 minutes of hiking. The fifth crossing can be done over the rocks. This part of the trail skirts around protected frog habitat, and winds down to meet Sespe Creek after about 1 mile. The trail follows the north bank for about 4.5 miles before dumping out on a sandy beach with boulders and Sycamore trees. This is the first river crossing, it's wide, swift and rocky so grab a good stick. During spring months the creek can be hip—waist deep, so be prepared. The river is too rocky and slippery to cross barefoot so have river shoes or sandals with you for crossings. On the opposite bank the trail leads up a small, steep, rocky chute and then heads left. Follow the trail for about 15 minutes until you reach the large landslide. The trail disappears at this point, so you'll have to climb over rocks to get past the slide which is a couple hundred yards long. At the end there's a heavily eroded slope to climb. It's loosely dried mud and sand and can be scary for inexperienced hikers (even worse on the way back going down the slope).

Once you reach the top of the landslide area the trail goes a little way and then seems to dump hikers at another rocky beach with no clear crossing point. Stop and look around, the trail actually goes up the hill behind you. It's hard to see through the foliage, but there are stone stairs that lead up the hillside to connect with the trail on the south bank. Follow this for another mile before crossing at another deep, swift ford. You'll stay on the north bank now for several miles. Watch for a sign for Ladybug Campground; at this point you're opposite Red Rock Canyon which is hard to miss. Within 1 mile you

Scott Harwood

will reach another sandy beach and you'll be able to see the tin roof of a small building up near Willets. This is the last set of river crossings. Cross over to the south bank and trudge through the side streams until you pick up the trail. Continue about 0.25 miles until it seems like you've gone past the cabin. There's a very obvious crossing point at a rocky beach which will take you back to the north bank, even though it's hard to see the trail on the other side. Once you get over there you'll be able to see it. From here go through the reeds and cross the last side stream to the trail which will lead to the cabin. The tin roof you can see from the trail is just an old building in ruins; the cabin is further east.

To reach the hot springs, follow the trail from the cabin heading west, and stay above the fence line as it passes the tin shacks. Continue on this trail and watch for the stone fireplace, a faint trail forks right and begins to climb up through the grass. Take this right fork and continue uphill (more switchbacks) for about 15 minutes. You will be well above the side creek. The trail goes up several hundred feet to the very top of the canyon. When you reach the lone campsite and firepit, drop your backpacks and follow the little trail another 100 feet under the tree and up the creek to the tub.

GPS. N 34 34.920 W 119 02.640

Wonder how in the world somebody got this big tank installed way up there. Rumor has it, the tub was air lifted in by helicopter.

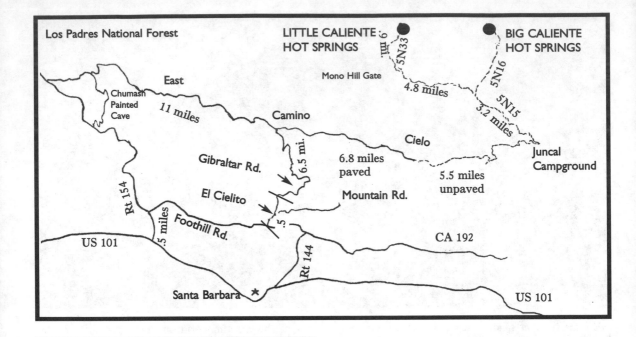

Los Padres National Forest

LITTLE CALIENTE HOT SPRINGS

BIG CALIENTE HOT SPRINGS

Mono Hill Gate

Chumash Painted Cave

East

Camino

0.9 mi.

5N33

4.8 miles

5N16

5N15

3.2 miles

Juncal Campground

11 miles

Cielo

Gibraltar Rd.

6.5 mi.

6.8 miles paved

5.5 miles unpaved

El Cielito

Mountain Rd.

Rt 154

.5 miles

Foothill Rd.

.5

US 101

Rt 144

CA 192

Santa Barbara ✳

US 101

---

723   THE HOURGLASS

213 W. Cota   805 963-1436

☐   Santa Barbara, CA 93101

Private spa and rental facility located on a creekside residential street near downtown Santa Barbara. Open evenings, Thursday through Sunday.

Three private indoor rooms with pools and eight private outdoor enclosures with pools are for rent to the public. Gas-heated tap water treated with chlorine is maintained at 104°.

A private sauna, a juice bar, and massage are available on the premises. Visa and MasterCard are accepted. Phone for rates, reservations, and directions.

---

724 A   LITTLE CALIENTE HOT SPRINGS
(see map)

● **Near the city of Santa Barbara**

Two small volunteer-built pools in a rocky canyon at the end of a wooded, winding, unpaved Forest Service road. Elevation 1,600 feet. Open all year, subject to fire season and rain/mud closures.

Natural mineral water flows out of a spring at 105° and through a pipe into the upper six-foot by six-foot by eighteen-foot rock and cement soaking pool. From here it spills over into the lower slimy-bottom rock and mud pool where the temperature cools a degree or two. The pipe in the upper pool can be detached to stop the inflow

and control water temperature. Remains of a volunteer-built wooden sunning deck and red wooden benches along the lower pool have collapsed due to erosion. The apparent local custom is clothing optional.

No services are available on the premises. It is one mile to a pack-in campground, six miles to a primitive National Forest campground, and twenty-seven miles to all other services.

Directions: See the directions to Big Caliente. At Juncal Campground, turn left on 5N15 for 3.2 miles where the road forks. Bear left for 4.8 miles where the road forks again. Bear right and drive another 0.9 miles to the parking area. At the upper end of the parking area, use the makeshift wooden steps to cross the creek and continue walking 100 yards to the spring. The brush becomes gradually greener as you get closer to the springs. Before heading to Little Caliente, it is advisable to check with the ranger station for information on road conditions and where to park. At times several of the gates are locked, (which may require more hiking), but generally the gates are open and you can drive to the spring.

Source map: *Los Padres National Forest*.
GPS: N 34 32.430 W 119 37.176

> Important Note: According to the sign at the springs all parked vehicles must display a Forest Adventure Pass which is available in town at places like Big 5 Sporting Goods, Mountain Air Sports, Far West Gun and Supply, and Dodge City Gun and Supplies. Be sure to get yours before you take the drive up there!

724 B   BIG CALIENTE HOT SPRINGS

(see map)

● **Near the city of Santa Barbara**

A concrete pool provides a soak at this hot spring located in a sparsely wooded canyon reached via ten miles of very windy, rocky gravel road. Elevation 1,500 feet. Open all year, subject to fire closure and road conditions during rainy season. Check with Los Padres National Forest Ranger Station, 805 967-3481.

Natural mineral water flows out of a bluff at 115°, then through a faucet-controlled pipe to a six-foot by ten-foot concrete pool. Water temperature in the pool can be controlled by diverting the inflow hose or shutting off the faucet. Please close the valve and divert the hose out of the pool when leaving, to prevent scalding others. When the valve is open, hot water showers into the pool. Continual flow-through keeps the water clean. A galvanized pipe ladder leads into the pool, and concrete decks and benches are on two sides. The apparent custom is clothing optional by mutual consent, although it is advisable to keep bathing suits handy in case the rangers check. Since you can drive right up to the pool, it is handicap accessible with assistance.

A second primitive soaking pool is at creek level below the source spring. From the far end of the parking area, a marked trail leads off toward Big Caliente Debris Dam. Across the creek, water seeps down the mountain from a source spring under a cottonwood tree to the primitive 105° pool at creek level, which fills up with silt and mud and needs to be dredged periodically. This pool can be reached by rock-hopping where a pipe is visible underwater, approximately 100 yards from the trailhead.

Facilities include nearby changing rooms, clean pit toilets across the level parking area, and a picnic table under the trees. A trail from the changing rooms leads down to the cold creek, which has small waterfalls and several small sunning beaches. Several primitive Forest Service campgrounds are within three miles, and it is twenty-five miles to all other services in Santa Barbara.

Directions: Coming from the south on Hwy 101 in Santa Barbara, take Milpas St. exit (Rte. 144). Follow Rte. 144 east through city residential streets, and a five-point roundabout, for a total of 6.3 miles, to the end at Rte. 192. Turn left on Rte. 192 (Stanwood Dr.) for 1.2 miles to El Cielito Rd. At 0.3 miles, El Cielito crosses Mountain Dr. Continue straight uphill on El Cielito 0.5 miles to Gibraltar Rd. Turn right and follow Gibraltar for approximately 6.5 miles to the end at East Camino Cielo. Turn right on very windy East Camino Cielo which is paved for the first 6.8 miles, then unsurfaced for the next 5.5 miles. At Juncal Campground, turn left on 5N15 for 3.2 miles where the road forks. Take the right fork (5N16) 2.5 miles to the spring. (The left fork goes to Little Caliente.)

Coming from the north on Hwy 101, take Rte. 154 exit, heading east for 0.5 miles to Rte. 192 (called Foothill Rd.). At 4.7 miles is a reservoir (Foothill has changed to Mountain Dr. and again to Mission Ridge). At 0.1 miles past the reservoir, Rte. 192 makes a sharp left at a fire station and becomes Stanwood Dr. Follow Stanwood to El Cielito Rd. and continue as described above.

Source map: *Los Padres National Forest.*
GPS: N 34 32.352 W 119 33.876

Little Caliente (above) and *Big Caliente* (below) are the only natural hot springs accessible to the public in the Santa Barbara area.

Photos by Soakers Bible

725   LAS CRUCES HOT SPRINGS

(see map)

● **Near Gaviota State Park**

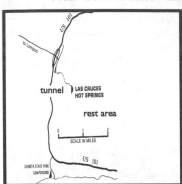

Two primitive, mud-bottom pools on a tree-shaded slope a few miles from the ocean. Elevation 500 feet. Open all year for day-use only.

Natural mineral water emerges at 96° directly into a shallow, knee-deep rock and mud soaking pool with relatively clear water, large enough for six to eight people. The overflow forms a waterfall over the earthen retaining wall into the larger lower pool, which averages 80° and has a slimy bottom. The water is murky. Clothing is optional with the mutual consent of those present.

There are no services available on the premises and overnight parking is prohibited in the parking area at the trailhead where a day-use self-parking fee is charged. Rangers check frequently and cite vehicles without valid parking receipts. It is three miles to a campground with RV hookups and six miles to all other services.

Directions: On Hwy101 approximately 35 miles north of Santa Barbara is Gaviota State Beach with its landmark railroad bridge. From here it is 3 miles to the turnoff for CA 1, west toward Lompoc. Directly across from this turnoff is the small road paralleling the highway and heading south to the parking area for Las Cruces. After Gaviota State Beach you will pass a rest area and go through a tunnel. It is 1 mile past the tunnel to the turnoff.

From the parking area, follow the steep dirt 4WD trail to where it forks at a white sign saying "no horses past this point." Bear right on a narrow trail approximately 0.75 miles from the parking area to the pools.

Phil Wilcox

Avila Valley Hot Springs has been in the hot water business since 1907, continually updating what is offered to the public to keep up with the times.

726 A   AVILA VALLEY HOT SPRINGS
250 Avila Beach Drive   805 595-2359
■   San Luis Obispo, CA 93405
www.avilahotsprings.com

A fun family destination, great for parties, with natural hot mineral water situated between oak-covered foothills that keep the morning fog away and make a natural year round air conditioner. Elevation 40 feet. Open all year; closed Tuesday and Wednesday from December to February.

Natural mineral water flows out of an artesian well at 130° and is piped to the outdoor twenty-foot square soaking pool (105°) which is drained and filled daily and requires no chemicals. The fifty- by one-hundred-foot outdoor swimming pool (86°) is filled with tap water and treated with chlorine and with two small water slides. Bathing suits required.

Massage, snack bar, pizza kitchen, arcade, twenty new cabins, RV hook-ups, lawn tent spaces, and a small store are located on the premises. All guests are invited to use the shaded picnic area with barbeque pits and tables. Major credit cards accepted. It is eight miles to all services in San Luis Obispo.

Directions: From either north bound or south bound U.S. 101, take the Avila Beach Drive exit (NOT the San Luis Bay Drive exit), and travel west towards the ocean. They are the first business on the right hand side of the road.

Oscar Voss

726 B   SYCAMORE MINERAL SPRINGS

■   1215 Avila Beach Dr.   805 595-7302
San Luis Obispo, CA 93401   800 234-5831
www.sycamoresprings.com

Delightful upscale resort, Integrative Retreat Center, spa and hot tub rental, offering secluded redwood hot tubs out under the oaks and a private natural mineral spa on the balcony of every room. Located on a wooded rural hillside two miles from the ocean. Elevation 40 feet. Open all year from 7AM to 2AM. Reservations required.

Natural mineral water is pumped from a well at 110° and piped to the tubs on the hillside. The large lookout tub on the hill has hot and cold faucets to regulate the temperature. The swimming pool is filled with tap water treated with chlorine. The "oasis," a natural-looking rock spa that will hold thirty people, is located next to the pool. Bathing suits are required except in the hillside hot tubs. Some pools and areas are handicap accessible.

Facilities include a restaurant, hotel rooms and suites with hot tubs on the balcony, luxury suites with spas and fireplaces, a one bedroom cottage with its own hot tub in a private enclosure, dressing rooms, meeting space and wellness center, and gift shop. Several varieties of massage and facials are available. A half-hour soak in one of the outdoor tubs is included in each appointment. In addition to the many retreat programs, guided local hiking tours are offered. On request, directions to a nearby clothing-optional state beach will be provided. Major credit cards accepted.

Directions: From US 101 8 miles south of San Luis Obispo, take the Avila Beach exit, then go 1 mile west on Avila Beach Dr. and watch for the resort sign on the south side of the road.

Marjorie Young

727 A   PASO ROBLES INN
1103 Spring St.
Paso Robles, CA 93446
www.pasoroblesinn.com

805 238-2660
800 676-1713

Originally built in 1864 and featuring a hot mineral springs bathhouse. The Inn, now a member of the National Trust Historic Hotels of America, has been completely refurbished. Located on the main street in Paso Robles. Open all year.

A newly redrilled geothermal well supplies the hot mineral water to the Inn's hot springs wing which features a mix of personal therapy spas and larger, family jet tubs. The pools themselves sit on the balconies which can be closed off with canvas curtains for a private soak. There are fireplaces in each room. There is also a large swimming pool and hot tub. Most of the rooms overlook the beautiful garden court. There is an indoor dining room, as well as one outdoors and a coffee shop.

Thirty new spa rooms, eighteen in the garden area and twelve above the historic ballroom have been completed, along with the total restoration of the hundred-year-old Grand Ballroom. A full-service health spa and salon with indoor/outdoor mineral water plunge bath, and a state-of-the-art conference center and meeting space are in the planning stage. Phone for status of construction.

The Inn was a fashionable favorite among sports heroes, millionaires, political bigwigs and Hollywood movie stars in its heyday. Today it is being restored to its former glory. The Inn is set in a tranquil setting of lush gardens and oak trees.

Phil Wilcox

Phil Wilcox

The runoff from this hot pool supports a fish farm where you can be prepared to catch and release Large Mouth Bass, Catfish, and Bluegill. As this is a private lake, a fishing license is not required. Bring your pole!

Directions: From 101 southbound at Paso Robles take the 16th St. exit and turn left on Riverside Dr. Go 0.8 miles to 13th St. and turn left. 13th St. becomes Creston Rd. Continue 4.5 miles on Creston Rd. to the hot springs.

Directions: From 101 northbound at Paso Robles take the Spring St. exit and go right on Niblick Ave. Go 1.8 miles to Creston Rd. and turn right. Continue 2.3 miles to the hot springs.

727 B   FRANKLIN LAKES HOT SPRINGS
3010 Creston Rd.   805 712-5373
■   Paso Robles, CA 93446
www.franklinhotsprings.com

Soaking tub, swimming area, and fishing hole in the rolling hills outside Paso Robles. Be prepared to see many species of waterfowl, muskrat, beaver and even huge turtles. Open all year, 8 AM to midnight, every day. Small fee.

A two thousand-foot-deep well produces 110° water at over 3300 gallons per minute. A large insulated pipe will bring the hot water to the surface to fill the large pool with a sand and gravel bottom that is forty-feet wide and eighty-feet long. It is three feet deep at the well head and slopes to eight feet at the spillway. Pipes coming out from the well head provide a nice shower. The water is high in sulfur and has some sodium bicarbonate, potassium, fluoride and calcium. Bathing suits required. A private soaking pool is now open and several others are under construction. A twenty-four inch deep wading pool with three small slides has been specially built for the children.

Picnic tables and toilets are provided and there are changing rooms. RVs are welcome. Massage is available by appointment, and a paintball field is also open for use. Alcohol and smoking are prohibited.

727 C   RIVER OAKS HOT SPRINGS AND SPA
3725 Buena Vista Dr.   805 238-4600
■   Paso Robles, CA 93446
www.riveroakshotsprings.com

Nestled in the heart of Paso Robles Wine Country, with both indoor therapeutic mineral tubs and outdoor pools, River Oaks offers an intimate setting featuring a cozy fireside lobby, therapeutic mineral tubs, and lakeside gazebo for special events. Elevation 100 feet. Open all year.

An artesian well with a very mild mineral and sulphur content fills all of the tubs. The spa pavilion offers five patio spas which are cleaned and refilled daily, filtered every three minutes, and require only minimal chemical treatment. New outdoor tubs, filled with hot mineral water are located close to the main building. The indoor premises are handicap equipped, the tubs with assistance.

Innovative therapeutic massages, energy healing, and skin care are offered to help you reach greater levels of balance and awareness. Call for reservations. The lakeside setting offers a wonderful site for weddings and special events for up to 350 guests. Credit cards accepted.

Location: Conveniently situated off Hwy 46 East on Buena Vista Dr.

Courtesy of River Oaks

728   ESALEN INSTITUTE
Workshop, Room Reservations
Hwy 1   831 667-3000
■   Big Sur, CA 93920
www.esalen.org

Primarily an educational/experiential center rather than a hot spring resort. Located on CA 1, 45 miles south of Monterey. Elevation 100 feet. Open all year.

Esalen specializes in residential programs that focus on education, philosophy, and the physical and behavioral sciences. Access to the grounds is by reservation only for those wishing to take workshops or rent an available room. The hot springs are also open for up to thirty people each morning from 1 AM to 3:30 AM for a charge. To make a bath reservation, call 831 667-3047.

The bath house was constructed to both complement and highlight the natural setting. The hot mineral water flows out at 120° to gravity-fill the tubs and provide heating for both the shower water and the facility's radiant heat. The building has two main sections with a total of seven large tubs, three of which are partially covered and two that are outside, suspended above the rocks and ocean. Inside the bathhouse are several private claw foot tubs and four massage areas all facing the ocean. The bath facilities can accommodate sixty people comfortably. The upper level has an outdoor pool with a lift for handicap access, designed by the ADA.

Outside there are two areas: the "quiet side" and the "silent side." The "silent side" has two large tubs and two individual tubs. The "quiet side" has four single tubs and four larger tubs, two of which are perched on the edge of the cliff overlooking a rocky ocean beach. Some of the tubs are roofed over or partially roofed. The water temperature in all tubs can be individually controlled. No chemicals are necessary.

Facilities include housing and a dining room for registered guests. It is eleven miles to a restaurant, store, and service station. Massage is available on the premises. Credit cards are accepted for registered guests.

729   TASSAJARA ZEN MOUNTAIN CENTER
39171 Tassajara Rd.
Carmel Valley, CA 93924
Overnight Reservations   415 865-1899
Day Reservations   831 659-2229
■   Carmel Valley, CA 93924

Primarily a Buddhist Monastery with accommodations available to the public from late April to early September. Located in wooded mountains of the Ventana Wilderness southeast of Monterey. Elevation 1,500 feet.

Please, no drop-in visitors. Prior reservations are required. Guests are expected to respect the spirit of a monastic community.

Natural mineral water flows out of the ground at 140° into two large, enclosed soaking pools that average 110° and two outdoor pools at 106°. The water, which is not chemically treated, cools as it flows into nearby streambed soaking areas. The outdoor swimming pool is approximately 75°. There are also steambaths in the separate men's and women's bathhouses. Bathing suits are required in the swimming pool only and it is requested that robes be worn over bathing suits when walking around the grounds. Pools are handicap accessible with steps and handrails.

Rooms and meals are included as part of confirmed overnight reservation arrangements. The use of meditation facilities is also included. No credit cards accepted. It is ninety minutes to a store, cafe, and service station. The road is steep and dangerous, requiring good brakes and low gears.

(see map)

● **Near the village of Big Sur**

Four hot pools located at the end of a beautiful, ten-mile hike up the Big Sur River in the Ventana Wilderness Area of the Los Padres National Forest. During times of high water, some pools can become submerged and the Big Sur River will be more difficult to cross. Elevation 1,000 feet.

Four small soaking pools offer rest and relaxation after a long hike up the Big Sur River. Four friends can share the largest pool, which averages about 100° and overflows into a riverside soaker below. The largest pool sits up on a bluff above the river so it shouldn't be affected by the weather. However, the three other pools are all right on the river and will undoubtedly be washed out or filled with sediment from above every winter. The hottest of the pools is the second soaker on the river, a small grotto is sandbagged to separate the hot water from the cold. Hot water is piped down the steep bluff and directly into the tub through a hose. The spring is near one of the most popular hiking routes, so the distance is no assurance of quiet or privacy during the summer months, particularly on weekends.

If you decide to camp near the springs you can choose from Sykes or Pine Ridge campgrounds. All services can be found in Big Sur including several options for lodging and dining. Be sure to fill up your tank in Carmel, the gas in Big Sur is very expensive.

Soakers Bible

Directions: From Monterey head south on Highway 1. Park at the Big Sur Ranger Station where you can get recent trail information, a hiking map and a permit for your campfire and cook stove. Follow the Pine Ridge Trail from the east side of the parking area, as it parallels between the highway above, and campground below. You'll cross a small creek before the trail heads moderately uphill for the first several miles. Five miles into the trail you'll pass through Terrace Creek Campground, a lush area with downed old growth, fern covered banks and a fantastic waterfall. This is a good place to have lunch. Continue on to mile 7 where there's a sign indicating Barlow Flat Campground down along the river. Barlow Flat is a sideshot, so don't bother going down another hill unless you want to camp there. Instead, keep going straight another 3 miles through old growth madrone and cedars to a series of downhill switchbacks which will lead you to the Big Sur River. Once you reach the river go downstream about 50 yards to find a good crossing. You will have to cross over and back again to pick up the trail leading about 0.25 miles down to the pools. They are on the left just after a huge down tree crosses the river.

Source maps for trails: USGS *Ventana Cones, Partington Ridge* (springs not shown).

GPS: N 36 14.916 W 121 41.112

Note: This location involves a ten-mile hike on the Pine Ridge Trail, and a Wilderness Permit must be obtained from the Big Sur Ranger Station. The Forest Service issues a trail map to those holding Wilderness Permits, and on request, will mark the hot-spring location on that map. Check your preparations, including water supply, with the ranger.

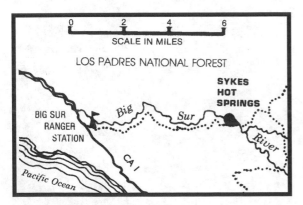

SCALE IN MILES
0   2   4   6

LOS PADRES NATIONAL FOREST

SYKES HOT SPRINGS

BIG SUR RANGER STATION

Big   Sur   River

CA 1

Pacific Ocean

Warren Vidrine

731 MERCEY HOT SPRINGS

62964 Little Panoche Rd. 209 826-3388
Firebaugh, CA 93622
www.merceyhotsprings.com

One hundred sixty acres of rolling hills in California's central valley is home to the only hot spring resort in this area. Spring and Fall are choice times to visit when you can spend warm days in the swimming pool and cool evenings in one of the hot tubs. Altitude 1,200 feet. Open all year from 9 AM to 9 PM for day use. Reservations for camping and cabins highly recommended.

Natural hot mineral water comes out of a spring at temperatures of 119° allowing seven outdoor claw-foot style bath tubs located on a deck to be filled at whatever temperature the soaker wants. Bathing suits optional in this area. A new artesian well now provides 110° water to the swimming pool allowing it to be regulated for an optimum swimming experience year-round. Minimal chlorine is used in the pool. Swim suits are required.

A variety of cabins with and without kitchens and fireplaces is available for rent. A newly renovated cabin will have its own private hot tub. There are also camping spaces with water and full RV hookups with water and sewer hookups. No electricity is provided. Day-use entitles you to the use of the picnic areas, swimming pool, and outdoor hot tub. Groups of ten or more get a ten percent discount. Gas and camping supplies can be bought thirty-five miles away in Los Banos. Ice and drinking water are available.

Directions: From the north—go south on I-5 for 24 miles past the I-5/Hwy 152 interchange. (Do not take the Mercey Hot Springs Rd. exit!) Continue 8 miles past the Mercey Hot Springs exit and get off at the Shields Ave./Little Panoche Rd. exit (J1), go right (west) for 13 miles.

From the south—go north on I-5 for 70 miles past Coalinga to the Shields Ave./Little Panoche Rd. exit (J1). Do not take the Panoche Road exit; go past the Panoche Rd. exit 11 miles to reach the Little Panoche Rd. exit. Take a left and drive west for 13 miles.

Courtesy of Kiva Retreat

732 A KIVA RETREAT

702 Water St. 831 429-1142
Santa Cruz, CA 95060
www.kivaretreat.com

Meditative and social areas set among trees, grass, and flowers lend a peaceful ambiance to this unusual, clothing-optional, hot-pool rental establishment. Located near the city center. No alcohol, drugs, smoking or glass.

A single day rate gives entry to the communal grass area, two large hot tubs, a cold-tub plunge, and a large sauna. Adjoining indoor dressing and social rooms are also available. Pools use gas-heated tap water and are treated with chlorine and ozone. Two outdoor private enclosures, rented by the hour, have water maintained at 102°, and include a shower, massage table, and servings of herbal tea. Whispers only are allowed in the large sauna. Towels and locks can be rented, or bring your own. Bathing suits are optional everywhere except in the front entry.

Massage is currently on the premises and spa services will soon be available. Major credit cards accepted. Phone for rates, reservations, and directions.

732 B   TEA HOUSE SPA
☐ 112 Elm St.   831 426-9700
Santa Cruz, CA 95060
www.teahousespa.com

Beautiful tiled hot pool and sauna rooms overlooking a Japanese bamboo garden, located in the heart of downtown Santa Cruz and available for rent by the hour.

Four private-space suites, consisting of a shower, changing area, and tub use bromine-treated tap water. The fiberglass pools offer a view of the garden and sliding shoji doors can be opened. Three of the suites also offer saunas. Water temperatures are maintained at 104°. Many of the tubs are handicap accessible. Herbal tea and large towels are provided.

Massage is available on the premises. Credit cards accepted. Phone for rates and reservations.

732 C   WELL WITHIN
☐ 417 Cedar St.   831 458-WELL
Santa Cruz, CA 95060
www.wellwithinspa.com

Beautifully appointed hot pool establishment with Japanese gardens, koi ponds, and waterfalls visible from the individual rooms. Located in downtown Santa Cruz and available for rent by the hour.

Four private indoor tubs and two outdoor tubs in private enclosures are maintained at approximately 102°. Two of the indoor tubs and both outdoor tubs have saunas which are cedar lined. The outdoor tubs can accommodate up to six people each and the gate between the two tubs can be opened to hold up to fourteen people. The tubs are treated with bromine. The entire facility is handicap accessible and one of the outdoor tubs is equipped with special railings.

A shower and changing area are found in each room. Towels and herbal tea are included. Massage and spa services are available by appointment. Credit cards accepted. Phone for rates, reservations, and directions.

733   GILROY YAMATO HOT SPRINGS

Sold to the Nature Conservancy of California.

734   GRAND CENTRAL SAUNA AND
HOT TUB CO.

376 Saratoga Ave.   408 247-8827
☐   San Jose, CA 95129

One of a chain of urban locations established by Grand Central, the pioneer in the room rent-a-tub business.

Twenty-one private indoor tubs are heated to 102-104° and treated with chlorine. The individual rooms each have a sauna and dressing room. Towels and soap are provided.

No credit cards or reservations are accepted. Phone for hours, rates, and directions.

735   WATERCOURSE WAY

165 Channing Ave.   650 462-2000
☐   Palo Alto, CA 94301
www.watercourseway.com

The beautiful oriental decor creates a comfortable and interesting environment, offering a variety of highly decorated rooms and experiences.

Pools for rent to the public use gas-heated tap water treated with chlorine. Nine individually decorated private rooms each have a different combination of hot pool, cold pool, sauna, and steambath. Water temperature in the pools is approximately 103°. To accommodate larger groups, two rooms can be joined.

Facials, spa treatments, massage (specializing in hot-stone massage) and gift store are available on the premises. Credit cards accepted. Phone for rates, reservations, and directions.

736 A   GRAND CENTRAL SAUNA AND
HOT TUB CO.

15 Fell St.   415 431-1370
☐   San Francisco, CA 94102

The first of a chain of urban locations established by Grand Central, a pioneer in the private room rent-a-tub business.

Pools in twenty-six private rooms, each with a sauna, are for rent to the public. The pools use gas-heated tap water treated with chlorine and are maintained between 102-104°. Towels and soap are provided.

Tanning booths are available on the premises. Credit cards are not accepted. Reservations are not accepted. Phone for rates and directions.

736 B   THE HOT TUBS

2200 Van Ness Ave.   415 441-TUBS
☐   San Francisco, CA 94109

One of the few stress-reduction establishments offering tile tubs and decks in a chrome and glass urban environment. Located on a main street just west of downtown.

Pools in twenty private rooms are for rent to the public. Gas-heated tap water treated with chlorine is maintained at 104°. A sauna, music, and rest area are included. Towels and soap are provided.

Massage and a juice bar are available on the premises. No credit cards are accepted. Phone for rates, reservations, and directions.

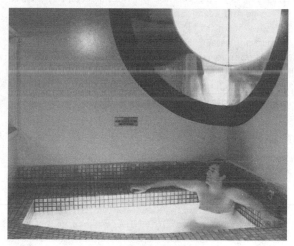

Hot Tubs of San Francisco welcomes you to "The Home of the 60-Minute Vacation, and "A Total Relaxation Experience." Sounds great.

737 F. JOSEPH SMITH'S MASSAGE THERAPY
158 Almonte   415 383-8260

☐   Mill Valley, CA 94941

www.josephsmithmassage.com

A Marin county healing center with two five-foot deep hot tubs nestled under redwood trees, located in a country setting.

Two private enclosures with chlorine-treated water and temperatures of approximately 104° are rented to the public. One of the tubs is available for communal use during the day. A cedar sauna is also for rent. Bathing suits are optional in the tub and sauna areas.

The prayer garden is open for relaxation and meditation. The crystal room also provides a space to meditate. Massage and advanced body therapy classes are available on the premises, as are chiropractic and acupuncture services. Massage classes and workshop space are available. Phone for rates, reservations, and directions.

738 SHIBUI GARDENS
19 Tamalpais Ave.   415 457-0283

☐   San Anselmo, CA 94960

An inviting blend of Marin County natural redwood hot tubs and lush landscaping. Located on a suburban side street.

Three privately enclosed hot tubs using bromine-treated, gas-heated tap water are for rent by the hour. Water temperatures are 101°. Enclosures are also equipped with cold showers. Bathing suits are optional inside the pool and sauna spaces.

A private indoor sauna is for rent on the premises. Massage is available. Phone for rates, reservations, and directions.

739 FROGS
10 School Street Plaza   415 453-7647

☐   Fairfax, CA 94930

May be the only nudist/naturist spa in the San Francisco Bay area. Located in a Marin County suburb and kept in pristine condition with clothing optional areas.

There are two outdoor hot tubs in private enclosures, plus a large communal hot tub and a cold plunge. There are two saunas, one completely redone in cedar, (and kept at the hottest temperatures in the Bay area) and a clothing-optional sundeck.

Voted "Best of Marin" for massage therapy, with therapists available until midnight. Walk-ins encouraged. Website offers links with naturist events and interests.

740 ALBANY SAUNA AND HOT TUBS
1002 Solano Ave.   510 525-6262

☐   Albany, CA 94706

www.albanysauna.com

Established in 1934 as one of the earliest rent-a-tub establishments in the Bay Area, it has since been extensively remodeled. Located two blocks west of San Pablo Ave.

Three outdoor, circular wooden tubs with jets enclosed pools for rent to the public use gas-heated tap water treated with chlorine and cleaned with a diatomaceous earth filtering system. Water temperature is maintained at approximately 105°. There are railings throughout the facility.

Four private, traditional Finnish-style rock-steam saunas, individually controlled for temperature with an outside air source for comfortable breathing, are available for rent. Eucalyptus scented towels are provided. Swedish-Esalen massage, and hair and skin care products are available on the premises. Major credit cards accepted. Phone for rates, reservations, and directions.

741 A THE HOT TUBS
1915 University Ave.   510 843-4343

☐   Berkeley, CA 94704

One of two urban locations in Berkeley and San Francisco.

Fourteen private rooms with pools use gas-heated tap water treated with chlorine. Water temperature varies between 102-104°. A sauna is included.

Towels and soap are provided. A juice bar is available on the premises. No credit cards or checks. Reservations are not accepted. Phone for rates and directions.

741 B   THE BERKELEY SAUNA
1947 Milvia St.   510 845-2341
☐   Berkeley, CA 94704

A stress-reduction establishment located a few yards north of University Ave.

Three private rooms with hot tubs, filled with gas-heated tap water. The bromine-treated water is maintained at temperatures from 104-106°.

Three private saunas are also for rent. Massage is available on the premises. Credit cards accepted. Phone for rates, reservations, and directions.

742 A   AMERICAN FAMILY SAUNA AND HOT TUB
2367 Pleasant Hill Rd.   925 472-0852
☐   Pleasant Hill, CA 94523
www.familyhottub.com

Outdoor establishment located near the intersection of Gregory and Pleasant Hill Rd. Closed Tuesday.

Ten private outdoor tubs in a garden setting, all with shower and dressing area. Some rooms are open to the sky. Gas-heated tap water treated with chlorine is maintained at 102-104°. Large, private Finnish-style sauna and therapeutic massage by our excellent staff available by appointment. Half price for half-hour tub before massage. Double and single massage rooms. Handicap accessible tubs available. Gift certificates. MasterCard and Visa accepted.

742 B   SUNSHINE SPA
1948 Contra Costa Blvd.   925 685-7822
☐   Pleasant Hill, CA 94523

Funky, fun-loving, rent-a-tub business that prides itself on its great massages. Located in the Pleasant Hill Plaza.

Pools using gas-heated tap water treated with bromine are for rent to the public. There are seven private rooms, each with an in-ground hot tub, shower, massage table, and mural. Pool temperatures range from 90-102°. Handicap accessible.

Massage is available on the premises. Major credit cards accepted. Phone for rates, reservations, and directions.

743   PIEDMONT SPRINGS
3939 Piedmont Ave.   510 652-9191
☐   Oakland, CA 94611
www.piedmontsprings.com

Urban rent-a-tub establishment situated in downtown Oakland.

Five private outdoor hot tubs, one in combination with a sauna, complete with redwood decks, changing areas, and showers. Water temperature is maintained at 102-104°. All tubs are ozone/chlorine treated. A dry Finnish sauna and a tiled private steam room are also available.

Massage, facials, body treatments, and other skin care services are offered. Phone for rates, reservations, directions, or a brochure. Credit cards accepted.

744   HOT TROPICS
17389 Hesperian Blvd.   510 278-8827
☐   San Lorenzo, CA 94580

Seniors, families, singles, and couples are welcome at Hot Tropics, just a couple of blocks off Hwy 880.

Fifteen private indoor rooms with tubs heated to 102-105° and treated with chlorine. Cool tubs are available in summer, or when requested. Seven rooms are also equipped with saunas, futons, showers, and radios. Saunas are large enough for two people to stretch out in and totally relax. Seven rooms do not have saunas but do have large skylights that roll open when the weather permits. Special minerals are added to the tubs. Handicap accessible.

No credit cards or reservations are accepted. Phone for hours, rates, and directions.

745   PARADISE SPAS
5168 Mowry Ave.   510 793-7727
☐   Fremont, CA 94538

Suburban rent-a-tub and tanning center located in a shopping center just off Highway 880.

Eight private rooms, including three with special black lighting, come complete with tubs and showers. The water is heated to 102-104° and is chlorine treated. Towels and radios are supplied.

Tanning booths are available. Credit cards accepted.

SOUTHERN CALIFORNIA

CA 190

■ 801 A-B

802 A ●
802 B-C ■ ■ 803 A-D
● ■ 804 A-C
★ Tecopa

NEVADA

CA 178

US 395

CA 127

I 15

CA 58

Barstow ★

I 40

US 395

I 15

CA 138

CA 247

805 ●
San
Bernardino ★

CA 62

Colorado

ARIZONA

■ 818
□ 819

Los Angeles ★

820

I 10

■ 806 A-Y
■ 807

Palm ★
Springs
■ 808

I 10

CA 111

817

San Juan Capistrano ★

I 15

I 5

CA 79

CA 86

■ 809 A-D

River

814 ■

CA 78

Salton
Sea

816 ■

CA 78

813 ■

810 ●

815 □

I 8

S 2

El Centro

I 8 ● 811

San Diego ★

812 ■

MEXICO

Pacific Ocean

This map was designed to be used with a standard highway map.

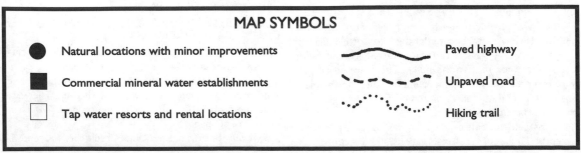

MAP SYMBOLS

● Natural locations with minor improvements

■ Commercial mineral water establishments

□ Tap water resorts and rental locations

〜 Paved highway

- - - Unpaved road

······ Hiking trail

Courtesy of Furnace Creek Resorts

Debbie Johnson

801 A FURNACE CREEK INN RESORT
PO Box 1   760 786-2345
■ Death Valley, CA 92328
www.furnacecreekresort.com

An historic resort built around a lush oasis on a barren hillside overlooking Death Valley. Elevation, sea level. Open mid-October to mid-May.

Natural mineral water flows out of a spring at 89°, into two outdoor pools, and through a large, palm-shaded arroyo. The swimming pool maintains a temperature of approximately 85°, and the flow-through rate is so great that no chemical treatment of the water is necessary. Bathing suits are required. Pools are for the use of registered guests only.

Facilities include two saunas, lighted tennis courts, rooms, two restaurants, live entertainment, dancing, and a bar. Major credit cards accepted.

801 B FURNACE CREEK RANCH RESORT
PO Box 1   760 786-2345
■ Death Valley, CA 92328

A family setting, the Furnace Creek Ranch was the home of the original "20-mule team." Located just down the hill from the Furnace Creek Inn in a green oasis setting surrounded by Death Valley National Park. Elevation 214 feet below sea level. Open all year.

Water from a natural warm spring is piped down from the 89° spring serving the Inn to a swimming pool at the ranch. The rate of flow-through is so great that a temperature of approximately 85° is maintained and no chemical treatment is necessary. The pool is for the enjoyment of registered guests only. Bathing suits are required. Most facilities are handicap accessible; handicap rooms are available.

Other amenities include 224 guest accommodations, three restaurants, a saloon, three retail shops, a service station, an eighteen-hole golf course, tennis courts, basketball courts, a children's playground, and horseback riding (October-May). Massage therapy is also offered. For those of you who want to fly in, there is a small airstrip located near by. All major credit cards accepted. Contact resort for further information.

Sally Jackson

Soakers Bible

802 A   WARM SPRINGS

● **North of Shoshone**
In Death Valley National Park

Fig trees, bamboo, mesquite, oleanders, cottonwood trees, tamarisk, and lots of grapevines line the trail to this warm spring located in a rocky canyon near several abandoned buildings and mines. Open all year, weather dependent.

Natural mineral water trickles out of the rocks at the top of a canyon creating a small pool about four-feet wide, six-feet long, and maybe a foot deep. The water temperature is 94°. The cooler water in this very hot climate would be great on one of those baking desert days.

No services on the premises but camping is not prohibited. All services are back in Shoshone.

Directions: One and one-half miles north of Shoshone, turn west on SR 178 heading toward Badwater. Continue 28 miles past Ashford Junction to West Side Rd. Turn west on this good gravel road for 3 miles, then turn left on Butte Valley Road and go 11 miles. It gets worse and worse the closer you get to the springs. You will travel through an abandoned talc mine as you head west through a canyon just before the turnoff to the springs. On the left at the base of the mountains are some large trees and the parking area.

GPS: N 35 57.995 W 116 55.918

802 B   SHOSHONE INN
■ Box 67   760 852-4335
Shoshone, CA 92384
www.shoshonevillage.com

Older resort located on CA 127 in desert foothills near the southern entrance to Death Valley. Elevation 1,600 feet. Open all year.

Natural mineral water flows out of a spring at 93° with such pressure that no pumps are needed to push it through the pipes to the outdoor swimming pool. The rate of flow-through is so great that a temperature of 92° is maintained and no chemical treatment of the water is necessary. A waterfall at the end of the pool cools the inflow for pool use in the summer. Pool use is available only to registered guests. Bathing suits are required.

Sixteen rooms, some with kitchenettes, include phones and cable TV, Crowbar Cafe and Saloon, general store and gift shop, and service station. RV hookups and overnight camping spaces are available at the ShoshoneRV Park (802 C). Major credit cards are accepted.

Location: Shoshone is 28 miles south of Death Valley Junction and 27 miles north of Pahrump on CA 127.

Note: Shoshone Airport, available for fly-in customers. Call Bishop Airport for details, 760 872-2971.

Soakers Bible

Lynn Foss

409   MELANIE HOT SPRINGS

●   **North of Silver City**

Rock soaking pools along the banks of the Middle Fork Gila River located below streams of hot water cascading from the face of the cliffs above and, depending on river level, in overhangs along the river's edge. Elevation 5,900 feet. Open all year; accessible only during low water flow as you will be fording the river eight to twelve times before reaching the spring.

Natural mineral water flows out of many rock fissures at 102°, twenty feet to forty feet above river level, and runs across a steep slope before dropping directly into the pool at the river's edge. During low water, three pools are found under the edge of the rocks, with hot water dripping from the ceiling at temperatures ranging from 98-101°. The pools are shallow and a shovel to dig them out would be a good idea. Clothing optional.

There are no services at the location. Camping is permitted at the Forks Campground where the trail starts and there is a shady camping area about a five-minute walk up river from the springs. All other services can be found one and one-half miles north on Hwy 15 at Doc Campbell's Post.

Directions: From Silver City drive north on Hwy 15, and just north of milepost 38 watch for Forest Forks Campground on the right. Follow the dirt road down to the banks of the Gila River, and park there. The road quickly deteriorates and heads into the river. Follow it downstream, crossing almost immediately. Next cross a side stream, then under the bridge back to the south bank. This third crossing, as well as fourth and fifth are deep and swift, even when the river level is low, use a walking stick for support. Only 3 more fords after this, leaving you on the north (left) side of the river. The trail heads through a forested area, which leads you then to the rocky beach. About 10 minutes since you last crossed the Gila, keep your eyes out for orange colored cliffs on the left, surrounded by greenery including grasses, yuccas and prickly pear cacti. Two soaking pools lie at the base of the cliff, their runoff leads to the river.

When fording rivers, one can only hike about 1mph. Melanie is about 1.5 miles downstream, so it really will take you 1–1.5 hours to get there by foot.

GPS: N 33 97.440 W 108 12.516

Note: Vehicles pulling trailers, busses, and RV's are not allowed north of the junction of Hwy 35 and Hwy 15 as Hwy 15 becomes incredibly narrow, steep and has very tight turns. You may be able to park at a campground at Lake Roberts, leave your trailer there and continue north in a passenger vehicle.

Courtesy of Wildwood Hot Springs

410   WILDWOOD RETREAT AND
■   HOT SPRINGS   505 536-3600
Gila Hot Springs, New Mexico
www. gilanet.com/wildwood

Four miles from the Gila Cliff Dwellings National Monument, Wildwood offers individuals and groups the perfect opportunity to relax in a spacious retreat cabin, camp in beautiful wooded surroundings, and soak in comfort. Elevation 5,600 feet. Closed in the winter. Call or email for information. Wildwood@gilanet.com.

Hot springs flowing from the Gila River are routed into hot pools of different temperatures. The temperatures range from 100-108° depending on the pool and the season. The fenced in bathing area is surrounded by trees with a patio space for sunbathing and is clothing optional after sunset.

Wildwood Retreat, located in the heart of the Gila Wilderness, has over twenty-five camping sites, including several car-camping sites along the beautiful West Fork of the Gila River, all under a cover of ponderosa pine and cottonwood trees. Most sites are just a short walk from our modern restroom with hot showers and flush toilets. There is also a private outdoor shower. Wildwood can rent you tents and camping gear. There is also a cozy camper kitchen/lounge with propane stoves for people wanting to cook their own food and spend leisurely time.

The spacious, private retreat center/cabin has a master bedroom with a double bed. The second bedroom has two single bunks. There is a hide-a-bed in the living area. (Linens not included.) The cabin has plenty of floor space and is ideal for small groups and workshops. It is also the perfect getaway for singles, couples or families who would like all the amenities of home. The full kitchen is stocked with pots and pans, dishes and toaster oven. It has an electric stove and full size fridge. The modern bathroom has a

shower/bathtub combination. The cabin is available for day or overnight use, short and long term rentals available.

The group facility, ideal for large gatherings, includes a complete kitchen with full size gas range, refrigerator, microwave, toasters, coffee makers, dishes, pans and silverware located along the beautiful Gila River. It includes a stage area with lawns for gatherings. The picnic area includes large picnic tables, BBQ's, and a fire pit.

There are options to rent all or part of the Wildwood Retreat with reasonable daily, multi-day or weekly rates. They give discounts to groups. Contact them for reservations and more information. wildwood@gilanet.com

Directions: There are two routes to Wildwood from Silver City. One route travels through Pinos Altos and is very windy. This route is not recommended for RV's and vehicles over twenty feet long. Drivers of large vehicles would be well advised to take the alternate route through the Mimbres Valley.

Through Pinos Altos: From 180 in Silver City, go north on Hwy 15, 38.9 miles. Stay on Hwy 15 past Pinos Altos, and continue down the road through the Gila National Forest. After the Lake Roberts turnoff, you will climb over Copperas Pass and down into the Gila River valley. Approximately one mile after you pass Forks Campground, turn right on Access Road, and then right on Jackass Lane. Wildwood is near the end of Jackass Lane.

Through Mibres Valley: From Silver City, travel east on highway 180 to Santa Clara. Turn left (east) on Hwy 152 towards San Lorenzo. Turn left (north) on Hwy 35 and go past Lake Roberts until you intersect Hwy 15. Turn right (north) on 15 and head on over Copperas Pass, down into the Gila River valley. Approximately one mile after you pass the Forks Campground, look for Access Road and the sign for Wildwood Retreat on the right.

Soakers Bible

411   THE WILDERNESS LODGE AND HOT SPRINGS

Jackass Lane   **505 536-9749**

■   **Gila Hot Springs, NM**

www.gilahot.com

Formerly a school house in Hurley, this hundred year old lodge was completely dismantled and moved to its present site. Located on the West Fork of the Gila River, four miles south of the Gila Cliff Dwelling National Monument. Registered guests only.

Deep hot pools, fed by natural mineral water, are built of local stone bedded in bentonite clay, and surrounded by vegetation and an adobe privacy wall.

A two-bedroom suite with a private bath is on the first floor. Five bedrooms with a shared bath are on the second. Fresh coffee, home-baked breads and muffins served in the morning. There are two large rooms suitable for meetings and workshops, weddings, and reunions. Communal kitchen.

Directions: From Silver City take Hwy 15 north to Gila Hot Springs. Turn right on Access Rd. (0.25 miles south of Doc Campbell's Post), then turn left on Jackass Lane. Wilderness Lodge is the only house on the left.

Miles and miles of hiking area in the Gila Wilderness are within close proximity. It is recommended that you purchase the USDA Forest Service *Gila Wilderness* map before setting out. To order call 505 536-9344.

Soakers of all ages enjoy soaking in the pools and the great hospitality.

412 A GILA HOT SPRINGS VACATION CENTER

Gila Hot Springs, Rte. 11   505 536-9551
■ Silver City, NM 88061
www.gilahotspringsranch.com

An all-year vacation center providing multiple services, located in the middle of the Gila National Forest. Elevation 5,000 feet. Open all year.

Doc Campbell's Post offers a country store with groceries, snack bar, ice, gas, fishing and hunting licenses, supplies, gifts, laundromat, showers, and most important, knowledgeable advice about the area. Arrangements can be made for half-day and full-day horseback rides, pack trips, fishing and hunting trips, youth group trips, drop camps, and pack stock for backpackers. Reservations for lodging are also made here. Credit cards are accepted at the store.

Lodging includes two downstairs apartment units and a spacious upstairs apartment, all equipped with kitchenettes, and a completely furnished trailer all using natural hot springs water for drinking, showers, and baths. The RV park has hot and cold taps at all hookups. Hot springs water can be hooked up to your trailer, or you can use the RV Park showers and hot tub. A picnic pavilion offers grill and fire ring, plus a children's playground.

Note: Allow two hours for the thirty-nine mile drive from Silver City along scenic route NM 15, a two-lane mountain road which twists and winds through the Gila National Forest.

412 B GILA HOT SPRINGS—RIVER
● CAMPGROUND

Shady, primitive area with hot pools beside the river. Natural mineral water flowing at 150° from the springs on the east bank of the Gila River is piped to the riverside camping area. The existing pools have been dug out and restructured, offering a much nicer soak. The first pool is quite hot at 110°. The other two pools cool to 105°. The bathing suit issue seems to be decided by those who are camping there, although official policy is bathing suits required. Ground is fairly level, so could be handicap accessible with caution.

All that is provided is a water spigot with safe drinking water, and nearby rest rooms. There are seven rustic campsites for tents and self-contained vehicles only.

Directions: Located right off of NM 15, the main road into the area. Watch for signs on your right (before you get to Doc Campbell's store). There is a small fee.

Photos courtesy of Gila Hot Springs

A perfect place to camp on the way to view the Gila Cliff Dwellings. If you need supplies or directions you can stop at Doc Campbell's Post just up the road. This whole area is surrounded by beautiful wilderness and is well worth a visit.

413 A   MIDDLE FORK HOT SPRING

●   North of the Gila Visitors Center

A series of shallow rock and sand soaking pools on the Middle Fork of the Gila River, one-half mile from the Gila Visitors Center and the Indian Cliff Dwellings. Elevation 5,800 feet. Open all year, subject to high water in the river, which must be forded twice each way.

Natural mineral water flows out of the spring on the east side of the canyon at 130°, directly into several shallow pools next to the river, where the water gradually cools as it flows through the pools. Other pools can be found up stream. Bathing suits advisable during the day.

All services are back at the Gila Hot Springs Vacation Center.

Directions: To reach the trailhead, go to the far end of the visitor center parking lot and turn right. There is a special parking area for hikers up the hill on the left. Walk down the road past the gate to the bottom of the hill. The main trail (157) continues toward the canyon, crossing the river almost immediately. The pools are on the east (right) side of the canyon after the second crossing At the second crossing, a feeder stream comes in from your left. The water is only warm, but it is shady and more secluded. Continuing upstream you can find several grottoes where the water is deep enough for floating. Check at the ranger station before starting out.

GPS: N 33 14.014 W 108 14.059

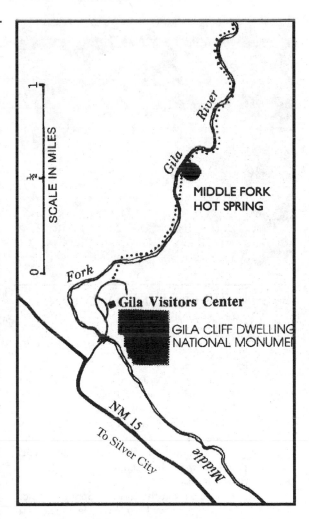

Ysabel Luecke

During years of heavy rain, the river bed often changes its course requiring that new pools be dug out.

Note: Allow two hours for the forty-four mile drive from Silver City along scenic route NM 15, a two-lane mountain road that twists and winds through the Gila National Forest.

For further information contact:
The Gila National Forest Service,
3005 E. Camino del Bosque, Silver City, New Mexico 88061
505 388-8201
or
Silver City Ranger District
505 538-2771

Photos by Soakers Bible

413 B   HOUSE LOG CANYON (JORDAN) HOT SPRINGS

● **Northwest of the Gila Visitors Center**

Remote, unimproved hot springs on a tree- and fern-covered hillside in the Gila Wilderness where the canyon meets the Middle Fork of the Gila River. Elevation 5,900 feet. Accessible only during low water in the river.

Natural mineral water flows out of several springs at 100° and cascades directly into two rock-edged, sandy-bottom pools large enough to hold ten people. The upper pools is about twenty-five by fifeen feet and at least thigh deep. Clothing optional.

All services are back at the Gila Hot Springs Vacation Center. Check with the very knowledgeable people here about trails, etc. as they have hiked this area for years. Make sure you have sufficient water and supplies.

Directions: To begin the 8-mile hike, park at the Middle Fork trailhead (trail 157). Follow the trail past the locked gate and straight upstream into the canyon. The trail follows the river for 6 miles until it joins with the trail from Little Bear Canyon. Immediately cross the Middle Fork and head upstream. Including this first crossing, there will be 15 more crossings before you reach the springs on the northeast side of the canyon. Continue a bit further and look for a marshy area with hot water seeps. It is abut 2 miles to the hot springs from the junction of Little Bear Canyon and the Middle Fork. A mile farther up the Middle Fork beyond Big Bear Canyon, are more warm springs called The Meadows at the mouth of Indian Creek Canyon. (See next entry.)

GPS: N 33 17.568 W 108. 16.236

413 C   MEADOWS WARM SPRINGS

● **Northwest of the Gila Visitors Center**

Warm springs fill frog ponds and small streams throughout the south end of a large meadow along the Gila River, accessible only by foot. Elevation 6,360 feet. Best time to go is late spring through November, but be sure to check water levels in the Gila River due to the many crossings necessary to reach the meadow.

Warm water flows out of the ground in several places forming pools and streams throughout the thick grassy meadow. The main pool is about thirty feet by twelve feet at it's widest. The water is only about 80°, which is a great environment for all sorts of frogs, fish and underwater plants. Hikers could float around in the pond during the hot summer months, but it's not a place to swim or bathe. Lots of other warm water streams through the grasses.

There are no amenities at the spring. The nearest services are at Doc Cambell's Post near Visitors Center. You can camp anywhere. About a quarter mile past the warm springs there are several nice campsites with log benches and fire pits; this is a great area to watch wildlife.

Directions: Follow directions to Jordan Canyon Hot Springs. From here you must continue upstream for another 39 crossings, which is 5.5 miles to Meadows Warm Springs. After that 39th crossing, it's still a couple hundred yards to the pool. When you reach a clearing you'll see a pool on the right side of the trail.

Do check the website for updated river level information before you set out on this journey. http://waterdata.usgs.gov/nm/nwis/uv/

GPS Coordinates: N 33 18.414 W 108 19.410

Note: A wilderness permit is required before entering this area. While obtaining your permit from the ranger at the Gila Visitors Center, check on the adequacy of your provisions and on the level of the water in the river. Source maps: *Gila National Forest*, USGS *Woodland Park*. (Springs not shown on either map.)

Steve Heerema

414 A   TURKEY CREEK HOT SPRINGS
(see map)
●   North of the town of Gila

Several truly primitive hot springs accessible only via a challenging and rewarding hike into the Gila Wilderness. Elevation 5,200 feet. Not accessible during high water in the Gila River.

Natural mineral water (approximately 160°) flows out of many rock fractures along the bottom of Turkey Creek Canyon and combines with creek water in several volunteer-built soaking pools. Temperatures are regulated by controlling the relative amounts of hot and cold water entering a pool. Be careful, as many of these pools are quite hot. The apparent local custom is clothing optional.

There are no services available, but there are a limited number of overnight camping spots near the hot springs. Visitors have done an excellent job of packing out their trash; please do your part to maintain this tradition. All services are a long seventeen miles away in the town of Gila.

Michele Sullivan

Directions: Starting at the end of the 4WD road, Wilderness Trail FS 724 crosses the Gila River several times before reaching Wilderness Trail FS 155, which starts up Turkey Creek Canyon. Approximately 2 miles from the trail junction, FS 155 begins to climb a ridge separating Turkey Creek from Skeleton Canyon. Do not follow FS 155 onto that ridge. (If you encounter switchbacks you've gone the wrong way.) Instead, stay to the right in the bottom of Turkey Creek Canyon, even though there is often no visible trail. Another half-mile will bring you to the first of the springs. This is a very arduous hike, often entailing climbing over boulders and following almost non-existent trails.

Source maps: *Gila National Forest, Gila Wilderness and Black Range Primitive Area*, USGS *Canyon Hill*. (Note: Springs are not shown.)

GPS: N 33 06.480 W 108 28.980

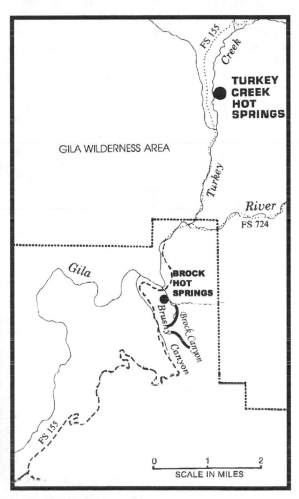

Camilla Van Sickle and Bill Pennington

414 B   BROCK CANYON HOT SPRINGS
(see map on page 103)
● **North of the town of Gila**

Several hidden pools bubble up through the sandy floor of a small canyon near the Gila River located near Turkey Creek Hot Springs. Elevation 5,000 feet. Not accessible during high water as there could be road washouts; best visited during cooler weather.

Natural hot, 110-115° mineral water, fills the six foot in diameter, sandy bottom pool that is on the other side of a small cottonwood tree. About a foot deep, the water is very clear. The second pool is just a bit farther up the canyon hiding in a small grove of Aspens. The water is a more comfortable 103°. Be prepared to clean this one out as it is often partially silted in. There's been a report that oil (smelling like crankcase oil) has been found in the lower pools, but not in an upper pool up on the right side of the canyon where the hot water source comes directly in from the side.

You can car camp within 500 yards of the hot springs, or pack your things into the wash. Beware of monsoon weather and do not camp in the wash during the rainy season. Be sure to bring everything you need with you as the nearest source of supplies is back in Gila.

Directions: From the town of Gila, New Mexico, just east of US 180, take SR 153 north. The state road ends and becomes FR 155, the Turkey Creek Road, where high clearance is a must and 4WD is a good thing to have. Follow FR 155 for 7 very scenic, very bumpy miles until it goes down to the Gila River. The road makes a sharp left bend at that point—on the right is a road leading into Brock Canyon which a 4WD vehicle can easily negotiate. At one point the road splits into two obvious fors. The right fork is really steep, the left curves around an easier route, but they meet again within a half mile. About 150 yards up the canyon, old mine shafts are visible on the left, and just beyond that are two very small soaking pools filled with tepid, algae laden water. A bit farther up the canyon on the right wall is a very hot sandy bottomed pool, too hot to soak in during the summer but would probably be great in much cooler weather because the slow flow doesn't vary. Another 75 yards up the canyon are two more soaking pools. One is nearly filled in and the other one had the distinct odor of crankcase oil; bubbles of it floated on the surface.

Source maps: *Gila National Forest, Gila Wilderness and Black Range Primitive Area*, USGS *Canyon Hill*. (Note: Springs are not shown.)
GPS: N 33 03.504 W 108 29.904

Camilla Van Sickle and Bill Pennington

Soakers Bible

The pools almost always flood each year. Bring a shovel with you to dig out some new ones.

415 A   SAN FRANCISCO (BUBBLES) HOT SPRING—UPPER

● **South of the town of Pleasanton**
(Information provided by the Glenwood Ranger Station)

A large, warm water pool and a smaller hot pool are located under a spectacular cliff on the west side of the San Francisco River's flood plain. The hot springs are located two miles south of Pleasanton. Forest Service Signs identifying access will get you to the trailhead. A bulletin board provides visitor information and restrictions (NO nudity!!). The hot springs, pool, and the surrounding area are a day use only recreation site, although camping is allowed for seven days south of the trailhead. Elevation 4,500 feet at the pool. High water can occur during all four seasons making the fording of the river very dangerous.

A large, warm water pool and a smaller hot pool are located under a spectacular cliff on the west side of the San Francisco River's flood plain. Natural mineral water flows up through the sandy pool bottom at approximately 106°, maintaining the larger pool at 96-100° depending on air temperature. The smaller pool maintains a higher temperature, up to 104°. The pool flushes and cleans itself during high water and flows out over a small dam. Watch out for rattlesnakes!

Directions: South of mile marker 58 on US 180 go over the cattle guard to the west and follow the dirt road (Forest Road 4229) for approximately 0.5 miles. The road terminates in a parking area and trailhead that includes a vault toilet and an information bulletin board. The trail starts near the bulletin board and is approximately 1.5 miles to the pools. The trail is only slightly improved and goes across the slope to the southwest and drops to a river crossing. The trail is very steep the last 0.5 miles, so caution and good walking boots are advised. You can see the big pool from the edge of the cliff before the steep descent. The hike can take a good hour, particularly on the return.

IMPORTANT NOTE: Before you set out to the springs, it is strongly recommended that you contact the Glenwood Ranger Station, Gila Nation Forest, at 505 539-2481 or email bodonnel@fs.fed.us.

GPS: N 33 14.321 W 108 52.842

There are tent camping spaces, and sixteen RV spaces with full hookups available. Spaces are divided by natural rocks and vegetation. Bring a shade cloth. There is one standard bathhouse with a shower, toilet and sink. There is also a laundry room which you can use for a small fee. It is sixty miles to a major city, Silver City, and four-and-one-half miles to Glenwood where there is a country store for basics, a cafe and gas. Groups can rent the entire site. No credit cards accepted.

Directions: Mile marker 56 is the turnoff for FR 519 (The only indication for FR 519 is a binocular sign #42.) This road winds up at the gate to the property.

Photos by Camilla Van Sickle and Bill Pennington

415 B   SUNDIAL HOT SPRINGS
■   PO Box 152   505 539-2712
    Glenwood, NM 88039
    www.sundialsprings@ gilanet.com/sundial springs

This private campground, hot springs and wildlife sanctuary is located on thirty-nine acres, surrounded by National Forest and perched above the San Francisco River. The pinons, grassland, junipers, and mesquite complete this high desert landscape. There is much wildlife in the area and particular effort should be made not to disrupt any of the big horn sheep, particularly. Elevation 4,700 feet. Visits by reservations only—twenty-four hours in advance.

Natural water comes up at 110° through a fifty-foot well that taps a fault in a large river geothermal source. It is pumped at 105° into several rock and mortar pools in the summer, and one pool in the winter. The first pool, located under the junipers, is 150 square feet and will comfortably hold three to four people. The second will hold three people. Pool three flows directly into pool four and is big enough to be booked for a larger group. The pools are drained and refilled often and require onlylight chlorination in the summer. Overflow from the pools is used to irrigate dozens of interesting plants that surround the pools and line the paths. Decks surround the pools. You are required to bathe, using only organic soap, before entering the pools. Handicap accessible with help. Clothing optional.

If you want privacy and to soak all by yourself, this is definitely the spot.

The obvious trail continues about 2 miles, sometimes taking you away from the river, and then the old riverbed is the trail for the next 2 miles, (At this point you are paralleling private property. Do not trespass.) On the south bank, look for a pipe and sign for Frisco Box Spring. Follow a well-worn, slightly uphill path 75 yards to the concrete box. The box may be covered with vegetation.

GPS: N 33 49.860 W 108 48.180

---

416   FRISCO BOX HOT SPRING

● **North of the town of Reserve**

Shallow, concrete soaking pool with spectacular views, located in a scenic canyon at the end of a somewhat rugged but beautiful four mile trail, much of it along the San Francisco River. Elevation 6,800 feet. Open all year, subject to high water and flash floods.

Natural mineral water flows out of a spring at 100° and is piped to a four-foot by eight-foot by twenty-inch-deep concrete box located above river level. The apparent local custom is clothing optional.

Camping is permitted anywhere in the National Forest. It is twelve miles to groceries and gasoline and all other services in Reserve.

Directions: Start at the Reserve Ranger Station to obtain current information on weather conditions, river level, and a Gila National Forest Map. (505-533-6232). This area is subject to flash floods.

If you've been to this spring before, beware, the access has changed and you will trespass by taking the old route. South of Luna on Hwy 180, watch for a sign on the East Side of the road indicating San Francisco Warm Springs Trailhead (right around mile marker 14). This is Forest Service Road 35, located north of a scenic outlook. You won't see the sign if you're coming from the north so watch for the mile marker or vista point to avoid missing the turn. Follow this 4WD track 13 miles through gravel, fallen rocks and otherwise unimproved road, to the beginning of the trail.

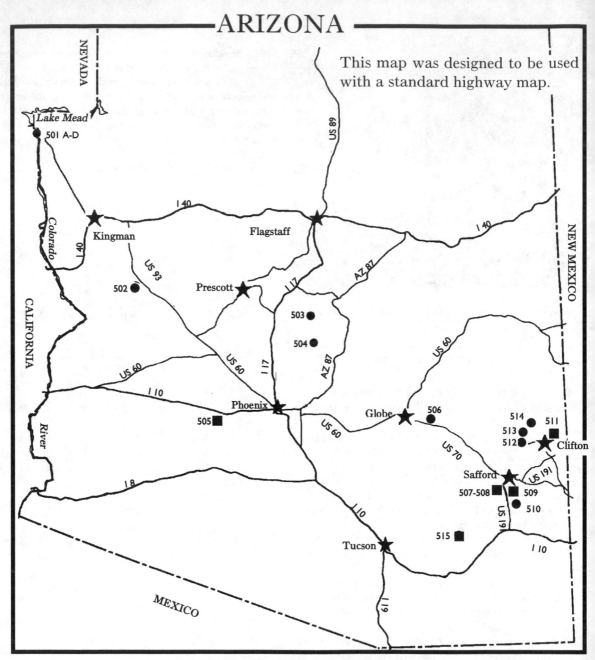

ARIZONA

This map was designed to be used with a standard highway map.

NEVADA

NEW MEXICO

CALIFORNIA

Lake Mead
501 A-D

Colorado

I 40

US 89

Kingman

Flagstaff

I 40

I 40

River

US 93

502

Prescott

I 17

AZ 87

503

504

US 60

AZ 87

US 60

I 17

US 60

I 10

Phoenix

505

Globe

506

US 60

US 70

514

513   511

512

Clifton

US 191

Safford

507-508   509

510

US 191

I 8

I 10

515

I 10

Tucson

I 19

US 191

MEXICO

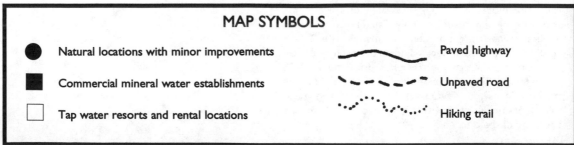

MAP SYMBOLS

● Natural locations with minor improvements

■ Commercial mineral water establishments

□ Tap water resorts and rental locations

〜〜 Paved highway

- - - Unpaved road

⋯⋯ Hiking trail

HOT SPRINGS OF THE LOWER COLORADO

Over many centuries, flash floods have carved hundreds of spectacular canyons that lead into the Colorado River. In three of these canyons, downstream from Hoover Dam, natural mineral water flows out of rocky sidewalls at temperatures up to 125°, then gradually cools as it tumbles over a series of waterfalls between sandy-bottom pools. The water is sparkling clear, with no odor and a pleasant taste. In all three of these canyons, volunteers continue to build rock-and-sand soaking pools, even though most of them are washed away every year by the floods. Elevation 800 feet. You can reach these pools all year; however, the extreme heat during the summer months may make this area unpleasant. It is also highly recommended that you check at Willow Beach regarding floods and high water during the rainy season.

Land routes to these springs range from the difficult to the impossible. Most visitors rent an outboard-powered boat at the Willow Beach Marina, which is located at mile marker 52, eight miles downriver from Arizona (Ringbolt) Hot Springs. Willow Beach also has a ramp for launching your own boat, gas for boats, and a store for supplies. There are no overnight facilities at Willow Beach. It is twenty miles to all services in Boulder City, Nevada. The access road to Willow Beach connects with US 93, fourteen miles south of Hoover Dam on the Arizona side of the river.

Rafters and kayakers can obtain a special permit from the Lake Mead National Recreation Area to put in just below Hoover Dam, float to the various hot springs, and take out at Willow Beach.

The National Park Service maintains pit toilets at the entrances to Gold Strike and Arizona (Ringbolt) Hot Springs.

Note: The amount of water being released from Hoover Dam is controlled by the Bureau of Reclamation and may change from hour to hour, substantially affecting the water level in the river. Therefore, it is important that you secure your boat or raft in a manner that will withstand such changes.

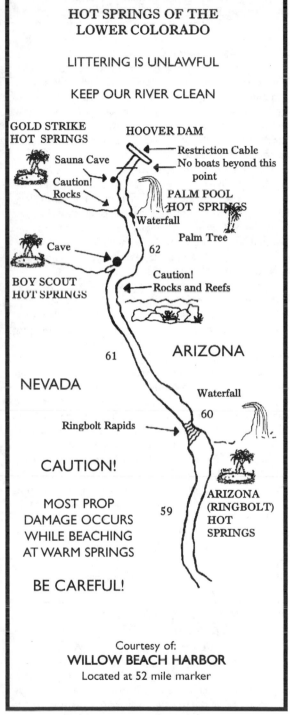

HOT SPRINGS OF THE LOWER COLORADO

LITTERING IS UNLAWFUL

KEEP OUR RIVER CLEAN

GOLD STRIKE HOT SPRINGS
HOOVER DAM
Sauna Cave
Restriction Cable
No boats beyond this point
Caution! Rocks
PALM POOL HOT SPRINGS
Waterfall
Palm Tree
Cave
62
Caution! Rocks and Reefs
BOY SCOUT HOT SPRINGS
61
ARIZONA
NEVADA
Waterfall
60
Ringbolt Rapids

CAUTION!

MOST PROP DAMAGE OCCURS WHILE BEACHING AT WARM SPRINGS

BE CAREFUL!

59
ARIZONA (RINGBOLT) HOT SPRINGS

Courtesy of:
WILLOW BEACH HARBOR
Located at 52 mile marker

501 A   ARIZONA (RINGBOLT) HOT SPRINGS

(see map)

● **Near Hoover Dam**

This is the most popular of the three hot springs because it is closest to Willow Beach and downstream from the turbulent water of Ringbolt Rapids. It is one-eighth mile downriver from mile marker 60, and two small warning buoys can be seen on a large submerged rock near the beach at the bottom of this canyon. There is no visible stream at the beach because the hot water disappears into the sand a hundred yards before reaching the river.

The long narrow canyon has beautiful rock formations and a few sections that require some scrambling ability. As you head upstream, you will often be walking in the streambed as well as climbing over sharp rocks, so be prepared with appropriate footwear. Barefoot is definitely not recommended. There is a ranger-installed metal ladder at the one major waterfall.

Source springs in the upper canyon run at 106° or more, depending on water flow, and volunteers have built a rock and sand soaking pool which can be very, very hot–be careful. The geothermal water is cooled down to approximately 95° by the time it flows over the twenty-five-foot waterfall.

There is a large amount of camping space in the lower canyon and on a dry sandy plateau just south of the canyon mouth. When you enter the canyon from the river, bear left when the trail splits inland from the beach. A pit toilet is near the camping area. This is the only spring along the river that has a practical overland route.

Hiking directions: From Hoover Dam, drive southeast on US 93 to mile post 4.2 and a dirt parking area on your right, at the head of White Rock Canyon. Follow this canyon downhill, through the wash, to the river. Then follow the edge of the river 0.25 miles south to the lower end of Ringbolt Hot Springs canyon and hike upstream to the springs. Distance 2.9 miles, with an 800-foot elevation change. The trail is rated moderately strenuous, so allow at least 2.5 hours each way. Watch for Bighorn sheep.

GPS: N 35 57.650 W 114 43.506

501 B   PALM POOL WATERFALL
●   HOT SPRINGS   (see map)

Past mile marker 62 (coming from Arizona Hot Spring) on the east side of the river is a lone, very dead, palm tree and an obvious waterfall splashing into the river. A difficult scramble up and around the falls brings you to the a very cozy two-person soaking pool right above the waterfall. It may take a little cleaning out as it is seldom used because of the difficult climb.

GPS: N 35 59.7300 W 114 44.2782

Photos by Chris Andrews

The above soaking pool can be reached by climbing the ladder located up the canyon from the landing beach at *Arizona (Ringbolt) Hot Springs.*

Palm Pool Waterfall: If you are lucky and the water level in the river is quite low, which is very unusual, you can actually get a hot shower at the bottom of the falls. The water temperature is a nice warm 100 degrees. Be sure to tie up your boat well or it may be downstream when you get through soaking.

Hot water seeping out of the rocks fills several soaking pools up and down the four mile canyon.

501 C GOLD STRIKE HOT SPRINGS

(see map)

● **Near Hoover Dam**

The beach at the bottom of this canyon is within sight of the warning cable stretched across the river just below the dam. One hundred yards up the canyon from the beach, natural mineral water flows out of cliff seeps at 109° into a series of volunteer-built soaking pools. The canyon is about four miles long with about two miles of springs creating multiple places to soak in water temperatures ranging from 98-110°.

As you head farther up the canyon, you will often be walking in the stream bed as well as climbing over sharp rocks, so be prepared with appropriate footwear.

The canyon includes several beautiful waterfalls, which can be bypassed only with some strenuous scrambling along smooth rock walls. Near the bottom of the first large falls is a sandy-bottom pool with a water temperature of 100°.

From the river, the landmark for this canyon is a pit toilet in the sandy area at the wide canyon mouth. In the river near the canyon mouth, there are some large underwater rocks that cause rapids. There are also large rocks in the shallow water close to shore, making it difficult to navigate into this canyon entrance. Space for overnight camping at the beach is very limited. If you do choose to camp, set up at the far inland edge of the sand, or the changing river levels may flood your site.

Note: Hiking overland to this spring is not recommended. It is extremely difficult and dangerous.

GPS: N 35 59.970 W 114 44.550

501 D BOY SCOUT HOT SPRINGS

(see map)

● **Near Hoover Dam**

A large cave, shaped like a human ear, can be seen on the west riverbank just upstream (north) from this canyon, whose entrance is protected by a land spit that blocks visibility from the south. When coming from the north, look for the bend in the river on the left past mile marker 62. Ahead is a layered rock formation. The canyon entrance and small beach sit in front of you before the river veers left. Landing on the gently sloping sandy beach is easy, but a sudden drop in river level could leave your boat many yards from the water.

The wide sand and gravel canyon mouth has a trickle of 70° water and plenty of camping space for a group. As you head upstream, the canyon narrows. You will often be walking in the streambed as well as climbing over sharp rocks, so be prepared with appropriate footwear. Barefoot is definitely not recommended. Remains of previously constructed cement dams and pipes are visible as you walk upstream into the canyon. There are several pools and waterfalls with temperatures up to 104° in the narrow upper canyon. The apparent local custom is clothing optional.

Note: There is no safe overland hiking trail to this hot spring.

GPS: N 35 58.968 W 114 44.898

Photos by Camilla Van Sickle and Bill Pennington

Photos by Camilla Van Sickle and Bill Pennington

502   KAISER WARM SPRING

● **Southeast of Kingman
and Wikieup (trailhead)**

A primitive sand-and-rock pool in a recently flooded desert canyon accessed by a fairly short, easy walk. Elevation 2,400 feet. Open all year, but recommended only October through April due to extreme summer heat. This area is also prone to flash floods.

Natural mineral water at about 100° flows out of a hole drilled into the rock on the side of the canyon wall into a sand-and-stone volunteer-built tub that never seems to get any hotter than 94°. The runoff flows over the edge onto the sandy canyon floor. Clothing optional.

There are no facilities at the springs. There is plenty of BLM land along US 93 where overnight parking is not prohibited. Pack-in camping is also possible on BLM land in the canyon. It is seven miles from the trailhead to Burro Creek Campground, which has rest rooms and RV dump, but no hookups. All other services are eleven miles from the trailhead in Wikieup.

Directions: From Burro Creek Campgrounds, take Hwy 93 north 5.5 miles to Kaiser Wash Bridge. Park off the pavement just north of the bridge and walk southwest down into the canyon for 1.5 miles to the spring. Or, drive under the bridge (nice shaded parking) and walk down the canyon. If you have a high clearance vehicle and 4WD, head south 0.1 miles south of mile marker 134 (which is north of the bridge), go right (southwest) on a dirt track across a cattle guard. Go 0.1 miles and turn left. Go 0.9 miles to the canyon. Park and walk down the canyon 0.7 miles to the spring on the left side of the canyon.

Source map: USGS Kaiser Spring.
GPS: N 34 33.838 W 113 29.893

Recent catasrophic floods wiped out the previous pools and lowered the floor of the canyon as much as ten feet in placeS. The floor of the canyon at the spring was lowered three feet. Volunteers have made a new sand and rock pool.

Camilla Van Sickle and Bill Pennington

Oscar Voss

Two different source springs feed the outside pool and the indoor pool. The entrance pictured on the right is part of the remains of an old resort.

---

503   VERDE HOT SPRINGS

● **Near the Town of Camp Verde**

Small cement soaking pools, all that remains of an historic resort which burned down years ago, are decorated with artwork and historic paintings, including one of the springs resort as it appeared in its heyday. Located on the west bank of the Verde River in a beautiful, high desert canyon. Elevation 2,800 feet. Open all year, subject to river level and bad-weather road hazards.

Natural mineral water flows out of several riverbank springs at 104° and into a small indoor cement soaking pool. A larger outdoor cement pool is built over another spring and averages 98°. Twenty feet below, at low-water level, are several more springs that feed volunteer-built, rock and sand pools. Fifty feet upstream from the large cement pool is a 104° pool in a riverbank cave. The apparent local custom is clothing optional. Conscientious visitors have done a superb job of packing out all trash. Please respect this tradition.

There are no services available on the premises, and it is more than twenty miles to the nearest store, service station, and market. Parking and camping are permitted only in a Forest Service campground located on the abandoned site of the hamlet of Childs. Therefore, it is a one and one-half mile hike to the river ford at Verde Hot Springs. Check at the ranger station in Camp Verde regarding road conditions and river level before attempting to reach this site.

Directions: Exit off 17 at exit 283 (Cottonwood, Payson, Camp Verde). Turn right on Hwy 260 and follow this road through the town of Camp Verde. Just outside of town, cross over a bridge and continue approximately 6 miles. On the right hand side of the road is a sign saying "Fossil Creek Rd. Verde River" (Forest Road 708). Turn right. In about 16 miles you will come to a "Y" (it's easy to miss)–take the right fork onto FR 502 and continue about another 7 miles to the parking area above the Childs Power Plant.

Follow a trail down to the river on your left marked with stone pilings. The hot springs are across the river, visible from the jeep road. Look for palm trees across the river and a stone wall along the riverbank. Depending on the river level, it may be necessary to ford the river twice, first to an island and then to the springs.

Important Note: These directions keep you on public land. Please do not enter any private property. When the Verde River level is high after heavy rains or spring runoff, be sure to check at the ranger station before attempting to cross the river.

Source maps: *Coconino National Forest,* USGS *Verde Hot Springs.*

GPS: N 34 21.420 W 111 42.600

Soakers Bible

504   SHEEP BRIDGE WARM SPRING

●   **Southeast of Prescott**

Cement tub on a ledge above the Verde River, surrounded by a dense growth of bullrushes. Elevation 1,400 feet. Open all year; be aware of flooded roads.

Natural mineral water flows out of a spring at 99° and is piped to a masonry pool close to the river. Other natural pools may be found, depending on water level, below the tub. Clothing optional.

There are no services available on the premises. A level camping area is seventy-five yards upstream. It is fifty miles to all other services in Black Canyon City.

Directions: From I-17 north of Black Canyon City, take the Bloody Basin off-ramp and drive southeast on FS 269 for 37 miles. This road crosses several streambeds that are usually dry. The first 16 miles to Summit (elevation 4,500 ft.) is a good gravel road. The remaining 21 miles is a poor dirt road, but it is passable by a high-clearance 2WD vehicle. From a parking area at the bridge, walk 75 yards upstream to the soaking tubs.

To locate the closest campground, drive 0.3 miles back up from the bridge and look on the north side of the road for the remains of a building foundation. A steep path (4WD only!) leads 150 yards down to a level camping area by the river. The soaking tub is 75 yards downstream.

Alternate: From the intersection of Cave Creek Rd. and Tom Darlington Rd. in the town of Carefree, go east on Cave Creek Rd. Pass Horseshoe Rd and continue toward Seven Springs. Set odometer to zero where pavement ends and the road is now FS 24. At 7.5 miles is Seven Springs Campground. A small fee is collected. At approximately 21 miles you arrive at the intersection of FS 24 and FS 269 and turn right on 269. Sign says "Verde River 12 miles." Rough, high clearance road continues straight toward Sheep Bridge. At 33 miles you have arrived. Best to park (camp at old cement slabs and walk down rough stone road toward the river. Stay right and walk downstream about 75 yards past the bullrushes along the riverbank where there is an opening in the bullrushes. Duck through and find the pool

Source maps: *Mazatzal Wilderness, Tonto National Forest;* USGS quads, *Brooklyn Park, Bloody Basin, Chalk Mountain.*

GPS: N 34 03.755 W 111 42.439

505   EL DORADO HOT SPRINGS
■
PO Box 39   623 386-5412
Tonopah, AZ 85354
hotsprings@el-dorado.com
www.el-dorado.com

At El Dorado Hot Springs, odorless, tasteless, crystal clear hot mineral water, combined with years of hard work, has created a verdant desert oasis surrounded by palm trees, bamboo and distant mountain views. Elevation 1,123 feet. Open 365 days a year. In summer, misting nozzles, shade cloths, and cooled spring water make for a refreshing soak even on the hottest days. Common areas are free of smoke, alcohol, and pets.

El Dorado Hot Springs is available for personal retreats and small conferences with fourteen beds in four accommodations, as well as tent and van space.

Natural mineral water is pumped from an enormous subterranean hot spring. The 112° water flows to nearly two dozen outdoor and indoor pools, some with moveable shade and natural mineral water showers. Six private areas (thirteen soaking tanks total) can be rented hourly, by the half-day, or overnight. Each private area has a hot pool and a cool pool and each is different; one is beside a tropical fish pond, one has a 100 year old giant cast iron bath tub, while another has gorgeous views of the mountains, the sunset, and the stars at night. Semi-private soaking can be by the hour or by the day. No chemicals are necessary in the single tanks. One of the toilets, the whole tenting area, and two soaking pools are handicap accessible. Free dump station and water fill-up with a soak.

Massage by appointment. Tent space, fire rings, firewood, washer/dryer, hot springs guidebooks and cold water and soda for sale. All rentals include soaking; most include coffee and tea service. Motel California has a full bath, microwave, and fridge. The historic Old Post Office was built over another hot spring and has an ancient masonry tank where the mail workers used to soak. The Last Resort offers a bed and upper bunk and will soon have a private outdoor shower and soak.

All other services, including delicious meals at world famous Tonopah Joe's Restaurant, truck stop, as well as a full services campground, are available within walking distance in 'downtown' Tonopah, which consists of five buildings. Free phone for email and toll free calls. Credit cards welcomed. Hiking, mountain biking, four wheeling, petroglyph and wildlife viewing, old gold mines, rock climbing, free fourteen day camping, are available on 900,000 acres of public land beginning only 2.5 miles away. View the web site, email or phone for additional information.

Directions: At exit 94 on I-10 between Quartzite and Phoenix, go south on 411th Ave. Turn right on Indian School Rd, just before Tonopah Joe's and go west one quarter mile. El Dorado is on the left (south) side of the road at number 41225, surrounded by ever growing bamboo. (See photos next page.)

EL DORADO HOT SPRINGS

Tonopah (which means "hot water under the bush" in the local Native American language) is rich in mineral bath history and once boasted five hot spring emporia Even the old post office next door has two hot mineral water soaking tanks.

506   SAN CARLOS WARM SPRINGS

● **East of Globe**

A series of pools in the slow-flowing San Carlos River on the San Carlos Apache Reservation. Located in a tree-covered canyon with an abundance of wildlife. A permit is an absolute requirement. Elevation 3,500 feet. Open all year; pools may be under water during high runoff.

Natural mineral water bubbles up from several spots in the bottom of the river at temperatures between 85-95°. Warm spots can be found both upstream and downstream, but most are above the ford in the river. You can also follow the trail of green algae to where the warm spots are. Clothing optional would be all right during low use times, or head upstream for more private areas, but suits seem to be mandatory on weekends and holidays.

There are three campgrounds on the reservation (make arrangements at the Recreation Department). Gas is available one mile west of the Recreation and Wildlife Department along US 70. The business center on the Reservation has a market. All other services are 20 miles away in Globe.

Directions: From Globe, take AZ 70 and go 20 miles east to the San Carlos Recreation and Wildlife Department, where you must stop and buy a permit. From the headquarters, continue east 4 miles to Hwy 8. Turn left (north) and continue 15 miles. Turn left on an unmarked gravel road (Indian Hwy 3). At four-way intersection turn left onto Road 1500 (marked with small sign by the fence) for 3.5 miles to where the road ends at the river. It is possible during low water for 4WD vehicles to cross the river and explore the other side.

Camilla Van Sickle and Bill Pennington

WATSON WASH HOT WELL
THATCHER HOT WELL

Permanetly dismantled and closed.

507   ESSENCE OF TRANQUILITY
■   6074 S. Lebanon Loop   520 428-9312
     Safford, AZ 85546   877 895-6810

This spiritually uplifting retreat is surrounded with mesquite, eucalyptus, desert willow, salt cedar, tamarack, and palm trees. Elevation 2,990 feet. Open all year. Tubs are rented by the hour or for day use. Office is open Tuesday-Saturday, 8 AM to 6PM—call only at this time.

Natural 108° mineral water flows from a 1,632-foot artesian well into six stone and concrete tubs: one open, communal (clothing required), and five private (clothing optional). The continual flow-through requires no chemicals. Temperatures range from 98-105°. No bathing in tubs, a shower is available. No smoking in tubs. Facilities are somewhat handicap accessible with assistance.

Primitive and tepee campsites are available by reservation only. Camping fees include unlimited use of the mineral springs, and communal kitchen/livingroom area. There is a day use area with tables, small barbecue, and refrigerator. Various forms of body treatments available by appointment only. No food is provided on the premises, but there is a soda/juice machine. Two convenience stores are within three miles, and it is seven miles to Safford.

No RVs, no credit cards, no alcohol, no glass, no open nudity. Minimal noise. Well supervised children. Dogs on leash okay.

Directions: Starting in Safford at the intersection of US 70 and US 191, go south 6 miles on US 191. Turn right at Lebanon Rd. and follow road 0.5 miles to a 90-degree curve onto Lebanon Loop. Continue 0.6 miles further. Establishment is on the right.

From I-10 go north on US 191 approximately 29 miles to mile marker 115. Turn left on Cactus Rd. Approximately 0.5 miles west, turn right (north) on Lebanon Loop. The establishment is 0.25 miles on the left. Park in front. Call for days, hours, appointments, and reservations.

Photos by Phil Wilcox

508   KACHINA MINERAL SPRINGS SPA
■   1155 W. Cactus Rd.   928 428-7212
     Safford, AZ 85546
     www.kachinasprings.com

Therapy-oriented bathhouse, serving the community of Safford for over forty years. Elevation 3,000 feet. Open all year.

Natural mineral water flows out of an artesian well at 108° and is piped into six large, tiled, sunken tubs in private rooms where the water temperature measures around 104-106°. The pools are drained, cleaned, and refilled after each customer so that no chemical treatment is necessary. Two large soaking pools, a hot one at 104° and a cold one large enough for eight to ten people are in a covered spa room. Bathing suits are needed in the communal tubs.

A staff of six masseuses provide a variety of massage techniques, foot and hand reflexology, Sacro-cranial massage, body wraps, and aromatherapy. Credit cards accepted. Phone for rates and reservations.

Directions: From the intersection of US 70 and US 191 in Safford, go 6 miles south on US 191, and just past milepost 115 turn right onto Cactus Rd. for 0.25 miles.

Phil Wilcox

This seems to have become a party spot. Help keep it clean by removing trash and bottles. Thanks.

509 ROPER LAKE STATE PARK
Route 2, Box 712   520 428-6760
Safford, AZ 85546

A small, neatly constructed outdoor soaking pool in a popular state park surrounded by rolling desert hills. Elevation 3,100 feet. Day-use fee. Open all year

Geothermal mineral water flows from an artesian well at 99° directly into a stone and cement pool large enough for six to eight good friends. The water flows through continuously, so no chemical treatment is needed. There is a fifteen-minute limit when other people are waiting. Bathing suits are required. Access to the tub is ramped, with stairs and a handrail leading into the tub. The light over the tub goes off each night about 8 PM and the pool is drained into the lake each evening about 9 PM.

Facilities at the state park include camping and RV spaces, rest rooms, changing rooms, day-use picnic ramadas, a swimming beach, two stocked lakes for fishing, a boat ramp, and nature trails. A mini-mart and gas are available four miles north and all other services are approximately six miles away in Safford.

Directions: From Safford, drive south on US 191 for 6 miles, turn left (east) at the sign for Roper Lake State Park, and continue 0.5 miles to the park entrance.

510 HOT WELL DUNES

● Southeast of Safford

Two fenced-in soaking pools and one shallow pond surrounded by hundreds of acres of Bureau of Land Management (BLM) desert sand dunes open to, and popular with, off-road vehicles. Elevation 3,450 feet. Open all year, subject to flash floods.

Geothermal mineral water flows out of an artesian well at the rate of 200 gallons per minute and a temperature of 106° into two fenced soaking tubs. Overflow from the tubs spills into an adjoining shallow sand-bottom pool that provides soaking at a lower water temperature. Bathing suits are required, although not always worn.

A few developed tent or RV camp sites, fire grills, trash can, and vault toilets are available on the premises. Two weeks of camping are permitted on the level ground in this desert area, except where indicated right near the tubs. You will need to bring all your own supplies, including water. It is thirty-two miles to all services in Safford.

Directions: From intersection of Hwy 191 and US 70 in Safford, follow US 70 east for 8.1 and turn right (south) on Hackel Rd. Continue for 25 miles and turn left at the sign for Hot Well Dunes. This is open range country, so watch out for cattle.

Camilla Van Sickle and Bill Pennington

Photos by Phil Wilcox

511 POTTER'S AZTEC BATHS BED AND BREAKFAST

PO Box 1325   928 865-4847

■ Clifton, AZ 85533

A beautiful B&B, originally built by the current owner's grandfather in 1901. Located in the heart of Arizona's mining and ranching district. The Potter Ranch is on the National Register of Historic Places. Day use, if available.

Two fiberglass tubs are outside in the back and are filled with hot mineral water pumped from the riverside well. Lattice separates the two tubs providing some privacy. Water temperature is adjusted to 102° from the 150° at the source. The tubs are emptied after each use requiring no chemicals. Suits are optional based on preference of those present.

An overnight stay in one of the three bedrooms includes a full Mexican or American breakfast. Call for further information and reservations.

Primitive seeps along the San Francisco River on the Potter property have been used for years by soakers who build simple rock and mud pools that get washed out and rebuilt every year. They are located a quarter-mile south of the B&B where the three branches of the San Francisco converge. The pools collect the slow seeping hot water which mixes with cold river water. Move the rocks around to adjust the pool temperature. Bring a shovel, they require some work.

Note: Potter Ranch management doesn't mind if the public uses these pools, but please call ahead to let them know you are coming, and for directions. Also, please stay on the trail to protect the eroding riverbank.

512 GILLARD HOT SPRINGS

● Near the town of Clifton

Remote hot springs along the Gila River in the Black Hills area of southeastern Arizona. Located at the end of a six-mile drive on unpaved roads and a one-mile walk through a sandy wash. Elevation 3,500 feet. Open all year, subject to road washouts due to heavy rain.

Natural mineral water seeps from underground at over 183° along the northeast bank of the Gila River. Following each year's high water and spring runoff, the primitive rock and mud pools must be redug. Water temperature is controlled by mixing in cold river water. Due to the slow rate of flow, it may take some patience to achieve the proper soaking temperature. Clothing optional.

There are no facilities on the premises, but there is plenty of BLM land where camping is permitted. There are also areas for car camping along Old Safford Rd. near the Gila River. North of the bridge, a road heads down to the river where you can park under the trees. From here it is three miles to the hot springs by the river. Fifty feet downstream from the hot springs is a deep swimming hole. Oozy river mud makes natural mudbaths.

Directions: Drive 35 miles northeast of Safford, AZ on US 70 and US 191 to Three Way (where Hwys 191, 75, and 78 meet). Or, from US 70 in Lordsburg, NM, drive 55 miles northwest through Duncan to the Apache ranger station at Three Way. From Three Way, continue north toward Clifton on US 191 for 5.5 miles. When the divided highway ends, make an immediate left (west) on Black Hills Back Country Byway (also called Old Safford Rd.). Drive 3.5 miles to a primitive dirt road on the right with a sign to Gillard Hot Springs. Turn right onto this unmaintained road for 1 mile to a three-way intersection. Follow the middle fork for 0.3 miles and park on the right adjacent to the wash on your left. Walk down the wash until you come to a closed gate. Use the pedestrian access and continue down the wash to the Gila River. The seeps are on the northeast bank near the end of the wash. Look for hot steam rising.

Note: There may be washouts and detours due to flooding. The rough and sandy road can be maneuvered by passenger vehicles with a knowledgeable desert driver. A 4WD is recommended.

Source map: USGS *Apache-Sitgreaves National Forests* (springs not shown).

GPS: N 32 58.260 W 109 21.000

Skip Hill

The rough, difficult roads and the long hikes to get to the springs almost guarantees you a private soaking spot at *Gillard Hot Springs, Hannah,* or *Eagle Creek,* pictured above.

Soakers Bible

513   HANNAH HOT SPRING

● **North of the town of Morenci**

A large soaking pool nestled into a canyon wall above Little Blue Creek, in a remote area in the Blue Range Primitive Area. Late Spring through November. The access road passes through many deep washes and should not be attempted during monsoon season. The hike and canyons should be avoided during rains.

Note: Don't bother going to Hannah with kids, arthritis or any joint problems. Get a good walking stick (or two), and be sure to plan five hours for the hike each way. This is not a day trip; you will be sore from twisting your ankles and walking on rocks all day.

Natural hot water seeps out of the canyon wall above Little Blue Creek. Water emerges at about 120 ° as it flows down into a lovely soaking pool about twenty-feet long. Tall grasses grow along the sides, obscuring the pool. However it's easy to tell that the creek water is much cooler above the springs, so you'll know if you miss it. The pool is several feet deep at one end, but only eight inches or so at the hotter end. The cement and river rock pool is located about ten-feet above the creek so it can usually withstand seasonal flooding without being destroyed. It can become silted by debris. The easiest and lightest scoop to use to clean in out is a milk jug with the top cut off and holes cut in the bottom.

There is room for one small tent directly across the creek from the hot spring. There is also room to camp above the spring if you can scurry up a game trail about fifty feet downstream from the pool. A nice flat, shady spot with a fire pit and tent space offers camping safely out of the canyon. All services are back in Morenci.

Directions: From Morenci head north on Highway 191 for a lovely half-hour drive to a right turn onto Juan Miller Road. Follow this road as it curves through forest and offers many nice campgrounds. After 14 miles turn left onto Fred Fritz Road which is signed to the XXX Ranch, (also called FR475C and it follows the Blue River north). This road is high clearance recommended, rocky and rough, and passes through many deep washes. Follow it around an old green barn to the end of the road—a small parking area in the grass.

The Hike: From the parking area there is a small sign to the north. A path leads from here and almost immediately crosses the Blue River; from here on out there's no trail at all. Make a mental note of this first crossing or build a cairn at this point so you'll be able to find your car on the way back. Head up river and stay as close to the water as you can at all times. All the vegetation out here is thick with burrs and thorns, flood debris and beaver dams. If you veer from the river you will get backed up in swamps or thwarted by razor sharp grasses. You will cross the river countless times, or just walk in it completely when there is not much bank. Within 10 minutes or so the water forks around a large outcropping of rock. Stay to the right and continue to follow the river north. You will walk for about 3 hours to cover 3.5 miles as the rocks shift under your feet and make this hike slow going.

Keep your eyes out for some bright orange cliffs to the right. There will be fence line that was an old corral, and only the chimney is left from an old ranger station. Shortly after this another canyon opens up to the right, which is Little Blue Creek Canyon. There should be water flowing making this turn obvious. Continue up Little Blue for 2 miles or so (another 1.5-2 hour hike) and eventually you will want to turn right again into another narrower canyon carved out by Hannah Creek. There is water running here too, but the entrance to the canyon is narrow and you will have to climb around boulders and wade through waist deep water to get through. The next obstacle involves scaling a steep cliff to the left of a waterfall that can't be crossed any other way. We suggest taking off your backpack and scouting this route before going for it. You'll have to slide down on your butt once you get over the hump, right above the waterfall. This is made easier if one person is already on the other side and the second hiker lowers the backpacks down to them. This is the hardest part of the hike. Once you make it through this point hike up the canyon for another ten minutes until you reach the hot pool on the left side of the canyon.

About 200 feet past the hot springs, Hannah Creek Canyon narrows down to about 8 feet wide, and the creek is chest deep with no easy way through other than wading. The canyon is spectacular beyond this point but don't try it with a backpack on, you'll have to get wet and climb rock walls. Good luck!

GPS: N 33 24.018 W 109 9.156

514   EAGLE CREEK HOT SPRING

● **Near the town of Morenci**

Hot water seeps up from the ground in several spots high on a ridge above Eagle Creek in the remote high desert of Eastern Arizona. Elevation 4,000 feet. Open all year, subject to river flooding.

Hot 116° water seeps out of the ground and flows through a shallow gully where it cools substantially until it pours over a precipice as a trickling cold waterfall. A soaking pool could be built at the source, which is currently a watering spot for cattle and wildlife. (The entire Eagle Creek canyon is private Phelps Dodge property. Officially visitors should sign in at the P.D. security desk before entering Eagle Creek.) Clothing optional.

There are no facilities at this location except level areas for pack-in and car camping on nearby BLM land. Bring plenty of water or a filter for Eagle Creek water.

Directions: (See directions for #512 as far as Clifton.) From Clifton, follow US 191 to Morenci. Turn right at the first traffic light in Morenci and go 1.5 miles to a "Y" at Mine Rd. Stay on US 191 another 3 miles to a small cemetery on your right. Opposite the cemetery is Eagle Creek Rd. (unmarked), a wide gravel road with yellow highway markers. Follow this road for 5.3 miles to a power plant at the creek. Unless you have a 4WD, park here. You will cross the river back and forth 5-6 times to reach Hot Springs Canyon, on your right.

Hike about 1 mile south, past the farmhouse, along the dirt road adjacent to Eagle Creek and look for Hot Springs Canyon on your right. Or, with a 4WD, cross the river by the power plant and immediately cross again. With a high-clearance 4WD, depending on water level, you may be able to do the river crossings and park opposite the mouth to Hot Springs Canyon (the first large canyon on your right). Due to flooding, river patterns and crossings may change seasonally. Best landmarks are the canyon walls. When the river level is low, all crossing can be done on foot. Just before the entrance to Hot Springs Canyon, Eagle Creek opens up into a large 5-foot deep swimming hole.

Once you reach Hot Springs Canyon cross the creek and head up the wash. On the right is a 35-foot, warm, trickling waterfall. Look back to the right against the rocky wall where the water is seeping. The springs are up above here. The dark green areas have the seeps. If you make a sharp left as you start to climb and look uphill you will find a small warm-water cave. It's a short, prickly climb.

Source map: USGS *Copperplate Gulch.*
GPS: N 33 02.760 W 109 26.400

515   MULESHOE RANCH

■ 6502 N. Muleshoe Ranch Rd. 520 212-4295
Willcox, AZ 85643
www.muleshoelodging.org

Owned and managed jointly by The Nature Conservancy, Coronado National Forest, and the Bureau of Land Management in order to conserve and enhance unique ecosystems, and endangered species and their habitat. Closed June, July, and August.

The odorless, natural hot mineral water fills two livestock tanks under a canopy of trees and are only available to those people staying at the ranch. Bathing suits required.

Accommodations include a mix of original and renovated historic buildings dating from the late 1800s. Each unit is fully equipped, containing bath, kitchen, furnishings and linens. Bring your own food.

The Visitors Center provides information about hiking trails, back country safety, and road conditions. Horse corrals available for lodging guests. Credit cards accepted.

Directions: From Tucson take I-10 east to Willcox exit 340. (Pick up any needed supplies here.) After exiting turn right. Turn right again and follow Bisbee Ave. past the high school to Airport Rd. Turn right. After driving about 15 miles, take the right fork at junction right past the mailboxes, and continue on Muleshoe Rd. approximately 14 miles. After you cross the entrance to Muleshoe follow the signs to the HQ gate. After heavy rains a 4WD vehicle may be necessary.

Camilla Van Sickle and Bill Pennington

NORTHERN CALIFORNIA

This map was designed to be used with a standard highway map.

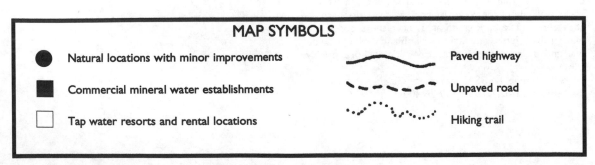

MAP SYMBOLS

● Natural locations with minor improvements

■ Commercial mineral water establishments

□ Tap water resorts and rental locations

⎯⎯ Paved highway

▬ ▬ Unpaved road

• • • Hiking trail

601 A   GLEN AND CHICKEN HOT SPRINGS

● **Near the town of Cedarville**

Undeveloped cluster of hot springs on a barren slope along the east side of Upper Alkali Lake. Glen Hot Springs is located partly off and partly on Leonard's property. Elevation 4,600 feet.

More than a dozen source locations at about 190° spread out over about 100 feet. As it flows along, the water becomes cooler, allowing for basic soaking opportunities in several locations. By the time the water flows under the public road that bisects the property, it has cooled to about 100°, depending on the season.

Directions: From Cedarville at the intersection of SR 299 and CR 1, go north on CR 1, Surprise Valley Rd. (the main street) for 5 miles. Go right (east) on Fortynine Lane. Travel 4 miles and turn right (north). The remains of the resort at Leonard's Hot Spring are across the road on the south side of the road. To reach the best cool-weather soaking are, go a short way east to a point just before where the the year-round flow of spring water passes under the road.

Three hot springs close together with a combined total daily flow of more than half a million gallons.

Directions to Chicken: turn left (north) off Fortynine Lane 0.5 miles before Leonard's and follow it 0.8 miles to the spring on the right, 0.2 miles up a narrow dirt track to the several sources.
Source map: *USGS Cedarville*.
GPS: N 41 38.945 W 120 06.210

601 B   LEONARD'S HOT SPRING

● **Near the town of Cedarville**

Abandoned and deteriorated old resort on a barren slope along the east side of Middle Alkali Lake. Elevation 4,500 feet.

Natural mineral water flows out of the ground from several springs at a temperature of 150°. Near the old resort remains is another spring of about 100°. Like Glen Hot Springs, it is way too hot to soak in and there currently are no pools to get into. Turn left (north) with the hot creek on the right, proceed north and find the best soaking temperature in any of several makeshift soaking pools on the right. Be very careful as the ground is often very unstable.
Source map: *USGS Cedarville*.
GPS: N 41 36.000 W 118 50.555

Photos by Camilla Van Sickle and Bill Pennington

602   SURPRISE VALLEY HOT SPRINGS
PO Box 458   877 927-6426
■ Cedarville, CA 96104   530 279-2040
www.surprisevalleyhotsprings.com

Destination get-a-way with accommodations that include private hot tubs is set in a picturesque valley bordered by the majestic Warner Mountains. Elevation 4,600 feet. Open all year. Call about day use. (Pilots, note the special packages for you.)

Private hot tubs on the deck of each room are filled with natural mineral water coming out of an artesian well at a temperature of 208°. The water cascades into the pools over your very own waterfall. The hot water is cooled with water from a cold artesian well to make the tubs a comfortable 104°. Since the tubs operate on a flow-through basis, minimal amounts of chlorine are used only for cleaning when the tubs are drained and refilled. Pipes using the hot water run under the cement decks to keep them warm in the winter. And, using a system created by the first member of the Rose family to own the property (they are now in the fourth generation), the place is geothermally heated.

Accommodations offered include four deluxe villas (with a complete kitchen) that can sleep at least four. The six standard villas have a refrigerator and microwave and sleeps two. Each villa features a private hot tub fed by a cascading waterfall. Catch and release fishing can be done in the pond right on the property. Nearby are opportunities for hiking, biking, fishing, horseback riding and golf. Massage in the garden spa area is by appointment only. A 6,000 square foot conference center with geothermally heated floor is under construction.

Fly-and-Soak packages include a car for your use waiting at the airport, and a half-hour massage for the pilot or one of his lucky guests.

Location: Five miles east on Highway 299 from the town of Cedarville. Four miles from the Nevada border and 3 hours from Reno, Nevada, Redding, California, and Medford, Oregon.

603 A   EAGLEVILLE HOT SPRING

●   **South of the town of Cedarville**

Shallow, primitive soaking pool and tub with a commanding view of Surprise Valley and surrounding mountains. Elevation 4,600 feet. Open all year. As the water is so very hot, cooler weather or nighttime makes for a better soak.

Natural mineral water flows out of two PVC pipes in the road embankment at 111°. One pipe goes to a shallow volunteer-built, shallow rock and sand soaking pool that will hold about six, and the other goes to an adjacent five-foot redwood tub. The pools are barely visible from the road, so the apparent local custom is clothing optional. Local custom also expects new arrivals to await the departure of those already there.

Both hot springs are just up the road from the Nevada state line where there's a very large, uninhabited area with dozens of side roads for quiet, solitary camping and hiking. There are no services available on the premises. It is seven miles to Eagleville, although there are no services there, and twenty-three miles to all services in Cedarville.

Directions: From Cedarville, on Modoc County Road 1 (Surprise Valley Rd.), drive south 15 miles to Eagleville. From the post office, drive 7.7 miles. You will pass two houses on your left with a crumbling stone wall. Drive 1 mile further to a dirt drive on the east side which goes down about 0.1 miles to a parking lot. Walk 135 yards north (down hill) to the pool and tub. If you come to an abandoned cement house 0.1 mile further on the east side of the street, you've gone too far. However, this is where Wild Mint Hot Spring is. (See 603 B)

GPS: N 41 12. 370 W 120 03.270

603 B   WILD MINT HOT SPRING

●   **South of the town of Cedarville**

A delightful soak can be had in this cement tub adjacent to an abandoned cement house, offering wonderful views of the surrounding mountains. Named after the abundance of wild mint growing in the vicinity. Elevation 4,600 feet. Open all year.

Natural mineral water is piped through six small PVC pipes bringing 108° water from the source into the four-foot by eight-foot by three-foot deep cinder block pool. A small drain near the bottom of the tub must be plugged with a towel or like device to allow the tub to fill to the top. A wooden deck and two wooden chairs are the only amenities on the place. Custom seems to be clothing optional, but the tub can be seen from the road.

Both hot springs are just up the road from the Nevada state line where there's a very large, uninhabited area with dozens of side roads for quiet, solitary camping and hiking. Services can be found twenty-three miles away in Cedarville.

Directions: See directions to Eagleville Hot Spring (603 A). To reach Wild Mint, walk 200 yards south of the parking lot. About twenty yards past the abandoned cement house, between the house and the road, is the hot spring. It can also be reached via a dirt drive 0.1 miles south of the drive that leads to the parking lot at Eagleville.

GPS: N 41 12.494 W 120 03.340

Three different views of one of those hot springs found out in the middle of not much else, except open space and the smell of fresh mint. Not too bad!

Soakers Bible

604 WEST VALLEY RESERVOIR

● **South of the town of Alturas**

A small A-frame style shack offers shade from the sun and a little bit of privacy for a bath, in a lovely concrete soaking pool near the banks of West Valley Reservoir. Open year round, although roads may be impassible during wet weather; high clearance vehicles are necessary at all times. Elevation 4,765 feet.

Hot springs emerge in a field well above the reservoir. The hot water is trenched for a short distance while it cools, before dumping into an inground soaking tub sheltered by a ramshackle A-frame. There are a few benches in the shack, and both sides are open so bathers can still enjoy the scenery. The water in the tub measured 120°— way too hot for a soak. However, there is a diversion board in the trench so that once the tub is filled, you move the board and the water flows around the shack allowing the bath to cool. We suspect that through proper manipulation of the hot stream, visitors could have soaking room for eight to ten folks at once.

Camp here for free. Cars, and even some trucks will get stuck in the mud bog. High clearance vehicles are definitely necessary. To camp at the springs you'll need to either backpack, bike, ride a horse or an ATV. RV's can use the Likely RV Park on Jess Valley Road. There are no services at the spring. Some services can be found in Likely, but your best bet is to shop in Alturas.

Directions: From Alturas head south for 19 miles to the tiny town of Likely. Turn left onto Jess Valley Road which is signed for NFS access. Follow Jess Valley Road for 6.1 miles to a right turn signed for West Valley Reservoir (this isn't the first sign for the reservoir, so be sure to go the entire 6.1 miles before turning). Travel south for 1.8 miles on this gravel road which heads uphill, peters out and then dips down again through a really rough wash. The road gets worse from here on so park and walk if you don't have high clearance. After 1.8 miles the road forks, take the right fork which almost immediately forces you to go around a huge chuckhole. Another good place to leave your truck and walk. Follow this sandy road down to a dry wash then up a short hill to another fork. Stay left as the road goes down and forks again, keep left and the road will take you through a boggy area with deep ruts (which are easy to walk past but not so easy to get your truck out of). Continue up to a rocky flat area. Several roads loop around but all lead to the next meadow, where if you continue you'll see the metal shack on the right within a couple hundred yards.

GPS: N 41 11.682 W 120 23.358

Privacy, shade, and a view of the reservoir all come together to offer a very hot, soothing soak.

Soakers Bible

126

605 STEWART MINERAL SPRINGS
4617 Stewart Springs Rd.   530 938-2222
■ Weed, CA 96094
www.stewartmineralsprings.com

Therapeutic mountain rustic retreat available to individuals for special events or seminars. Located on a mountain stream in a green canyon northwest of Mt. Shasta. Elevation 3,900 feet. Open all year, weather permitting. Phone for open hours.

Natural mineral water is pumped from a well at 40° and is propane heated. There are fifteen individual bathtubs in private rooms with relaxing music piped in. Tubs are drained and sanitized after each use, so no chemical treatment of the water is necessary. A huge wood sauna completes the purifying process. Wide wood decks overlook Parks Creek which has a small beach area. Clothing optional. Sheets are provided for coverage in public areas.

Lodging includes cabins, apartments, a large A-frame that will hold up to ten, camping and RV spaces, and tepees. There is also a restaurant for your dining pleasure. Various massage and spa services are by appointment. A sweat lodge is held every Saturday. Credit cards accepted. It is seven miles to a store, service station, and public bus. Pickup at the bus depot and at the Weed airport can be arranged.

Directions: Take the Edgewood exit on I-5 north of Weed. Turn north on the west side of I-5 and take the first left onto Stewart Springs Rd. Drive 4 miles to the resort at the end of the road.

The usual custom is to soak in a tub, experience the sauna, and take a dip in this cold mountain spring. This is repeated four times—once for each compass direction.

Camilla Van Sickle and Bill Pennington

As of this printing, *Big Bend* is closed and up for sale. Try the phone number listed below for updated information.

Phil Wilcox

Just one of the many pools at *Big Bend*.

606 A   BIG BEND HOT SPRINGS
196 Hot Springs Rd.   530 337-6606
PO Box 116
■ Big Bend, CA 96011

A series of pools in different places on this tree-shaded property, located fifty miles northeast of Redding on the bank of the Pit River. Elevation 2,000 feet. Open all year; in winter check first as the road may be snowed in. Springs are closed for entry between 10 PM and 8 AM. No liquor, smoking or dogs allowed at or near the baths although they are welcome on the grounds. Always call ahead for camping reservations or for day use. Elevation 1,820 feet.

Natural hot mineral water flows out of a springs at 170° cooling as it runs under a stone deck, is aerated, and then piped to cement-and-stone pools on the edge of the river. Cold and hot water pipes may be adjusted to desired temperature. Stairs lead down into other pools and seats where you can admire the view. No chemical treatment is necessary. Handicap accessible with assistance.

There are natural pools arranged along the Pitt River four-tenths of a mile further down the gravel road known as Indian Springs. Clothing is optional here and everywhere on the grounds.

There are four campground areas and a few spaces for small RV's with electricity and portable toilets. There is a cedar building available for groups during inclement weather. There is a small store [Pitt Stop] one mile away in the nearby Hamlet of Big Bend with gasoline and propane available. There is also a small café that is open weekends during the summer only. No other amenities are available at the springs.

Always call ahead for road conditions as well as pool and camping availability.

Photos by Phil Wilcox

606 B   HUNT AND KOSH HOT SPRINGS

● **Near the town of Big Bend**

Delightful rock-and-cement soaking pool situated on Kosh Creek close to where it joins the Pitt River. Located in a beautiful river valley south of Mount Shasta. Elevation about 2,000 feet. Open all year subject to road conditions.

Hunt: Natural hot mineral water flows out of several hillside seeps, often at more than 170° and cools on its way down to the creek. There are three pools, flowing one into the other, close to the river. The top pool, closest to the bank is much too hot, the next pool is generally about 104°, and the bottom pool is much cooler. These pools along the river seem to get the most use as temperature-wise they are easier to regulate. Best to bring a bucket to carry cold creek water to the hot tubs or hot water to the cooler pools.

Kosh Creek Pool: Natural mineral water flows out of a rocky cliff above the creek at a perfect 104° and flows directly down into a charming rock pool just big enough for two which is usually around 86°. Other pools are built along the river and washed out and rebuilt every season. These pools are often used by rafters and fishermen. Clothing optional.

There are no services available at either of the locations, but there is plenty of space where camping is not restricted. A general store, gasoline, propane and a café (summers only) are two miles back at the town of Big Bend.

A wonderful few days could be spent in the area visiting Big Bend Hot Springs, the Indian Pools along the river, and hiking into *Hunt Hot Springs* property.

Directions: Exactly one mile from the North edge of the bridge over the Pitt River, on paved road FS 11, past FS 37 on the right, turn left on to a rough dirt road (painted sign on tree with arrow says P15). Take right fork downhill, at 0.2 miles, for 1 mile off paved road, past the Wright Native American Cemetery, to parking/camping area at 2.0 miles. Springs along river bank will be visible directly in front of you. This one mile of dirt road is very rough. Although regular passenger cars have made it, a high clearance vehicle is suggested. 4WD is best. Or leave your vehicle at the store and take your ATV to the springs.

Directions to the Kosh Creek Pool: Climb the steep, well-used trail immediately behind Hunt to the other side of the hill and back down to Kosh Creek. The tub will be visible as you descend. Or, you can walk down the riverbed until you get to it on the east bank of the creek.

Note: Although all of the pools are on private property, legally, anything below the high water mark is open to public use. This includes the camping spots. If they are above the high-water mark, you are on private property and you are trespassing. Rules for wilderness camping should be strictly followed (see the Introductory Section in the front of the book for these guidelines). Please respect the property and carry all trash out with you.

GPS: N 41 01.885 W 121 55.967 (Kosh)

Several hot source springs are used to feed the swimming pool at *Drakesbad Guest Ranch* which is located in beautiful Lassen Volcanic National Park.

---

607 DRAKESBAD GUEST RANCH
c/o California Guest Services, Inc.
2150 Main St. #5   916 529-1512
■ **Red Bluff, CA 96080**

A rustic mountain ranch/resort, by reservation only, with a mineral-water swimming pool, plus horses and guides for riding and hiking. Registered guests only. Located in a superb mountain meadow within the boundaries of Lassen Volcanic National Park. Elevation 5,700 feet. Open first part of June to first part of October.

Natural mineral water flows out of two springs at temperatures between 140-150° and is piped to the pool. The swimming pool is maintained at 95° during the day and 105° at night by mixing the two hot water flows. Minimal amounts of chlorine are added to control algae growth. The lodge is handicap accessible. Bathing suits are required.

Facilities include lodge, rooms, cabins, bungalows, and dining room. Saddle horses and guides are available by the hour. Visa and MasterCard are accepted. Telephone for reservations.

Directions: From CA 36 in the town of Chester, take Warner Valley Rd. northwest 17 miles to the resort, which is at the end of the road. The last 3 miles are a combination of a dirt/gravel road.

---

608 TERMINAL GEYSER HOT SPRINGS

According to information received from the United States Department of the Interior, National Park Service regulations prohibit soaking in the hot springs. And I quote, "The reason for this prohibition is that 'bathers,' both through manipulation of water flow to form pools and by the very act of soaking in the pools, disrupt the natural biologic and geologic processes which the National Park Service is mandated to protect. Persons in hot pools observed by Park Rangers will be issued a violation notice and will be subject to either a fine or a court appearance, depending on the individual circumstances."

---

609 WOODY'S FEATHER RIVER HOT SPRINGS
● **Twain, CA 95984**

A great, clean, scenic soak, including a railroad train chugging up the canyon on the opposite side of the river. There is a sign telling you to enjoy the springs, take good care of them, and please leave a donation if you can. Reports are that the place is kept very clean, so someone must be taking care of it.

Natural mineral water from two different source springs high up in the mountains is piped into the two cement, sandy-bottom pools where temperatures can vary from 90-102°. The apparent local custom is clothing optional.

Camping is available at the Crystal Springs RV Park, just up the river.

Directions: On CA 70, go 4 miles west from the Quincy-Greenville "Y" at the junction of Hwy 89 and Hwy 70. Located at mile post 28.

610　SIERRA HOT SPRINGS

■

PO Box 366　　　　530 994-3773
Sierraville, CA 96126
www.sierrahotsprings.org

A 680-acre resort/community surrounded by secluded forests, meadows, and streams in a beautiful Alpine valley. A nominal membership fee and usage fees may be paid on arrival, or advance reservations for rooms and/or health services can be made with a credit card. Elevation 5,000 feet. Open year-round. No alcohol, pets, open fires or drugs allowed.

Natural mineral water flows out of several springs on a wooded slope at temperatures up to 112° into several terraced pools and waterfalls which range in temperature from 98-110°. The Temple Dome area has a full dressing room facility, a sandy-bottom circular hot pool with adjacent cold plunges, a larger warm pool and sun deck, and a small dry sauna. Another seasonal warm pool is available just beyond the Alpine Meadow camping area, and the Phoenix Baths offer both a private soaking tub and spa services. No chemicals are needed in any of the pools. Clothing is optional in all pool areas.

The rustic lodge has rooms and a dormitory, a large porch, and a communal kitchen. A seasonal restaurant (ask about the hours) and a cozy living room with a glass-doored wood burning stove complete the amenities. A two-night minimum is required at the Lodge for weekend and holiday stays. No reservations are required for camping and/or day visits.

Sierra Hot Springs also owns the historic Globe Hotel in Sierraville, less than one mile from the property. Staying there will get you a pass to soak at the pools. Major credit cards accepted.

Directions: From the junction of CA 89 and CA 49 in Sierraville, follow CA 49 east (toward Loyalton) for just 0.25 miles and turn right onto Lemon Canyon Road. Go another 0.25 miles and turn right onto Campbell Hot which runs along the east edge of the airport, to the main lodge which is first large building on the right hand side. Information on the airport can be found at www.airnav.com. The small airport is within walking distance of the springs.

Top and middle photos by Chris Andrews
Bottom photo by Camilla Van Sickle and Bill Pennington

Photos by Phil Wilcox

611 FAIRMONT SONOMA MISSION INN & SPA

PO Box 1447   707 938-9000
■ Sonoma, CA 95476
www.sonomamissioninn.com

Luxurious, upscale resort undergoing extensive renovations providing multiple beauty and health packages for your benefit and enjoyment in a lovely, romantic setting. Elevation 100 feet. Open all year.

Mineral water flows out of the source at 135° and is piped to a large swimming pool kept at 82°, a Watsu pool at 98°, a spa pool at 92°, and an outdoor whirlpool kept at 104°. All pools are lightly treated with bromine and refilled daily. Mineral water showers are also available in the spa. All pools are handicap accessible.

Beautifully appointed guest rooms, conference facilities, a gourmet four-star restaurant, a cafe/market, coed exercise and spa facilities, and an eighteen-hole golf course are available on the premises. In addition, over forty different spa treatments are offered. Major credit cards accepted.

612 MORTON WARM SPRINGS RESORT

■ 1651 Warm Springs Rd.   707 855-5511
Glen Ellen, CA 95452
www.mortonwarmsprings.com

A summertime neighborhood recreation facility in the middle of Jack London's famed Valley of the Moon. Elevation 100 feet. Open May to October; closed Mondays.

From a natural artesian spring located one-hundred feet below Sonoma Creek, mineral-rich natural mineral water (pure enough to drink) at 88-94° fills a diving pool, a three-foot to five-foot deep family pool, and a two-inch deep baby pool. All pools are lightly treated with chlorine and 94° natural sand-filtered artesian mineral water is added. Bathing suits are required.

The Wappo campground has barbecue grills and picnic seating at each site, with access to water source. Sites in the back meadow have electricity. A secluded creekside grove of trees in the back meadow is ideal for weddings and other events. Catering can be arranged for groups of over fifty. They welcome special events such as company picnics. Massage, Ayurvedic spa treatments, and yoga in the meadow are offered. Softball, volleyball, horseshoes, bocce ball and basketball are available, as are swimming lessons. Credit cards accepted.

Marjorie Young

Photos by Phil Wilcox

613 WHITE SULPHUR SPRINGS INN & SPA
3100 White Sulphur Springs Rd.
■ St. Helena, CA 94574 707 963-8588

A restored forty-five acre historic spa-retreat nestled in its own tranquil wooded canyon with its own cathedral redwood grove and waterfall in the heart of the Napa Valley. Elevation 400 feet. Open all year. Call about availability for day use.

Several sulphur mineral springs flow naturally in and out of an outdoor rock-lined soaking pool. The water is not chemically treated and is naturally warm at about 85-87°. Also available is a large outdoor jet tub with treated spring water at about 103° and a swimming pool at ambient temperature. All pools and grounds are for the use of overnight guests, and spa guests are encouraged to build a day around their treatments. Bathing suits required.

Three types of lodging are offered: a row of small one-room Creekside Cottages and two small inns with fourteen rooms each. The Inn has private bathrooms and the Carriage House has men's and women's shared bathrooms down the hall. All of the rooms are very small and simple without phones, televisions or refrigerators. While breakfast is served, you must order in for other meals.

Guests have access to phones and a refrigerator, microwave, fireplace, and hot beverages in a Hospitality Lounge. Rooms are sleeping rooms (quiet time after 10 PM) with amenities found outdoors, including lounge chairs, hammocks, shaded picnic tables, lawns, redwood grove, pools, and a connection with nature. Spa service is also available offering a full range of body treatments. Private outdoor massage for two can be enjoyed under the trees by a babbling brook (weather permitting).

Reservations can be taken only within thirty days of the requested date. All reservations are prepaid and non-refundable. Credit cards accepted.

This lower photo is of the natural hot mineral pool which requires no chemical treatment.

Courtesy of Meadowlark Country House

Relax with a picnic under the ancient oaks and firs with majestic views of the surrounding mountains and horses sporting in the pastures around the inn.

614 A   MEADOWLARK COUNTRY HOUSE
601 Petrified Forest Rd.   707 942-5651
■   Calistoga, CA 94515   800 942-5651
www.meadowlarkinn.com

Beautiful clothing optional country estate located on twenty-acres one mile north of Calistoga. Surrounded by fine restaurants and wineries, offering elegance and privacy. Open all year. Stay of two nights required on weekends. Children not recommended for safety and privacy reasons.

Natural mineral water fills a large swimming pool and hot tub surrounded by spacious flagstone terraces. The use of an ozonator precludes use of chemical treatment of the water.

Tastefully furnished rooms and suites with views, most with decks or terraces, and queen sized beds. Two separate guest houses are also for rent. A full gourmet breakfast is served. In-house massage. Dogs okay with prior approval. Credit cards accepted.

Enjoy the freedom of clothing optional vacationing at pool side.

CALISTOGA SPAS
Calistoga Chamber of Commerce
1458 Lincoln, Ste. 9 Calistoga, CA 94515
707 942-6333   www.calistogafun.com

All of the following locations are in or near the charming town of Calistoga, adjacent to the Napa Valley wine country. These facilities are open all year and stores, restaurants, etc., are available in the town.

Each of the locations has its own hot wells which are used to supply the water to the soaking and swimming pools. Chlorination of the pools is a state regulation. Soaking tubs in bathhouses are drained and filled after each use so no chemical treatment is necessary. Unless otherwise noted, resorts with pool facilities are available for day use except during peak times and holidays. Bathing suits are required in all public areas. Major credit cards accepted.

614 B   CALISTOGA OASIS SPA
■   1300 Washington St.   707 942-2122

Destination Day Spa providing private Mud and Mineral Bath areas for couples and singles from their naturally-sourced geothermal hot springs. The four mud tubs are heated to approximately 100° and are filled with an exclusive blend of volcanic ash, imported peat moss and hot spring water. There are four whirlpool tubs. This soothing retreat is also the place to experience healing massage and facials. The spa is renowned for providing the highest quality massage therapists in a comfortable and nurturing environment. Seasonally changing innovative spa specials and packages are available daily. The spa is located on the grounds of the Roman Spa Resort just one-half block from downtown. Reservations are recommended.

614 C   CALISTOGA SPA HOT SPRINGS
■   1006 Washington St.   707 942-6269

Resort motel with separate men's and women's bath areas. Offers volcanic ash mud baths, mineral baths, steam baths, blanket wraps, and massage.

Resort has four naturally heated mineral baths: outdoor soaking pool, 100°; outdoor swimming pool, 83°; outdoor wading pool, 90°; and a covered hydropool, 105°. Area surrounding pools has places to lounge and a refreshment stand. Indoor men's and women's bathhouses each contain individual tubs, two mud baths, and three steambaths.

All rooms are equipped for light housekeeping. Aerobic classes, workout rooms, and a conference room are available on the premises.

614 D   CALISTOGA VILLAGE INN AND SPA
■   1880 Lincoln Ave   707 942-0991

Offers a wide range of affordable lodging, some with Roman tub or whirlpool in room. Spa offers traditional mud bath, therapeutic massage, salt scrubs, facials, and reflexology.

Spa has an outdoor swimming pool at 80-85°, wading pool at 90-95°, and enclosed hydropool at 100-105°. Indoor men's and women's bathhouses, each containing two hydrotherapy tubs, two mud baths, two steam cabinets, and a sauna.

Facilities include forty-one rooms, conference meeting rooms, and an on-site restaurant serving all meals.

614 E   CARLIN COUNTRY COTTAGES
■   1623 Lake St.   707 942-9102

Fifteen cottages, seven with a two-person, in-room spa, are decorated with an Irish and Shaker country theme. Pools for registered guests only.

Mineral water outdoor pool is maintained at 90-95° in winter and 85° in summer. Outdoor hydropool is 104°. Cottage pools are controllable to 104°.

Continental breakfast served buffet style; can be taken to the poolside or to your room.

614 F   COMFORT INN
■   1865 Lincoln Ave.   707 942-9400
       Spa number   707 942-4636

Fifty-four beautifully decorated rooms. Complete spa facilities offered across the street at Calistoga Village Inn and Spa (see above).

Large geothermal outdoor swimming pool is maintained at 85-90°; one whirlpool is 104°. Sauna and steamroom are also available.

Complimentary continental breakfast included with room. Facilities include a meeting room and non-smoking and handicap rooms.

614 G   DR. WILKINSON'S HOT SPRINGS
■   1507 Lincoln Ave.   707 942-4102
    www.drwilkinson.com

One of the original locations (since 1946) offering massage, mud baths, blanket wraps and skin care.

Two outdoor mineral pools are 82° and 92°; one tropical-foliage indoor mineral pool is 104°. Indoor men's and women's bathhouses each contain four individual tubs, two mud baths, and a steambath. Handicap access.

Forty-two rooms, contemporary or Victorian style lodgings, some with kitchenettes. Massage and facial salon.

614 H   EUROSPA AND INN
■   1202 Pine St.   707 942-6829

Luxurious full-service spa surrounded by poolside gardens with a view of mountains and vineyards.

Outdoor unheated mineral water pool and heated whirlpool are 103-105°. Three gas-heated, tap water hydropools allow customers to control temperatures.

Thirteen nicely decorated rooms available. Massage and facials.

614 I   GOLDEN HAVEN HOT SPRINGS
         SPA AND RESORT
■   1713 Lake St   707 942-8000

One of only two spas in town offering coed mud and mineral baths as well as massage. Spa open to the public. You need not be a guest at the resort.

Enclosed mineral water swimming pool is 88°; covered hydropool is 102°. Handicap accessibility dependent on services used.

Rooms, some with private sauna or hydropool, some with kitchenettes, are available.

614 J   HIDEAWAY COTTAGES
■   1412 Fairway   707 942-4108

Seventeen cottages for adults only. Spa facilities at Dr. Wilkinson's (see listing). Nonsmoking facility.

Outdoor swimming pool is 82° and hydropool is 104°. Reserved for registered guests; no day use.

Various accommodations include some non-smoking rooms some with kitchens. A conference room for up to twenty-five people is also available.

614 K   INDIAN SPRINGS
■   1712 Lincoln Ave.   707 942-4913

California's oldest continuously operating pool and spa offering mud baths, soaking tubs, steam room, massage, and facials. Three active geysers on the premises supply the hot mineral water.

Outdoor, Olympic-size swimming pool is 90-102°, depending on the season. Men's and women's bathhouses, each containing five one-person mud or mineral water soaking tubs and a steam room. Only this spa uses pure volcanic ash, no additives. Pool is handicap accessible.

Comfortable bungalows have recently been restored. Clay tennis court, shuffleboard, bicycle surreys, croquet, and rose gardens are available on the premises.

614 L   LAVENDER HILL SPA
■   1015 Foothill Blvd.   707 942-4495
                                 800-528-4772

Two charming bath houses are nestled into a terraced garden hillside and allow one or two people to enjoy treatments in complete privacy. Choose from Volcanic Mud, Seaweed, Aromatherapy, Mineral Salt Baths, or Herbal Wraps. A few steps through the garden brings you to the main house where therapeutic massage, reflexology treatments, aromatherapy facials, and La Stone Therapy are offered

No lodging facilities.

614 M   LINCOLN AVENUE SPA
■   1339 Lincoln Ave.   707 942-2950

The Spa is located in a beautifully renovated historic stone building, and features salt scrubs, body mud treatments, herbal wraps and facials, and massage. Customers can use the hot mineral water swimming pool at Golden Haven Hot Springs at no extra charge.

No lodging facilities.

614 N   MOUNT VIEW SPA (AT THE MOUNT VIEW HOTEL)
■   1457 Lincoln Ave.   707 942-5789

Indulge yourself at one of the top-rated full-service spas in the Napa Valley. Located on the ground floor of the Mount View Hotel, the Mount View Spa offers a tranquil environment, treatments by professional therapists and licensed estheticians, and service that pampers our guests.

Spa services are designed to eliminate everyday stressors and help our guests unwind through time-honored healing techniques that promote peace of mind, health and well-being, a prelude to your activities and adventures in the wine country. Gorgeous and relaxing garden courtyard with outdoor heated pool and Jacuzzi. Elegantly decorated rooms and cottages with a wonderful restaurant and wine bar on site. Complimentary WIFI internet access.

614 O NANCE'S HOT SPRINGS
■   1614 Lincoln Ave.   707 942-6211

One of Calistoga's original spas offering mud baths, mineral baths, blanket wraps, facials, and massage.

Indoor mineral pool is 103°. The bathhouse is in the process of being rebuilt and will include tubs, mudbaths and steam baths. Call for updates.

Quality lodging features kitchens and rooms for the handicapped.

614 P ROMAN SPA
■   1300 Washington St.   707 942-4441

This three-diamond property has natural mineral pools and well-appointed rooms set amidst an exquisite garden setting of arbors, fountains, and flower-filled courtyards. Calistoga Oasis Spa is on the premises.

Outdoor swimming pool is 92-95°, the outdoor hydrotherapy whirlpool is 104°, and the indoor hydrotherapy whirlpool is 100°. There are separate men's and women's saunas.

Attractive lodgings with each room having TV, air conditioning, and a refrigerator. Suites are available, as are rooms with large roman tubs piped with untreated mineral water. All rooms are non-smoking, some have kitchens, and two rooms are handicap accessible.

Courtesy of the Roman Spa

614 Q SILVER ROSE INN HOT SPRINGS AND SPA
■   351 Rosedale Rd.   707 942-9581

Discover the Wine Country's only Resort Winery. The Silver Rose offers the personal service and intimacy of a B&B inn at the same time offering the comforts and amenities of a resort. The entire property is supplied with hot mineral water. The spa provides four massage rooms and two water treatment rooms for singles or couples. A full range of body, facial, and hydrotherapy treatments, including a Grape Seed Mud Bath or a Champagne Facial and Body Treatment is offered. The Spa is open to the public.

Two large outdoor pools are kept over 80° and two outdoor whirlpool tubs at 102°. Many facilities are handicap accessible.

Twenty guest rooms are each decorated around a theme. Almost all rooms have incredible mountain and vineyard views. The award winning winery is also on site and guests are offered a barrel tasting each day at 11 AM.

The property also offers several facilities for events from a state-of-the-art conference room to an elegant candle lit dinner in the winery's barrel room.

Courtesy of Silver Rose Inn

615   HARBIN HOT SPRINGS

■   18424 Harbin Springs Rd.   707 987-2477
Middletown, CA 95461
www.harbin.org

Surrounded by 1,700 acres of secluded forest, meadows, and streams, this historic resort is constantly being improved by a nonprofit residential community in the spirit of preserving the springs as a place to come for rest and renewal. Located in a rugged foothill canyon south of Clear Lake, north of Calistoga. Elevation 1,500 feet. Open all year.

Two natural hot mineral water springs (one sulphur, one iron) flow out of the earth at 120°, and the water is piped to an enclosed cement pool that has an average temperature of 110-115°, and an adjoining cement pool, fed by the overflow, that has an average temperature of 95-98°. The heart pool, cold plunge, and swimming pool are filled with pure cold water from the same springs that feed the drinking supply. The temperature of the heart pool is maintained at 95-98°. The temperatures of the cold plunge and the swimming pool depend on the weather. All pools operate on a frequent cleaning and flow-through basis combining sand filters, peroxide and ozone injections, and ultra-violet sterilizers. Clothing is optional everywhere within the grounds except in the front office, in the kitchen and dining room, and on the main roads where public access is allowed. Inquire about handicap accessibility for the pools and the rooms.

Facilities include day use of pools, camping, dorm rooms, private rooms, cottages, several conference buildings for the many retreats and workshops offered, one general store, a book store, a cafe by the pools, an espresso bar, a guest kitchen, and a communal restaurant with a wonderful view where freshly prepared, mostly organic meals (breakfast and dinner) are served. The camping area has flush toilets and showers.

Rooms are beautifully and comfortably decorated, and three elegantly appointed cottages are just perfect for a romantic getaway. Free movies, dances, and daily yoga programs are available. A wide range of massage techniques are offered including Harbin's own Watsu (water shiatsu). State accredited training in massage and Watsu is available on the premises. Credit cards accepted. It is four miles to a service station in Middletown. Phone for rates, reservations, and directions or visit the web site.

Elaine Marie

To really take advantage of the atmosphere of the turn-of-the-century hotel, bring your own food and be prepared to stay for at least a weekend. Hike on the grounds, swim in the pool, or soak in the hot tubs.

The solar-powered hotel has a large, commercial kitchen and personal cupboard and refrigerator space for each room. Guests bring their own food. Accommodations include the nineteen room hotel and an apartment with its own kitchen and bathroom, an eleven-bed bunk room and two campsites that are available seasonally. The hotel has a large community room with musical instruments, billiards, two dining areas, and a cozy library. Hiking and biking trails abound in their 1,800-acre nature reserve. Massage is available daily. Guests are welcome to come for the day, although reservations are required. For more information visit their website.

Location: Just off Hwy 20 between Hwy 5 and Clearlake.

616   WILBUR HOT SPRINGS

3375 Wilbur Springs Rd.   530 473-2306
Williams, CA 95987
www.wilburhotsprings.com

A self-styled "Health Sanctuary" these springs are twenty-two miles from the nearest town. Wilbur boasts an abundance of hot mineral water, hiking trails, and comfortable places in which to relax. The restored turn-of-the-century hotel is located in the remote foothills of Colusa County. Elevation 1,350 feet. Open all year.

Natural hot mineral water flows out of the ground into three large concrete tubs approximately twenty-feet long, five-feet wide and about two feet deep. These tubs are housed in a quiet open-air covered bathhouse. A fourth tub is nestled between a creek and fresh water swimming pool. A perfect setting for stargazing. Tub temperatures range from 98-112°. The mineral water is not chemically treated. A dry sauna, plenty of deck chairs and lounging areas are also available around the tubs. Clothing is optional behind the screened-in tub area, required everywhere else.

617 VICHY HOT SPRINGS RESORT AND INN

2605 Vichy Springs Rd. 707 462-9515
FAX 707 462-9516

■ Ukiah, CA 95842
www.vichysprings.com
vichy@vichysprings.com

The only Vichy baths in North America. Historic, beautifully restored resort in the Ukiah Valley foothills of Mendocino County. Famous for its warm and naturally carbonated mineral water. Guests are invited to explore the 700-acre ranch where wildlife abounds. Elevation 800 feet. Open all year.

Naturally carbonated mineral water flows out of the million-year-old springs at 90° and through redwood pipes to ten enclosed, two-person concrete soaking tubs from the 1860s. Tubs are drained and filled after each use, so no chemical treatment is necessary. One large, communal soaking tub in which the water is treated with ozone is heated to 104°. The Olympic-size swimming pool contains ozone-treated mineral water maintained at approximately 80° during the summer. All tubs and pools are available to the public for day use and to registered guests at any time. Pools, public area and two cottages are ADA handicapped accessible. Disabled guests are able to use all non-accessible facilities with assistance.

Facilities include a tree-shaded, five-acre central lawn ringed by country style cottages and rooms, overnight parking for self-contained RVs, a tree-ringed pond, a running stream, and a thirty-minute hike to a lovely waterfall. Massage, facials, and bed and breakfast are available by reservation on the premises. Credit cards accepted. It is five miles to a campground and four miles to Ukiah.

Phone, fax, or email for more information.

Photos courtesy of Vichy Hot Springs

Built in 1854, this cottage is the oldest structure in all of Mendocino County. *Vichy* has hosted such famous persons as Mark Twain, Jack London, Ulysses Grant, and Teddy Roosevelt. This historical landmark provides fun and relaxation.

Beautiful hiking trails meander through the grounds and often lead to the soaking tubs (pictured on right) which were originally built in the 1860s.

618　SARATOGA SPRINGS RETREAT CENTER
10234 Saratoga Springs Rd.

800 655-7153

Upper Lake, CA 95485

www.saratogasprings.com

Beautiful 5,200 square-foot conference center and lodge situated on 260 acres in a private valley covered with old oaks and black walnut trees in an area of plateaus, hills, and mountains. As you walk about the grounds you can't but help see the abundant wild life. Elevation 1,400 feet. Open all year by reservation only.

Twelve cold mineral wells supply water to the resort, the swimming pool maintained at ambient temperatures, and the eight- by seventeen- by four-foot hot pool where the water is boosted by propane heat. The hot tub is treated minimally with bromine and chlorine is used in the pool. Bathing suits are optional, depending on those present. A new building is handicap accessible.

Lodge, cabins, rooms, areas for camping, meeting rooms, fully equipped kitchen (you cook, or they do by prior arrangement), and sweat lodge are all available on the premises. The 2,000 square foot Heart Lodge is available for conferences, workshops, and seminars. Walk the labyrinth or the many trails on the grounds. All other services are in Upper Lake. Credit cards accepted.

Location: Four miles north of Upper Lake or 21 miles east of Ukiah on Hwy 20.

Courtesy of Saratoga Springs

This crystal clear soaking pool is filled with cold mineral water boosted by propane to make it a perfect temperature for you.

619   ORR HOT SPRINGS
13201 Orr Springs Rd.   707 462-6277
■   Ukiah, CA 95482

A small, tranquil resort nestled in the rolling hills of the Mendocino Coastal Range. Located on a wooded creek under Douglas fir and madrones, thirty-one miles inland from Mendocino. Elevation 800 feet. Open all year by reservations only for overnight stays and day use.

Natural mineral water flows out of several springs at 105° and is piped to two communal tubs, one indoors and one outdoors and six private tub rooms. The swimming pool averages 70°. The indoor tub and outdoor soaking pool are housed in a newly renovated bathhouse. All pools operate on a flow-through basis, so no chemical treatment is added. The excess heat from the hot water is turned into radiant heat and used to heat both dressing rooms and showers. The bathhouse, sauna and tub rooms are all handicap (wheelchair) accessible areas. Clothing is optional in all bathing areas.

Facilities include a fully equipped kitchen, rooms, hostel-style accommodations, small cottages with kitchens, tent spaces along the creek, car camping, one dry sauna and a steam room. Massage is available by reservation in three newly built massage rooms. No pets are allowed, and there is a strict policy regarding the child-to-adult ratio. Credit cards accepted. It is thirteen miles of steep and winding roads to all other services in Ukiah.

Directions: From Route 101 in Ukiah, take the North State St. exit, drive 0.25 miles north to Orr Springs Rd., turn west, and drive 13 miles to the resort.

> *Orr Hot Springs* was under construction when this book went to press so no new photos of the renovations were yet available.

620   SWEETWATER SPA AND INN

955 Ukiah St.   707 937-4140
☐   Mendocino, CA 95460
www.sweetwaterspa.com

A peaceful and comfortable combination of soothing redwood hot tubs, steaming saunas, fine woodwork, and stained glass. Elevation near sea level. Open all year.

Pools are for rent to the public and use gas-heated tap water treated with bromine. One private enclosure with a sauna can be rented by the hour. The water temperature is maintained at 104°. One communal hydropool is available at a day-rate charge. The water temperature is maintained at 104°, and a sauna is included.

Special features: One private suite can be rented by the hour and also by the night, and a sauna is included. One deluxe Oriental room with spa, ocean view, fireplace, and private sun deck offers privacy and romance. All room rentals include use of tubs. Bathing suits are optional everywhere except in the front office. Professional massage offering a wide range of body work is available on the premises. Credit cards accepted.

Sweetwater offers a wide variety of lodging options, including ocean view luxury suites, private cottages with hot tubs, and romantic water tower rooms. Also for rent is a three bedroom vacation house.

Phone for rates, reservations, and directions or visit their website.

621   FINNISH COUNTRY SAUNA & TUBS

5th and J St.   707 822-2228
☐   Arcata, CA 95521

A charming pond surrounded by grass-roofed Finnish style saunas, private outdoor hot tubs, and a European-style coffeehouse in a small Northern California coastal town. Elevation 50 feet. Open every day except Christmas and Thanksgiving.

Tubs are for rent to the public and use gas-heated tap water treated with bromine. There are six private wood hot tubs (two teak and four eucalyptus) rented by the half-hour and maintained at 104°. The conical tubs have benches all the way around and jets at three different levels. One hot tub and one sauna have handicap access. Clothing is optional in private spaces.

Facilities include two private sauna cabins and Cafe Mokka, a coffeehouse serving espresso and juices with live folk music on the weekends. No credit cards accepted. Phone for rates, reservations, and directions.

Located on a quarter acre, complete with pond, island, and outdoor seating area.

Camilla Van Sickle and Bill Pennington

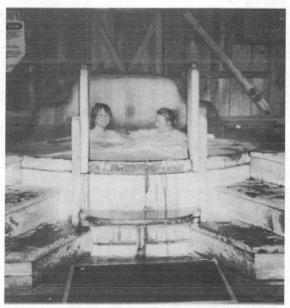

Marjorie Young

CENTRAL CALIFORNIA

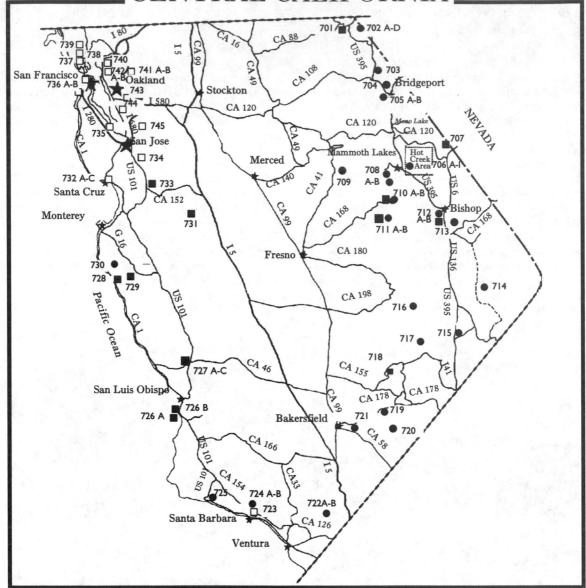

This map was designed to be used with a standard highway map.

MAP SYMBOLS

● Natural locations with minor improvements

■ Commercial mineral water establishments

□ Tap water resorts and rental locations

〜 Paved highway

- - - Unpaved road

········ Hiking trail

701   GROVER HOT SPRINGS

Box 188   **530 694-2248**
■ **Markleeville, CA 96120**

Swimming pool and soaking pool next to a major state campground and picnic area, located in a wooded mountain valley. Elevation 6,000 feet. Open all year.

Natural mineral water flows out of several springs at 147° and into a holding pond from which it is piped to the pool area. The soaking pool, using natural mineral water treated with bromine, is maintained at approximately 103°. The swimming pool, using domestic water treated with chlorine, is maintained at 70-80°. Domestic water is used to cool down the hot mineral water. Admission is on a first-come, first-served basis, and the official capacity limit of fifty persons in the hot pool and twenty-five in the cold pool is reached early every day during the summer. Bathing suits are required. For handicap accessibility there is a ramp to the pool, although there is not a ramp into the pool. Bathrooms and parking spaces are provided.

Campground spaces are available by prior reservation, as with all other California state parks. Cross-country skiers are encouraged to camp in the picnic area during the winter and to ski in to use the soaking pool. The road is also plowed during the winter making for easy access. It is four miles to the nearest restaurant, motel, and service station in Markleeville.

Location: On Alpine County Road E4, 4.5 miles west of Markleeville. Follow the signs.

Photos by Mark Gillespie

In summer, as big as this hot soaking pool is, it fills up very quickly. In winter, skiing or driving in lets you soak almost by yourself.

Wonderful hot springs with beautiful mountain views are to be found along the banks of the East Fork of the Carson River in Toiyabe National Forest. The springs are accessible during the rafting season, approximately May through July, depending on water flow. Elevation 5,000 feet.

There are no services available at any of the hot spring sites, although the BLM has installed out-houses at the major springs. While the apparent local custom at the pools is clothing optional, please be respectful of those people already there. These springs are not shown on any Forest Service or USGS map but are well known to raft trip guides.

While you can navigate this river yourself if you are an experienced kayaker, for a real treat, one-day and two-day raft trips (Class 2 rapids) are available through commercial outfitters.

Note: It is possible to access this spring by car from Gardnerville, however, according to all reports, it is at the end of "seven of the most miserable miles a 4 WD can handle." It also takes you across a working ranch; during the months of April to November they really do not want you on the property. During the other months you must stay out of the fields and travel only on the road. The field hands will chase you out of the area. An extremely steep trail requiring the 4 WD vehicle puts you down at the river's edge where there is a campground and outhouse on BLM land. **River Run** is located directly across the river and in plain sight. During low water time in the summer you can walk or drive very carefully across the river. The spring is totally inaccessible during high spring runoff except by raft.

GPS: N 38 46.049 W 119 43.310

Marjorie Young

702 A   RIVERSIDE HOT SPRING

● **Near the town of Markleeville**

Approximately eight miles downstream from where you put into the water three small pools are visible from the river on your right (east). Natural mineral water flows into the upper pool at approximately 92° and then continues flowing into the lower pools. The lower tub has been lined with a tarp by some volunteers. During high water these pools are often underwater and need to be rebuilt annually.

Camping is possible near the springs.

702 B   HILLSIDE HOT SPRINGS

● **Near the town of Markleeville**

Just before you round the bend to get to River Run a small pool has been built of rock and cement that will hold four to six people comfortably. The water was 104° but varies with the ambient temperature.

Mark Gillespie

You can also get to this pool by hiking around the bend from *River Run Hot Springs*.

Debbie Johnson

Saturday nights find trucks crossing the river to get to *River Run* often making this pool "the party spot"—rather noisy and very crowded. Early in the morning it was lovely to find the pool almost empty.

702 C   RIVER RUN HOT SPRINGS

● **Near the town of Markleeville**

Natural mineral water emerges from several springs on the hillside at 110° or hotter and cools as it flows toward the river. The temperature of the water drops to approximately 100° by the time it reaches the large cement and river stone pool on the edge of an eight-foot cliff above the river. The large pool is equipped with fill spout and drain and is about four feet deep. The small upper pools are quite hot and should be approached with caution.

There is a large open area available for camping, but there are no facilities except an outhouse near the springs.

702 D   HOT SHOWERBATH

● **Near the town of Markleeville**

One mile downstream from River Run Hot Springs, a small pullout is visible on the left (west). Due to earthquakes and other natural phenomena the water only trickles over the embankment and the pool is barely ankle deep.

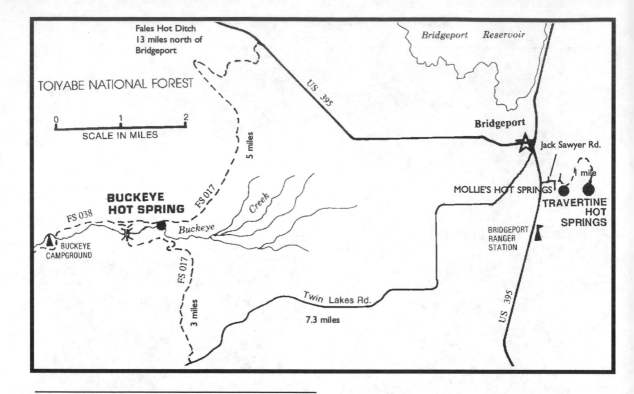

Fales Hot Ditch
13 miles north of
Bridgeport

TOIYABE NATIONAL FOREST

Bridgeport Reservoir

0   1   2
SCALE IN MILES

US 395

Bridgeport

5 miles

Jack Sawyer Rd.

FS 017

BUCKEYE
HOT SPRING

FS 038

Creek

Buckeye

1 mile

MOLLIE'S HOT SPRINGS

TRAVERTINE
HOT
SPRINGS

BUCKEYE
CAMPGROUND

BRIDGEPORT
RANGER
STATION

FS 017

3 miles

Twin Lakes Rd.

7.3 miles

US 395

703   FALES HOT DITCH

● **North of the town of Bridgeport**

A primitive pool on Hot Springs Creek in the sage-brush foothills of the Eastern Sierra. Elevation 7,200 feet. Open all year.

Natural mineral water emerges at 140° from a spring on the property of an old resort, now closed, and flows down Hot Springs Creek, gradually cooling as it goes. Volunteers have dammed the creek to form a thigh-deep, rock and sand pool, ten-feet by twelve-feet and four-feet deep on the east side of the highway 0.3 miles past the old resort (which is on the west side of the highway). Although the soaking pool is twenty feet below the highway and out of sight of passing vehicles, it is advisable to wear a bathing suit or have it close at hand.

There are no services on the premises. It is seven miles to a Forest Service campground and thirteen miles to all other services in Bridgeport.

Directions: From Bridgeport, drive north on US 395 for 13 miles to a boarded-up, fenced, brown wooden structure that used to be Fales Hot Springs Resort (on the west side of US 395). The gated property just north of the old resort is private and posted "no trespassing." However, from the old resort, drive 0.3 miles north and park along the shoulder of US 395 on the east side of the road. The pullout is right before mile marker 90. The creek and soaking pool are 20 feet below the highway (not visible until you park and look over the small cliff).

GPS: N 38.21.152 W 119 24.290

Marjorie Young

Jayson Loam

Along with these soaking pools by the river, there is a small cave (to the left under the overhang) where the water drips off the roof forming a soaking area.

---

704   BUCKEYE HOT SPRING

(see map on page 148)

● **Near the town of Bridgeport**

Delightful hot spring in a superb natural setting on the north bank of Buckeye Creek in Toiyabe National Forest. One of the best. Elevation 6,900 feet. Open all year; not accessible by road in winter.

Natural mineral water flows out of the ground at 135°, runs over a large cliff built up by mineral deposits, and drops into the creek. Volunteers have built loosely constructed rock pools along the edge of the creek below the hot waterfall. The pool temperature is controlled by admitting more or less cold water from the creek. A new dam and drain has been added to the upper pool.

There is another small outflow of hot geothermal water on the bluff near the parking area. Volunteers have dug a new, larager soaking pool that maintains a temperature of approximately 100°. It is near the foot of the only pine located in the upstream direction from the parking area. The apparent local custom at both pools is clothing optional, however during the day there are usually clothed families there with young children.

Three hundred yards upstream from the parking area are several acres of unmarked open space on which overnight parking is not prohibited. It is one mile to a Forest Service campground and nine miles to all services in Bridgeport. Twin Lakes, a bit closer, also provides gas, food, and a campground. There is a parking turnout on the south side of the road on the bluff above the springs.

Directions: (This is the easier route.) At the north end of Bridgeport, take Twin Lakes Rd. west for 7.3 miles to Doc & Al's Resort. Turn right (north) onto FS 017, a two-lane, graded, washboard road, for 3 miles to the second bridge over the creek, where the road intersects with FS 038 toward Buckeye Campground to the left. Branch off to the right for a few hundred yards up a short hill on the north branch of FS 017 to a large flat parking clearing on a big knoll. The upper pool is a few steps away (slightly downhill and to the right) under a tree, at the crest of the knoll overlooking Buckeye Creek. Several unofficial paths lead down the slope to the pools located along the creek at the foot of a large mound covered over by the mineral deposits.

Source maps: *Toiyabe National Forest*, USGS *Matterhorn Peak*.

GPS: N 38 14.384 W 119 19.568

Debbie Johnson

This pool on the hillside has recently been enlarged so that it will now hold at least four people.

Sally Jackson

Soakers Bible

Travertine Hot Springs is named after the mineral which has built up here to form this tufa mound. The area around the pools is carefully maintained so please stay on the trails to help conserve the fragile vegetation.

705 A   TRAVERTINE HOT SPRINGS
(see map on page 148)
● Southeast of the town of Bridgeport

An unusual group of volunteer-built soaking pools on large travertine ridges with commanding views of the High Sierra. Located two miles from the center of Bridgeport. Elevation 6,700 feet. Open all year; wet weather can turn road into a slippery slide.

The flow of natural mineral water (115-156°) out of several geothermal fissures can be interrupted or shifted to a new outlet by underground movement resulting from local earthquakes. The scalding water is channeled to a series of volunteer-built soaking pools in which the individual pool temperatures are controlled by temporarily diverting the hot water inflow as needed. The upper pool is handicap accessible with assistance. Clothing optional, but determined by who is there first.

At the upper ten- by five- by two-foot deep pool, scalding water issues out from a small hole and is directed through a stepped channel with a "bear claw" configuration at pool's edge. The source is diverted to control pool temperature. There is a plug for draining and cleaning the pool, which is done fastidiously by volunteers. Overflow goes into a small adjoining foot bath for rinsing off before entering the pool. Since you can drive right up to this pool it is handicap accessible with assistance.

Four lower wood, rock-and-cement pools, one-hundred yards below, are at the foot of a large travertine ridge the water is channeled along the top of the ridge into the pools at about 100°. A primitive 80° rock and mud pool nearby is fed by a separate underground source. The first and hottest small pool was built in the early 1900s for dipping sheep and original boards still exist.

There are no services and overnight camping is not permitted. Other primitive amenities include a large deck around the pools covered with old carpets for sunbathing, a picnic table, and "butt cans." There is no trash collection, so please pack it out. All other services are in Bridgeport.

Directions: From the ranger station 0.5 miles south of Bridgeport, drive north on Hwy 395 for 0.2 miles. Turn right on Jack Sawyer Rd., the first paved road on your right. At 0.4 miles the paved road makes a 90-degree turn to the right. Do not bear right. Continue straight ahead on the unpaved, ungraded road for approximately 1 mile to the pools. On the way you will pass a sign on your left to Bridgeport Barrow Pit; continue straight to the forest service sign on your left. If you continue straight, the second turnoff just ahead on the right leads to the lower pools. Or continue uphill to where the road curves around to the right to reach the upper cement pool.

GPS: N 38 14.729 W 119 12.323

705 B   MOLLIE'S HOT SPRINGS

(see map on page 148)

● Southeast of the town of Bridgeport

Carefully built to use all the available flow, this hot springs in built on public land by special people and offers great views in all directions.

Natural mineral water flows into a three- to four-person tub carefully built out of rock and with a squishy bottom. A wood bench offers a place to enjoy the view. Clothing optional.

Directions: From the lower pools at Travertine Hot Springs, walk due west toward US 395, angling slightly left toward the high travertine wall that also runs approximately west. After 100 yards, cross over that wall where it has crumbled nearly down to grade, heading approximately southwest. In a short time, a primitive road becomes visible, along with a tall pole due south of the road which runs approximately east to west. With the pole straight ahead, the pool is just on the south side of the primitive road, almost invisible in the surrounding white stones, mostly travertine. The large white board beam of a bench, nearly the same color as the rocks, may be easy to spot because its shape stands out from the rocks.

Pictures top and right by Camilla Van Sickle and Bill Pennington

Two of the regional contributors to this book, Petty Prange and Bill Pennington, enjoying a soak.

SoakersBible

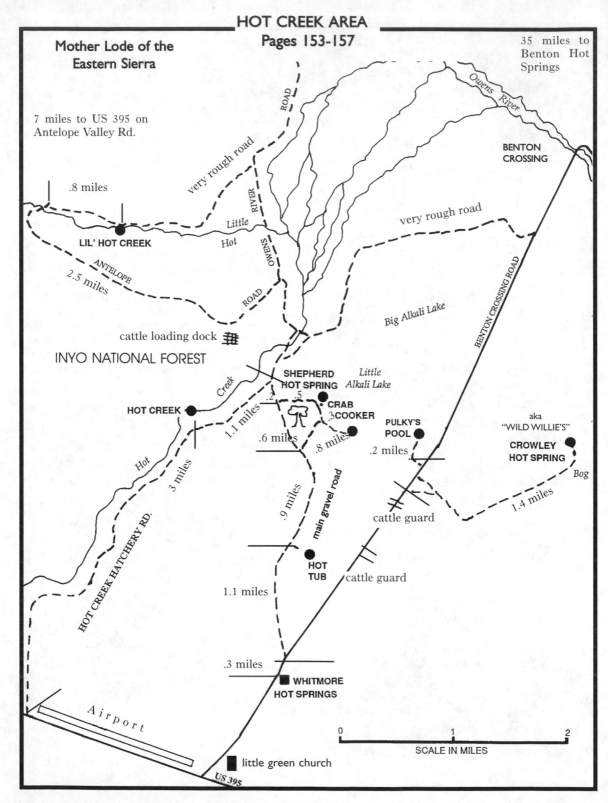

HOT CREEK AREA
Pages 153-157

Mother Lode of the
Eastern Sierra

35 miles to
Benton Hot
Springs

7 miles to US 395 on
Antelope Valley Rd.

.8 miles

LIL' HOT CREEK

ROAD

Little

Hot

OWENS

RIVER

BENTON
CROSSING

very rough road

Owens River

very rough road

ANTELOPE

2.5 miles

ROAD

Big Alkali Lake

cattle loading dock

BENTON CROSSING ROAD

INYO NATIONAL FOREST

Creek

SHEPHERD
HOT SPRING

Little
Alkali Lake

HOT CREEK

1.1 miles

.2

.5

CRAB
.3 COOKER

PULKY'S
POOL

aka
"WILD WILLIE'S"

.6 miles

.8 miles

.2 miles

CROWLEY
HOT SPRING

Hot

3 miles

.9 miles

main gravel road

Bog

1.4 miles

cattle guard

HOT CREEK HATCHERY RD.

HOT
TUB

cattle guard

1.1 miles

.3 miles

WHITMORE
HOT SPRINGS

Airport

0   1   2

SCALE IN MILES

little green church

US 395

152

At the time of this printing, Hot Creek is closed for soaking. No final decision has been made as to whether or not it will be reopened for public use.

Photos by Phil Wilcox

706 A   HOT CREEK

(see map on page 152)

● **East of the town of Mammoth Lakes**

Primarily a geologic observation and interpretive site with some limited use by bathers. Open daylight hours only.

Natural mineral water with a slight sulfur smell emerges from many fissures as steam or boiling water, and several danger areas have been fenced off for safety. Substantial amounts of boiling, geothermal water also flow up from the bottom of the creek. A bend in the creek provides a natural eddy in which the mixing of hot and cold water stays within a range of 50° to 110°. Those who venture into this confluence experience vivid thermal skin effects, but they must be careful to avoid the geothermal vents because of the danger of scalding. The trail from the main pool goes upstream 400-500 feet where cold water is diverted around other hot spots in the river. Bathing suits required.

In the past, night use of this location has resulted in many injuries and some fatalities, so the area may be used only from sunrise to sunset. Citations are issued by the Forest Service to anyone found there after sunset or before sunrise. During the winter, when snow blocks the access road, skiers and hikers may still enter the area during daylight hours.

Facilities include men's and women's changing rooms, pit toilets, and an asphalt parking area with a paved, fenced pathway down to the creek, making the area handicap accessible with assistance. Overnight parking is prohibited. It is ten miles to all services in the town of Mammoth Lakes.

Directions: From US 395, 3 miles south of the Mammoth Lakes turnoff, turn east on Hot Creek Hatchery Rd./Airport. At 0.5 miles, turn right at the sign to "Hot Creek Geothermal Area." From this sign, it is 3 miles to the parking area for Hot Creek. Only the first 1.2 miles are paved. Or, from Benton Crossing Rd., take 3S50, the main gravel road, for 2.8 miles. Turn left for 0.3 miles to the Hot Creek gate and another 0.8 mile to the parking area.

Source maps: *Inyo National Forest*, USGS *Mt. Morrison*.

GPS: N 37 39.629 W 118 49.700

Bill Franks

Dave Bybee

706 B   LIL' HOT CREEK

(see map on page 152)

● **East of the town of Mammoth Lakes**

A very hot flowing creek fed by a 180° geothermal spring. The name Lil' Hot Creek has been given to a large, squishy-bottom soaking pool, six feet across, located just below where the flow from several cold springs cools the hot stream to approximately 107°. The thigh-deep cement and rock pool, three feet deep, has tiered seats used as steps, so you can soak at different depths. Pool temperature can be controlled by opening or capping a four-inch plastic pipe that brings the water in from the nearby creek. There's a plug for draining and cleaning the pool. Spillover goes through a tiny channel back to the creek. As you leave, please shut the inflow of hot water so the next ones in will not be scalded—water can get up to 120-125°.

Wood benches and a boardwalk edge one side of the cement pool. Plenty of level ground, as well as hideaway spots among the pine trees in the nearby national forest, are available where overnight parking is not prohibited. The apparent local custom is clothing optional.

Directions: There are four routes, depending on your starting point.

1. (This is the best.) From the main gravel road (3S50, Benton Crossing Rd.), drive a total of 3.3 miles to the sign for Owens River Rd. (This is 0.7 miles past the turnoff to Shepherd.) You'll pass a cattle loading dock on the left just before Owens River Rd. Turn left for 0.7 miles to Little Antelope Rd. Turn left onto Antelope Rd. for 2.5 miles across a flat open area. At 2.5 miles, at the beginning of the pine forest, is a cattle guard. Make a sharp right just past the cattle guard and follow this very rough, ungraded

Hot water from the tub is recycled back into the hot stream. Water temperature varies greatly, often up to 120 degrees, so be careful! Nearby brooms and scrub brushes are evidence that volunteers continually maintain the pools.

dirt road for 0.8 miles to the springs on your right. Whenever the road forks, keep bearing right, following the fence until you come to a flat open area for parking. You'll see steam rising from the creek to your right as you follow the fence. At the parking area, look for a small wooden portion in the wire fence and a cattle-proof entrance. Go through the gate and over log planks across the creek to reach the hot soaking pool.

2. Take Hot Creek Hatchery Rd. from US 395 for 3 miles to the Hot Creek asphalt parking area. Continue past the parking area for another 1.1 miles to a fork in the unpaved road. Do not bear right, but continue straight ahead for another 0.1 mile to where the road ends at a wide gravel road. This is 3S50, the main gravel road. Turn left, and on your left you'll see the cattle loading dock mentioned above. Follow directions above.

3. A very beautiful but much longer drive begins at US 395. At the turnoff to Mammoth Lake, instead of heading west toward the lakes, turn east and follow the sign to Little Antelope Valley (not Chalk Hills). At 6.3 miles you will be at the cattle guard at the edge of the pine forest. Turn left onto the ungraded dirt road and follow the fence as described above to reach the soaking pool.

4. For those with 4WD vehicles, or at least with good clearance, continue past the turnoff to Antelope Rd. another 1.3 miles and turn left. Follow the washboard road 2 miles to the springs, which are now on the left.

GPS: N 37 53.416 W 118 50.555

Camilla Van Sickle and Bill Pennington

At present, there is no water in *Crab Cooker*. However, several people have offered to go in and replace the valve and piping to make it useable again.

Betty Prange

Crab Cooker overlooks a boggy meadow with mountains forming a stunning backdrop.

706 C   SHEPHERD HOT SPRING
(see map on page 152)

● **East of the town of Mammoth Lakes**

Natural mineral water flows out of a spring and through a plastic pipe to a twenty by twenty-four inch deep rock and cement tub. There are benches in the pool, which is large enough for three or four people. Pool temperature is controlled by diverting the hot water flow from the nearby source pool which can often be as hot as 130°. The white plastic inflow pipe has a ball valve to control the flow and if allowed to run the temperature in the pool can be very, very hot–be careful. There is a plug for draining the pool, capped with a tennis ball. However, local volunteers prefer emptying the pool with a bucket before scrubbing. A scrub brush is on site.

There are no facilities except a primitive campfire ring. A posted sign prohibits overnight parking. The apparent local custom is clothing optional.

Directions: From Benton Crossing Rd., turn north on 3S50 (the main gravel road) 0.3 miles past the Whitmore public swimming pool. Drive 2.6 miles to a dirt road on your right. Follow this across an open bog for 0.5 miles to the pool on your left.

From Crab Cooker, follow the dirt road back the way you came in for 0.5 miles to a four-way, dirt-road intersection. To reach Shepherd, turn right at this intersection and go 0.2 miles to the small clearing where the pool is located.

GPS: N 37 40.014 W 118 48.213

706 D   CRAB COOKER
(see map on page 152)

● **East of the town of Mammoth Lakes**

Natural mineral water flows out of a spring at over 120° and through a cement casing across the road to a rock-and-cement soaking pool. The pool temperature can be controlled by turning off a valve just outside the pool when the desired soaking temperature is reached. (Please turn off this valve when leaving so as not to scald the next soakers.) Do not tamper with the pipes in the nearby well, as special plumbing equipment is required to fix them.

There are no facilities on the premises. The apparent local custom is clothing optional.

Directions: Follow the main gravel road for 2 miles from Benton Crossing Rd. (0.9 miles past the turnoff to Hot Tub). Watch for a lone juniper tree on the right side of the road. The road to Crab Cooker is on the right just before this tree. Two separate roads appear to head off to the right, but they merge after a short oval and continue as a rocky, one-lane dirt road for 0.1 mile to a large white mound of rocks. Follow the road around the left side of these rocks for another 0.2 miles to a four-way dirt-road intersection. Continue straight for another 0.5 miles across cow pastures to where the road ends at a flat open area where you will see the pool.

GPS: N 37 39.775 W 118 48.507

706 E   DAVE'S WARM TUB

● **East of the town of Mammoth Lakes**

As of 1995, there was no longer a tub here and the existing water is only 80° in a shallow seep.

Marjorie Young

Debbie Johnson

706 F   PULKY'S POOL (HILLTOP)
(see map on page 152)

● **East of the town of Mammoth Lakes**

Natural mineral water flows out of a spring at 131° and through a PVC pipe to a free-form, rock and cement pool up on the plateau. This pool, with a temperature of about 107° features a very clear water and a plug in the bottom to facilitate easy cleaning. The hot water pipe (green) has a gate valve and a second pipe (red) admits cold water allowing for temperature control.

Primitive facilities include a small carpeted deck for undressing and sunbathing, and a cement bench. The area is posted for day use only; no overnight parking is permitted. The apparent local custom is clothing optional.

Directions: From US 395, drive 2 miles past Whitmore Pool over one cattle guard to the second cattle guard. The turnoff to Crowley, 706-G, is just past the second cattle guard on the right (south). For Pulky's, continue on Benton Crossing Rd. for another 0.4 miles to an unpaved road on the left (north). Follow this road as it curves around a large alkali field for 0.4 miles to a flat parking area and park by fence. The pool is up on the plateau. Caution: Do not attempt to drive to the plateau, stay on the road; even 4WD vehicles have become stuck in the soft ground. Road is very rough.

GPS: N 37 39.838 W 118 47.359

706 G   CROWLEY HOT SPRING
(ALSO KNOWN AS WILD WILLIE'S)
(see map on page 152)

● **East of the town of Mammoth Lakes**

Natural mineral water flows out of a spring and down a small creek channel at 110°, then into a cement and rock pool large enough for thirty people. Surface cooling keeps the pool temperature about 104° most of the year.

Fifty feet away, at the foot of a large rock outcropping, is a squishy, mud-bottom pool at approximately 100°. Natural mineral water flows from a separate source near the rock into this knee-deep pool. The pool is large enough for a half-dozen people. Clothing optional.

There are no facilities on the premises, but overnight parking is not prohibited in the large parking area.

Directions: From Benton Crossing Rd., drive 2 miles past Whitmore Pool. Immediately past the second cattle guard, two rough dirt roads cut off to the right. Take either one (they join up) and drive 1.1 miles to a large rock. Follow the road to the right side of the rock and take an immediate left at the fork. Drive 0.3 miles to a large level parking area bordered by logs. Do not attempt to drive any farther. To reach the pools, follow the walkway from the end of the parking area for approximately 250 yards to where it joins a trail from the opposite direction and a path leading down a small hill to the left. The primitive pool is under some trees near the big rock ahead on your left; the pool with the deck is ahead on the right.

Caution: Do not attempt to drive across the bog to the pool area. Even 4WDs have been trapped. A new wooden and gravel walkway has been constructed from the parking lot to the pools—please use it!

GPS: N 37 39.550 W 118 46.270

706 H   HOT TUB

(see map on page 152)

● **East of the town of Mammoth Lakes**

Natural mineral water flows out of a spring at 110° and through a black PVC pipe to a three-foot deep rock and cement pool. The pool temperature is controlled by diverting the hot water inflow whenever the desired soaking temperature has been reached. There is a plug for draining, and the pool is kept clean by a group of local volunteers. The thigh-deep pool can hold about six people comfortably.

There are no facilities, but there is plenty of level area surrounding the pool, and overnight parking is not prohibited. Campers, please be considerate of others. Park away from the tubs, and keep the noise level down. The apparent local custom is clothing optional.

Directions: From Benton Crossing Rd., drive 1.1 miles on 3S50 (the main gravel road) to the second one-lane dirt road on the right. Turn right and go for 0.1 mile to a clearing, then bear left for another 0.1 mile to the pool.

706 I   WHITMORE HOT SPRINGS

(see map on page 152)
904 Benton Crossing Rd.   760 935-4222
■ **Mammoth Lakes, CA 93546**

Large, conventional public swimming pool jointly operated by Mono County and the town of Mammoth Lakes on land leased from the Los Angeles Department of Water and Power. Open during the day, Monday through Saturday, approximately mid-June to Labor Day.

Natural mineral water is pumped from a well, propane boosted, and piped to the swimming pool where it is treated with chlorine. Depending on air temperature and wind conditions, the pool water temperature averages 82°. An adjoining shallow wading pool averages 92°. Bathing suits are required. Bathrooms, showers, and slidegate entrance are handicap accessible.

A small access fee includes showers (campers take note) and a barbeque area. A full aquatic schedule is available on the premises. Parking is permitted only during hours of operation. No credit cards are accepted.

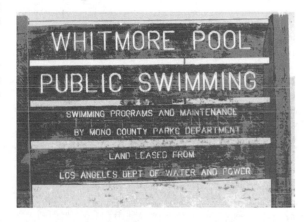

Photos by Phil Wilcox

707 THE OLD HOUSE AT BENTON HOT SPRINGS

55045 Hwy 120   (tubs) **760 933-2507**
■   **Benton, CA 93512**   (inn) **760 933-2628**
www.395/oldhouse.com

Two facilities next to door to each other: one houses the antique store and rents out the hot tubs in back by the day or hour; the other is the B&B that includes the use of the private tubs on that property with the room rental. Tubs are located in an oasis-type setting under cottonwood, Russian olive, tamarisk, and locust trees in high desert and sagebrush-type country along the eastern border of California near the Nevada state line, with views of Montgomery and Boundary Peaks (highest points in Nevada). Elevation: 5,500 feet. Open all year.

Natural, soft, silky mineral water flows out of a spring at 135° and supplies water to the entire town of Benton Hot Springs. A cooling/evaporation tank at The Old House provides the only cool water in town. There is no chemical treatment of the water in the tubs. A group of redwood tubs were cut from an old redwood pipeline that used to go to the generating plant. The four tubs, located under the trees, are drained and scrubbed after each use. Each tub has a hot and cold faucet to adjust water temperature. The five-foot diameter tubs are about three feet deep, have seats inside, and are large enough for four to six people. Bathing suits are optional in the tubs, except for one which is not screened. Owners operate on a body-tolerant basis.

Snacks and beverages are sold on the premises and there are also camping spaces. A small store in the town of Benton sells the basics, and a cafe offers meals.

Directions: From Bishop, take US 6 north for 36 miles to the tiny town of Benton. Turn west on CA 120 and drive 4 miles until you see the old green and white house on the north side of the street. Or, from US 395 in Lee Vining (Tioga Pass from Yosemite), take CA 120 east for 46 miles to Benton Hot Springs. If you are coming from the series of natural springs outside Mammoth, take Benton Crossing Rd. south of the Mammoth Airport for 36 miles to where it ends at CA 120. Take 120 east for 3 miles to Benton Hot Springs.

Each of the tubs at the two locations offer beautiful views and privacy. You can also adjust the temperature to your liking.

Top photo: Courtesy of Benton Hot Springs
Middle photo: Debbie Johnson
Bottom photo: Camilla Van Sickle and Bill Pennington

Steve Heerema

Scott Harwood

708 A   RED'S MEADOW HOT SPRINGS

● **In Red's Meadow Campground near Devil's Postpile National Monument**

Tin-roof shed with six cement shower-over bath tubs in six small private rooms, on the edge of a mountain meadow campground. Elevation 7,000 feet. Road open approximately Memorial Day to September 20. No charge is made for the use of the tubs, which are available on a first-come, first-served basis. Donations accepted.

Natural mineral water flows out of the ground at 114°, into a storage tank, and then by pipe into the bathhouse. Depending on the use, water temperature out of the shower heads will vary from 90-100°.

In summer, all water from the spring is diverted into the bathhouse. During the winter, the cement hot water storage tank is used for soaking and can only be reached by snowmobilers and cross-country skiers.

A Forest Service campground, open during the summer, adjoins the hot springs. It is four miles to a cafe, general store, rustic cabins, and pack station at Red's Meadow Resort, and twelve miles to an RV park and other services in Mammoth Lakes.

Directions: From the town of Mammoth Lakes, take CA 203 west to the end, then follow signs through Minaret Pass to Devil's Postpile National Monument and to Red's Meadow Campground. Note: During the day in summer, private vehicles are prohibited beyond Minaret Pass. A frequent shuttle bus service originates at Mammoth Mountain Inn.

Source map: *Inyo National Forest*, USGS *Devil's Postpile*.

GPS: N 37 37.080 W 119 04.440

708 B   IVA BELL (FISH CREEK) HOT SPRINGS

● **South of Devil's Postpile National Monument**

A delightful cluster of volunteer-built soaking pools, some with spectacular views of the wilderness. Elevation 7,400 feet. Open all year.

The pools adjoin the Iva Bell camp area that includes numerous camping sites separated by meadows and stands of pines. A 102° bottom-fed pool may be reached by following a path thirty yards across a meadow.

From the first pool, a path leads due east for fifty yards to a cozy campsite. From this site, a steep one-hundred-yard path leads up to four more pools, ranging in temperature from 101° to 110°. Two pools are carved into the face of the hillside with spring water cascading into them, and two more rock and log pools are on top of the hill near the 124° source. The nicest pool has a sandy bottom and is nestled on the back side of this ledge, where a 106° trickle flows out of a fissure slowly enough to maintain a 101° temperature in the summertime.

Note: In summer you must pay to enter Reds Meadow and take a shuttle to the area. You must also obtain a backcountry permit and a mandatory bear canister from the ranger station. Empty your car of anything that might entice a bear into boxes provided at the parking area.

Directions: Take the trail to Rainbow Falls and continue towards Fish Creek for 8 miles eventually dropping into Fish Creek Valley. Cross the bridge and continue upstream 4 more miles and turn left at the turn marked Fish Valley. The unmarked camping area and springs are just past this turn. Also check with the Mammoth Ranger District of Inyo National Forest, 760 873-2408.

Source map: *USGS Devil's Postpile*.

GPS: N 37 31.920 W 119 01.500

709   LEWIS CREEK WARM SPRINGS

● **North of the town of Oakhurst**

Spectacular scenery and a hot pool filled by warm water flowing out of the cracks in the rocks at the top of gorgeous Corlieu Falls. Situated in a heavily-wooded river valley surrounded by pine and madrone in the Sierra National Forest.

Natural mineral water fills a small two-person pool that has a temperature of around 85° and is located on the far side of Lewis Creek. Clothing optional. There is also a nice swimming hole you can access directly from the hot spring.

Large campsite nearby. All other services back in Oakhurst.

Directions: From the town of Oakhurst go north about 7 miles to the marked midpoint of the Lewis Creek trail. You will go about 0.25 miles on the trail and then down a few hundred feet to the river where you will see the campsite. Be careful and don't take the trail to the base of the waterfall as the spring is located at the top of the waterfall across from the campsite.

Map source: USGS *Poleta Canyon* Quad
GPS: N 37 16.000 W 118 16.340

While I don't have a picture of *Lewis Creek Warm Springs*, this is the type of habitat to be found in that area and would certainly make for a beautiful hike.

710 A   MONO HOT SPRINGS

(Summer) 7200 Hwy 168   559 325-1710
Mono Hot Springs, CA 93642
(Winter) PO Box 215   559 683-5857
Lake Shore, CA 93634
Northeast of Fresno
www.monohotsprings.com

A vacation resort offering fishing, hiking, and camping in addition to mineral baths with access across the river to several natural springs. Located on the south fork of the San Joaquin River near Edison Lake, Florence Lake, and Bear Dam in the Sierra National Forest. Elevation 6,500 feet. Open May to October for summer season;.call for winter snow packages.

Natural mineral water flows from a spring at 107° and is piped to a bathhouse containing four two-person soaking tubs in private rooms. Tubs have geothermal water only, measuring 100-105°. Tubs are drained and refilled after each use, so no chemical treatment of the water is necessary. An outdoor hydrojet pool is maintained at 103-105° and is treated with chlorine. Bathing suits are required except in private rooms. Facilities are available on a day-use basis, as well as to registered guests, and are handicap accessible with assistance.

On the south side of the river directly across from the resort is a series of springs and soaking pools that are open all year, but only to cross-country skiers and snow-mobilers in winter. Water from one spring feeds into a holding tank. From there it is piped across the river to the resort. Nearby is a cement soaking tub called "The Coffin" due to its size and shape. Above the riverbank are several cement soaking tubs that remain from an historic bathhouse. A rock and mud pool is near the cement tubs and another primitive pool, called "The Rock," is next to a large boulder ten feet up the hill from the cement tubs. Pool temperatures are approximately 101°. Bathing suits are advisable in the daytime.

Facilities include a restaurant, store, service station, tent cabins and cabins. A forest service campground is on the edge of the property. Massage is available on the premises.Credit cards accepted.

Directions to the resort: From the city of Fresno on CA 99, go 80 miles northeast on CA 168 to the ranger station at the northeast side of Huntington Lake. Inquire here about road conditions before attempting to drive in. The one-lane road is very narrow and winding. Allow at least one hour for this 15-mile stretch.

At 15 miles, you come to the High Sierra Ranger Station. Stop here for info and campfire permits, needed even for cooking in your van. One mile past this station the road forks. Bear left to Mono Hot Springs. At 1 mile, you will cross a small bridge. Continue downhill to a second green bridge. Mono is less than 0.25 miles past the bridge on your left.

To reach the soaking pools on the south side of the river, use the wooden bridge that starts at the forest service campground. "The Rock" is up a small hill to your left, the cement pools a few feet ahead uphill from the river.

Phil Wilcox

The cement pools are the remains of an old bathhouse located across the river from the resort. The pool below is only one of several in the area.

Scott Harwood

710 B   LITTLE EDEN
ROSE GARDEN

● **Northeast of Fresno**

A primitive, squishy-bottom, thigh-deep pool surrounded by grass and large enough for a dozen people, with a gorgeous view of the surrounding mountains and a real feeling that you are out in nature. Elevation 6,500 feet. Open all year; accessible only to cross-country skiers and snowmobilers in the winter.

Natural mineral water bubbles up through the sandy pool bottom at around 100°. Because of its large size, pool temperatures measure only in the nineties. The apparent local custom is clothing optional.

There are no facilities on the premises. Services are less than a mile away at Mono Hot Springs Resort.

Directions: Follow directions given for Mono Hot Springs to the High Sierra ranger station. 2.1 miles past the station, and 1.1 miles down the left fork at the "Y" is a steel bridge. Park at turnout on right just before bridge or on left just past the bridge. A steep, unofficial trail to the pool begins on the left (north), approximately 50 feet before the bridge, and goes around a large rock outcropping, through some marshy spots, and down to the pool at the base of the rocks. From the other direction, Little Eden is below the green bridge that is just past the spring that fills the Rose Garden and then flows over the road

GPS: N 37 19.313 W 119 11.172.

Note: A mushy bottomed dirt pool has recently been dug out located just across the road from the trail down to Little Eden. Called the Rose Garden for the obvious reason.

Scott Harwood

711 A   MUIR TRAIL RANCH

Lakeshore CA 93634
www.muirtrailranch.com

Located in a beautiful valley in the high mountains of central California east of Fresno, surrounded by soaring granite peaks and the John Muir Wilderness of the the Sierra National Forest. Near the John Muir Trail. Elevation 7,600 feet.

For information, write the owner, Adeline Smith, Box 176, Lakeshore, CA 93634 from mid-June to October, or Box 700, Ahwanee, CA 93601 from November through May. For more details check out their web site.

Over a thousand gallons per hour of fresh, hot water gushes out of a crack in the bedrock, flows along a streambed, then pours into a large pool that is surrounded by flowers and a beautiful enclosure. The pool is eight by ten feet and about two-and one-half feet deep. The 107° water flows through the pool sixteen times a day. This pool offers a magnificent view of granite peaks over the meadow. There is a place to wash up before entering the pool. They supply the soap and shampoo.

If that pool is too hot, there is a second one only a few feet away. It is enclosed too and has cooler water, about body temperature, coming in from a spring up the hill. There is a place to wash up here, also.

Muir Trail Ranch offers rustic log cabin comfort to organized groups on a bring-your-own-food basis, or hire a caterer from a list of cooks who have worked there in the past. There are three options if you want to visit the Ranch: Get a group of fifteen to twenty-plus people together and rent the whole place; stay a full week by joining another group; or stay for one night or more during our Short Stay periods in June and September. Horseback trips are available and range from half-day, full-day, or a several day pack packing trip. They encourage catch-and-release fishing and only fly fishing on the ranch. If you want to use lures or bait, fish anywhere off the ranch property. Only keep what your immediate family will eat. Get license before you come.

Directions: From the boat landing follow the yellow bricks to the sign board marking the trail. Be careful not to end up on the trail going back around the lake. Follow the trail to the Muir Trail Ranch and then either veer right at the private property sign through the ranch following the signs and fence to the springs or take the bypass and just after the first switchback take the trail to the right to the back country campsite. Cross the San Joaquin at the "No Camping Here" sign and follow the short trail to the spring and lake.

The eleven-mile trail from the road's end has an elevation gain of 500 feet and requires fording the South Fork of the San Joaquin River. In the summer it is possible to avoid five miles of walking by renting one of the boats to take you across the lake. From this part of the John Muir Trail it is only a hike of five miles down the Florence Lake Trail to reach the springs.

With all the hiking and physical activity on and around the ranch, soaking in one of the pools (cooler one on the top) would certainly feel good.

Photos by Bill Ralph

711 B   BLAYNEY HOT SPRINGS

● **Southeast of Florence Lake**

A combination hot springs and a mudbath in a grassy High Sierra meadow, nine- and one-half miles from the road's end at Florence Lake. Elevation 7,600 feet. Open all year.

While several springs flow across the meadow, hot mineral water oozes up through the squishy bottom of this large pool, surrounded my meadow grass, maintaining a temperature of approximately 102°. This pool is located across the river from the tent cabins at Muir Trail Ranch. While this pool is open to the public, it is not over-used. Be sure to check the water temperature at any of the other hot water sources as they can be quite hot. The apparent custom is clothing optional.

Near the natural springs across the river is Warm Lake, more like a large pond that is fed by both hot and cold springs. If you float on top, the water is warm, if you dangle your feet you can feel the chill. The lake is accessible in mid-to-late season when the river flow diminishes a bit and it's easier to get across. You will probably be sharing it with some fish.

There are no services at this location except nearby backpacker campgrounds. It is ten miles to a store and any supplies.

Source map: USGS *Blackcap Mountain*.
GPS: N 37 14.040 W 118 52.860

Scott Harwood

Phil Wilcox

Stephaine Turlow

712 A   KEOUGH HOT SPRINGS

■   800 Keough Hot Spring Rd.   760 872-4670
Bishop, CA 93514
www.keoughshotsprings.com

The Sierra foothills is home to this historical site where the original pool was built in 1919. Elevation 4,200 feet. Open all year.

Natural mineral water flows out of the ground at 128° and through an aerator at the end of the enclosed one-hundred- by forty-foot swimming pool (86-92°) and the twenty-four- by forty-foot wading pool (102-104°), using flow-through mineral water so that only minimal amounts of chlorine need to be added. Full-time lifeguard on duty. Bathing suits are required.

An RV campground with water and electric, tent sites, gift shop and snack bar are available on the premises. On-call massage is available. Credit cards accepted. It is seven miles to the nearest restaurant, motel, service station, and store. Call for schedule and rates.

Directions: Go 7 miles south of Bishop on US 395, then follow signs west from US 395.

712 B   KEOUGH HOT DITCH

●   **Near Keough Hot Springs**

Runoff from Keough Hot Springs cools as it flows through a series of volunteer-built rock pools in a treeless foothill gully. Elevation 4,100 feet. Open all year.

Natural mineral water flows out of the ground at 128° on the property of Keough Hot Springs, then meanders northeast for about a mile. (When the aerator is turned off at 7 pm at the swimming pool, the water that flows from the resort through the culvert jumps from 85 to 105°.) Volunteer-built rock dams create several primitive soaking pools and swimming holes on both sides of the road, each one cooler than the preceding one upstream. The apparent local custom is clothing optional.

No services are available on the premises. The land is posted for day-use only, no overnight parking, but reports are that parking for one night is not a problem as long as you leave nothing but tire tracks. Please do not bring any glass objects to the area, since broken glass is the biggest problem at Keough. It is one mile to an RV park and eight miles to a restaurant, store, and service station in Bishop.

Directions: Seven miles south of Bishop on US 395, turn west on Keough Hot Springs Rd. at approximately 0.6 miles. At the only intersection with a paved road (old US 395), turn north 200 yards to where a cold stream crosses under the road. (Note: There is an abundance of level parking space on the north side of the cold stream, but the stream must be forded with care.) Walk an additional 50 yards north to Keough Ditch. Either stream may be followed to where they form a series of warm pools.
GPS: N 37 15.340 W 118 22.440

Scott Harwood

713 "THREE DISH" WARM SPRINGS

● **East of the town of Big Pine**

This warm pond makes for an ideal soak on hot desert summer days. Open all year; spring and fall the best seasons.

Natural mineral water flows out of the vegetation-covered hillside at 85°. The high flow rate is able to maintain the pool at nearly the same temperature all year. Clothing optional.

There are no facilities on the premises other than a small fire ring and trash barrel. There is a small level place where overnight parking is not prohibited. The closest place for supplies is Big Pine, about nine miles away.

Directions: At the intersection of Hwy 395 and Hwy 168, just north of Big Pine, reset your odometer to 0. Head east on Hwy 168 for 1.9 miles to the remains of Zurich Station. Turn left on Leighton Lane heading for the huge "celestial" observation dishes. At 5.2 miles turn right at the "Caltech Owens Valley Radio Observatory" sign. Another sign read "Owens River 3." Proceed straight ahead 5.4 miles and veer left at 6 miles. The road becomes rather difficult, rutted, and hard to see towards the end. The spring is at 8.9 miles.

GPS: N 37 39.660 W 118 46.071

● **Northeast of the town of Olancha**

A sometimes crowded, spring-fed oasis located on a barren slope of land in a remote desert valley that was recently annexed to Death Valley National Park. Elevation 1,500 feet. Open all year, but access roads may become impassable at any time of the year due to heavy rainstorms or snow. Be sure to bring extra supplies of water and car repair tools.

Natural mineral water flows out of the main source springs at 107°, or hotter. Volunteers have installed pipes to carry this water to two cement and rock soaking pools.

Lower Warm: According to latest reports, the water is flowing again and the lower pool is filled all the time.

Palm Spring: Two pools are fed from this source.

Wizard Pool: With temperatures ranging from 105°-112°, this one's the hottest in Saline Valley. Built nearly thirty years ago by a determined group who took exquisite care to make this one a great soak. This hexagonal shaped rock and concrete pool is sunk into the ground with seating all the way around. The deepest spot is about three and one-half feet deep, and more than twenty people could squeeze in for an occasion although usually fewer folks makes it more enjoyable. Offers one of the best mountain views in the area.

Volcano Pool: Traditionally this is the kiddy pool due to its cooler temperature. An above ground tub fashioned from rock and cement, with a bench across one side. The pool is about fifteen feet by eight feet and three-feet deep and comfortably seats ten. Temperatures range from 98°-104°, warmer after a recent cleaning.

Upper Warm: Small squishy-bottom pool at about 102°, and cool pond. This spring is enclosed by a fence, installed to exclude predators when pupfish were transplanted from Death Valley in the 1970s. (The pupfish did not survive.)

All pools have valves and drains for controlling water flow and cleaning, except the natural upper warm spring. Most of the pools and facilities are handicap accessible with assistance. The area is currently designated as clothing optional by the Park Service.

Vault toilets have been installed by the Park Service. There is level space on which overnight parking is permitted, with a limit of up to thirty days per calendar year for the entire park. It is more than fifty-five miles, mostly unpaved, to a store or service station in Big Pine, and more than eighty-five miles to Olancha and Lone Pine. Everyone hauls out their own trash, as well as ashes from campfires, which are permitted in the existing firepans.

Temperatures regularly soar over the 110° mark in the summer, so this desert location with very little natural shade is preferred in the fall and spring. It becomes very crowded on major holidays and three-day weekends. The peace and quiet of the desert can best be enjoyed during the week.

Directions: The southern route via Olancha is shown on the map. The unpaved portion of the Saline Valley Road is county maintained. An alternate route starts just north of Big Pine on US 395. Drive northeast on CA 168 for 2.5 miles and turn right (southeast) on Death Valley Road. Drive approximately 15 miles and turn right on Waucoba-Saline Rd. Drive 32 miles south to a triangular intersection on the left (east) side of the road. Turn left (east) for 7 miles to the first group of springs. From US 395 it is at least a 3-hour drive via either route. All roads in are quite rough and a high clearance vehicle is recommended. The 2.2-mile road from the lower springs to the far upper springs is particularly rough. Either entrance route may be temporarily washed out by infrequent but severe flash floods, or blocked by snow. Inquire about road conditions before making the trip.

Source maps: So. CA Auto Club *Death Valley*, USGS *Waucoba Wash and New York Butte*.

GPS: N 36 48.346 W 117 46.404

Chris Andrews

Note: All visitors are expected to pay a park entrance fee, but no pay stations are available along either route into the Valley. Before entering, please purchase a $10 entrance permit, or an annual Park Pass, in Death Valley National Park, or at a designated Federal facility.

Photos by Skip Hill

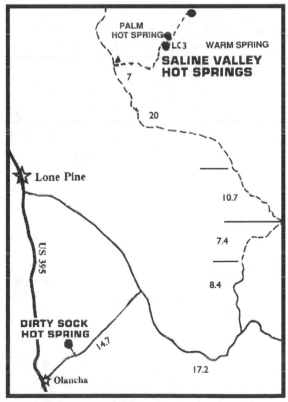

Scott Harwood

Miners from the now extinct silver mine of Cerro Gordo used to come down out of the surrounding hills to bathe here. The water is actually effervescent.

715 DIRTY SOCK HOT SPRING

● **Near the town of Olancha**

Large, shallow pool in an open desert area. Elevation 3,600 feet. Open all year.

Natural mineral water flows up through a large vertical pipe into the bottom of a circular, algae encrusted, cement-lined pool at 90° and flows out about a foot below water level at various temperatures, depending on wind and air temperature. Several sets of steps lead down to the somewhat slippery pool bottom. Word has it that it gets so scummy in the summer the fire department comes and sucks out the scum. Clothing optional.

No services are available on the premises, and there are no remaining buildings. There are many acres of unmarked level space on which overnight parking is not prohibited. It is five miles to the nearest restaurant, motel, service station, and store.

Directions: From the intersection of US 395 and CA 190, go five miles northeast on CA 190. There are no signs on the highway, so look for a narrow, paved road on the northwest side and follow it 300 yards to the spring.

GPS: N 36 19.750 W 117 56.900

716 KERN HOT SPRING

● **On the upper Kern River**

A small concrete soaking pool offering a truly spectacular view in return for a very strenuous three-day hike from the nearest road. Elevation 6,900 feet. Open all year.

Natural water flows out of the ground at 115° directly into a shallow soaking pool built at the edge of the Kern River. Water temperature is controlled by adding buckets of cold river water as needed. Bathing suit policy is determined by the mutual consent of those present.

There are no services available except a backpacker campground 100 yards away. The spring is 31.5 miles west of Whitney Portal and 37 miles east of Crescent Meadow. Situated in the mile-deep canyon of the upper Kern River, this spring has magnificent views in all directions. Detailed directions to such a remote location are beyond the scope of this book. We recommend that you purchase *Sierra South*, published by Wilderness Press, and also consult the Tule Ranger District of the Sequoia National Forest, 32588 Highway 190, Springville, CA 93265. 209 539-2607.

Source map: USGS *Kern Peak*.
GPS: N 36 28.680 W 118 24.280

Dave Bybee

717   JORDAN HOT SPRING

●   **Northwest of the town of Little Lake**

Hot water flows on Ninemile Creek have been formed into pools in the southernmost part of the Golden Trout Wilderness. Many buildings including a sawmill remain to be explored in the recently abandoned pack station. Elevation 6,500 feet. Open all year.

Natural mineral water flows out of a spring at approximately 120° down to the river where it may be mixed with cold creek water to form casual pools. Permanent pools are not legally permitted, however, someone packed in concrete and built a nice two-foot deep, three person tub, with a murky rock pool be low. Leave the plug out so the iron and algae don't accumulate in the upper pool. A clever system of dams allow you to control the temperature of the lower pool while the upper pool remains a toasty 109°. Clothing optional.

Directions: The trail starts at Blackrock Station where there is a pack station and small campground (no water). Follow the trail until it opens into a large meadow, then cross the creek and veer left heading down, down, down till you get to the springs at an abandoned pack station. The trail has an elevation change of 3,000 feet.

It is six miles to the nearest paved road at Sequoia National Forest Road 21S03, reached via County Road J41 from south of Little Lake on US 395.

Consult with the Mt. Whitney Ranger District of Inyo National Forest, Lone Pine, CA 93545. 760 873-2408.

GPS: N 36 13.740 W 118 18.120

Gateway to the Giant Sequoia National Monument.

718   CALIFORNIA HOT SPRINGS

42177 Hot Springs Dr.   661 548-6582

■   California Hot Springs, CA 93207

Historic resort that has been restored and expanded to offer family fun. Located in rolling foothills at the edge of Giant Sequoia National Monument. Elevation 3,100 feet. Open all year except Thanksgiving, the week before Christmas, and New Year's day.

Odorless natural mineral water flows out of several artesian wells at a temperature of 125° and is piped to the pool area where there are two large, tiled hydrojet spas maintained at 100° and 104°. A flow-through system eliminates the need for chemical treatment of the water. There is one large swimming pool containing filtered and chlorinated spring water that is maintained at 85° in the summer and 94° in the winter. Handicap access is at west end of pool. Bathing suits are required.

The restored main building houses the office, delicatessen, ice cream parlor, grocery store, gift shop, and dressing room facilities. With advance notice, meals can be arranged for groups. Massage is available on the premises by appointment only. Full-hookup RV spaces are adjacent to the resort area. Credit cards accepted.

Directions: From CA 99 between Fresno and Bakersfield, take the J 22 exit at Earlimart and go east 38 miles to the resort.

719   KERNVILLE WARM SPRINGS

● **Near the town of Kernville**

Another warm spring known only to the locals, offers a warm bath next to a cold plunge in the scenic Kern River. Elevation 3,512 feet. Summer is best after spring runoff as river must be low in order for the springs to emerge.

Warm springs flow out of the rocky banks on the far side of the Kern River where the water is channeled into a river rock pool. The springs are easy to spot due to the deep red residue on all the nearby rocks. Pools are reconstructed every season so the shape and size is always changing. During the last visit the pool measured 86° and had room for four adults. The valley gets so hot during summer that the river is practically overrun by swimmers, inner tubers and fishermen. You won't have the place to yourself, but you may be the only one interested in the warm water instead of the river.

Camp across the river at any of the nearby campgrounds or turnouts. There are many places to park where you can tote your tent and cooler down to the beach and sleep next to the river for free. McNally's Restaurant is open for dinner and cocktails; the burger bar serves up lunch. The hotel there has about a dozen rooms.

Directions: From Kernville go north on Sierra Way to McNally's on the left. Park here and follow the trail behind the motel, crossing the suspension bridge over the river. Head upstream along the bank for about 200 yards to the reddish orange rocks.

GPS: N 35 46.638 W 118 26.340

Photos by Soakers Bible

720   REMINGTON HOT SPRINGS

● **Near the town of Lake Isabella**

A delightful, two-person cement tub, an adjoining river-level tub and a one-person tub higher up on a hillside in an unspoiled, primitive, riverside setting of rocks and trees. Located in the Kern River Canyon down a steep trail from old Highway 178. Elevation 2,500 feet. Open all year, except during high water in the river.

Natural mineral water at 104° emerges from the ground at 3.5 gallons per minute. This flow comes directly up through the bottom of a volunteer-built, cement, two-person tub and provides a form of hydrojet action, maintaining the pool temperature at 105°. There is a second, larger tub adjacent to the first and further out into the river. An enlarged and deeper riverside tub, with steps leading to the river, is filled by a pipe and drained by pulling the plugs so it can be cleaned. A new cement and rock pool is filled with the overflow from the first pool along with a valve-controlled pipe and is around 98°. Twenty yards uphill is a drainable, one-person rock and cement pool that is fed by a smaller flow of 96° water, and has a valve for draining. The apparent local custom is clothing optional. However, don't be surprised by clothed people floating down river in rafts, inner tubes, or canoes.

There are no services available on the premises. It is six miles to a motel, restaurant, and service station and two miles to a Forest Service campground.

Directions: From Bodfish (by Lake Isabella) drive west on Kern Canyon Rd. (old CA 178, now CA 214) to Hobo Forest Service Campground. Continue west 1.5 miles to a large turnout on the right with a telephone pole in the middle. (This is the second turnout with a telephone pole.) Flat areas for camping can be found near the parking areas. From the parking area, two trails head

The ecosystem in this area is very fragile. Do not attempt to bring vehicles down to the river and please walk on already defined trails to help preserve the vegetation which in turn prevents erosion.

down toward the river, 300 yards below. A steep, narrow dirt trail on the left leads to a flat area along the river where camping is permitted. To reach the tubs, hike down the very steep trail to the right to the rock foundation of an old building. Do not attempt to bring a vehicle down this road as it is often muddy and vehicles can get stuck. Also, it is very destructive to the hillside area. Just before this foundation on your left is a footpath with some natural rock steps leading down toward the river. Under a tree on your left, a spur path leads to the shallow rock and cement pool. Follow the main path to the cement pools by the river. This is not a good area for children, please be careful. Help keep this special place beautiful by packing out all trash.

GPS: N 35 34.540 W 118 33.120

MIRACLE HOT SPRINGS

● **Near the town of Lake Isabella**

The pools have all been torn out and at this time there is no legal place to soak.

Phil Wilcox

Soakers Bible

721   PYRAMID HOT SPRING

● **At the lower end of Kern River Canyon**

A delightful but hard to find, natural pool beneath a giant boulder at the edge of the Kern River. Open all year but not accessible during the high water of spring runoff. Elevation 1,900 feet.

Natural mineral water flows out of the ground at 109°, under a giant boulder, and into a sandy-bottom soaking pool large enough for two people, where it maintains a temperature of 103°. The apparent local custom is clothing optional, but the site is visible to vehicles on CA 178.

There are no services available at the location. It is one and one-third miles east to a Forest Service day-use campground (Live Oak) and fifteen miles to all other services in Bakersfield.

Directions: From Bakersfield, go east on CA 178 to the beginning of the Kern River Canyon. Continue 2.5 miles east beyond dam and power plant to a paved turnout on the left with a 6-foot high pyramid-shaped boulder at its east end. Look across the river slightly westward to locate a large, cube-shaped boulder on the opposite bank. The pool is under that boulder. To reach it, follow the trail from the east end of the turnout to the large downstream boulder where you can hop across the river. Then follow a faint unmarked path upstream to the pool. Stay next to the river and beware of poison oak.

GPS: N 35 28.640 W 118 45.111

722 A   SESPE HOT SPRINGS

● **Near the Sespe Condor Sanctuary**

Note: An adventure pass is required to park at any trailhead leading into this area. You can pick one up at the Los Padres National Forest ranger station in Ojai (1190 E. Ojai Ave., 805 646-4348). A forest service fire permit is also required. Horses and mules are also allowed on the trails. Be sure to inquire at the Los Padres National Forest office about fire season closures, flood warnings, and the adequacy of your preparations for packing in and packing out. Make sure to get a map!

A remote, pristine hot spring river located in the rugged, desert mountains of a designated wilderness area. Elevation 2,700 feet. Open all year, subject to flash flooding and Forest Service closures.

Hot water streams down a hillside at near boiling temperatures, and cools as it flows down rocky channels and into seasonal rock pools. The mineral water is clear and clean, and offers a variety of soaking temperatures as it mixes with cool creek water. All pools are built by volunteers, and probably become washed out every year. Large boulders in the rocky streambed line the main soaking area, which must be scooped out every season. There are many seeps up and down the creek bed which aren't as hot as the main springs. Depending on the level of the cold creek water mixing with the hot and warm, many pools of different temperatures can be found. Be sure to explore the whole area. There's a hot waterfall and even a rock sauna near the source, but be careful, the water is very hot! Clothing optional.

Sally Jackson

this one has no swift current. There are some underwater ledges that aren't that deep, so again, scout out your route to avoid surprises. From here the trail goes up a hill and down to the last crossing back to the north bank.

Once on the north side you'll hike up an arroyo and through lots of scratchy brush on the narrow trail that leads up a long hill. Once on top you'll have a nice view of Coltrell Flat (watch for ticks throughout this section). The trail can be hard to follow through the flat meadow, but it basically skirts around the larger bushes and heads up to the left to go up the next hill where you can see the trail from a distance. The trail is still overgrown, and will lead up to another viewpoint; there's a sign up there with old trail numbers that points toward the east. The main path curves north and begins up Hot Springs Canyon. You will be in and out of the creek for the next mile as the trail meanders up the canyon—about 5 crossings, most of which you can hop rocks to cross. After the last crossing watch for the sign to Mutau Flat, there's a second trail that leads off to the right, under the Mutau Flat trail. Take the lower trail about 0.25 miles to the wide rocky canyon where you'll find palm trees and hot springs. Explore the whole area to find many soaking pools, a hot waterfall and rock sauna!

GPS: N 34 35.680 W 118 59.870

There are no services on the premises. You can get everything back in Ojai. Pack in everything you will need, and remember to camp a little ways away from the springs. There are several flat areas in the canyon near the hot springs, including a group of huge palm trees which shade a great camp spot.

Directions to Sespe: From Ojai take Highway 33 north for 14.3 miles to a right turn signed for Rose Valley. Follow this paved road for 3.1 miles and pass by the Rose Valley Work Camp. In another 1.4 miles you'll reach the end of the road where there's no place to camp, just the Piedra Blanca Trailhead parking area and pit toilets.

The Hike: Follow the directions into Willett's Hot Springs, which is a great place to camp for the first night out. From the cabin at Willet's follow the path across the first side stream and then cross Sespe Creek to the south bank. Follow the trail east for about 3/4 of a mile to the next crossing. This one can be swift during spring runoff so scout out the best route, probably just a little upstream. Follow the established trail past Hartman Camp to the next crossing. This one can be skirted by staying on the north bank. You'll have to clamber through some brush but it's not bad and won't take as long as changing into sandals for the crossing. Within a few hundred yards the trail becomes reestablished on the north side of the creek. After some smooth hiking you'll reach a big sandy beach and a beautiful, deep swimming hole. This is great during summer, but another deep crossing during spring. Probably waist deep in April, but at least

Soakers Bible

Sulphur springs emerge at 108° and flow down steep waterfalls where PVC pipe has been installed to divert the water into a huge soaking tank. The tank is about 8-feet wide and neck deep when sitting back and enjoying the scenery. It's perched at the very top of a side canyon well away from Sespe Creek, and the only water you'll hear flowing is that from the hot waterfalls cascading over the steep cliffs above. There is a drainpipe installed in the tub to drain off the top, but it's sometimes removed and soakers just plug the hole at the bottom—either way it only takes about fifteen minutes to fill the big tub. Because the sulphur water develops algae easily, leave the tub empty when you leave. Clothing optional.

There are no services on the premises. However, a pack group still maintains a drinking water spring, corral and barbecue area. While some of the cabins are in ruins, one is still available for use with four bunks, running water and an outdoor kitchen. Water has a sulphur taste. The outfitters often leave their tents up.

Directions: Follow driving directions to Sespe Hot Springs, from Ojai to the Piedra Blanca Trailhead up Hwy 33. From the trailhead the path leads downhill and almost immediately starts crossing Trout Creek. You will have to cross it 4 times within the first 30 minutes of hiking. The fifth crossing can be done over the rocks. This part of the trail skirts around protected frog habitat, and winds down to meet Sespe Creek after about 1 mile. The trail follows the north bank for about 4.5 miles before dumping out on a sandy beach with boulders and Sycamore trees. This is the first river crossing, it's wide, swift and rocky so grab a good stick. During spring months the creek can be hip— waist deep, so be prepared. The river is too rocky and slippery to cross barefoot so have river shoes or sandals with you for crossings. On the opposite bank the trail leads up a small, steep, rocky chute and then heads left. Follow the trail for about 15 minutes until you reach the large landslide. The trail disappears at this point, so you'll have to climb over rocks to get past the slide which is a couple hundred yards long. At the end there's a heavily eroded slope to climb. It's loosely dried mud and sand and can be scary for inexperienced hikers (even worse on the way back going down the slope).

Once you reach the top of the landslide area the trail goes a little way and then seems to dump hikers at another rocky beach with no clear crossing point. Stop and look around, the trail actually goes up the hill behind you. It's hard to see through the foliage, but there are stone stairs that lead up the hillside to connect with the trail on the south bank. Follow this for another mile before crossing at another deep, swift ford. You'll stay on the north bank now for several miles. Watch for a sign for Ladybug Campground; at this point you're opposite Red Rock Canyon which is hard to miss. Within 1 mile you

722 B   WILLETT'S HOT SPRINGS

● **Near the Sespe Condor Sanctuary**

> Note: An adventure pass is required to park at any trailhead leading into this area. You can pick one up at the Los Padres National Forest ranger station in Ojai (1190 E. Ojai Ave., 805 646-4348). A forest service fire permit is also required. Horses and mules are also allowed on the trails. Be sure to inquire at the Los Padres National Forest office about fire season closures, flood warnings, and the adequacy of your preparations for packing in and packing out. Make sure to get a map!

A remote and rarely visited hot spring located at the top of a side canyon above Sespe Creek, in the Los Padres National Forest above the remnants of an abandoned ranch. Elevation 3,000 feet. The best times to visit are summer and fall as there are many fords which are much easier after the creek level goes down. There are many long uphill climbs, so hot summer weather could be something to avoid.

Scott Harwood

will reach another sandy beach and you'll be able to see the tin roof of a small building up near Willets. This is the last set of river crossings. Cross over to the south bank and trudge through the side streams until you pick up the trail. Continue about 0.25 miles until it seems like you've gone past the cabin. There's a very obvious crossing point at a rocky beach which will take you back to the north bank, even though it's hard to see the trail on the other side. Once you get over there you'll be able to see it. From here go through the reeds and cross the last side stream to the trail which will lead to the cabin. The tin roof you can see from the trail is just an old building in ruins; the cabin is further east.

To reach the hot springs, follow the trail from the cabin heading west, and stay above the fence line as it passes the tin shacks. Continue on this trail and watch for the stone fireplace, a faint trail forks right and begins to climb up through the grass. Take this right fork and continue uphill (more switchbacks) for about 15 minutes. You will be well above the side creek. The trail goes up several hundred feet to the very top of the canyon. When you reach the lone campsite and firepit, drop your backpacks and follow the little trail another 100 feet under the tree and up the creek to the tub.

GPS: N 34 34.920 W 119 02.640

Wonder how in the world somebody got this big tank installed way up there. Rumor has it, the tub was air lifted in by helicopter.

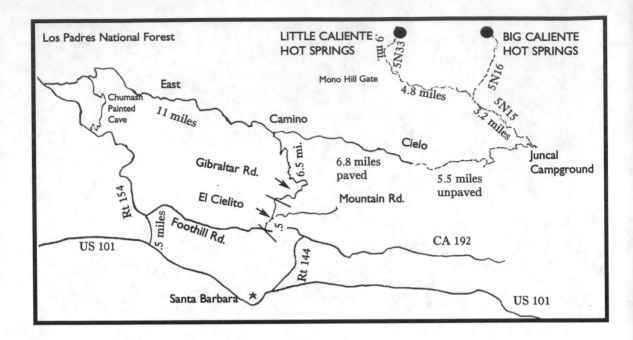

Los Padres National Forest

LITTLE CALIENTE HOT SPRINGS — .9 mi. — 5N33

BIG CALIENTE HOT SPRINGS

Mono Hill Gate

4.8 miles — 5N16

5N15 — 3.2 miles

East — Chumash Painted Cave — 11 miles

Camino

Cielo

Juncal Campground

Gibraltar Rd. — 6.5 mi.

6.8 miles paved

5.5 miles unpaved

Mountain Rd.

El Cielito

Rt 154

.5 miles — Foothill Rd.

US 101

Rt 144

CA 192

Santa Barbara ✱

US 101

---

723   THE HOURGLASS
213 W. Cota   805 963-1436
☐   Santa Barbara, CA 93101

Private spa and rental facility located on a creekside residential street near downtown Santa Barbara. Open evenings, Thursday through Sunday.

Three private indoor rooms with pools and eight private outdoor enclosures with pools are for rent to the public. Gas-heated tap water treated with chlorine is maintained at 104°.

A private sauna, a juice bar, and massage are available on the premises. Visa and MasterCard are accepted. Phone for rates, reservations, and directions.

---

724 A   LITTLE CALIENTE HOT SPRINGS
                                 (see map)

●   **Near the city of Santa Barbara**

Two small volunteer-built pools in a rocky canyon at the end of a wooded, winding, unpaved Forest Service road. Elevation 1,600 feet. Open all year, subject to fire season and rain/mud closures.

Natural mineral water flows out of a spring at 105° and through a pipe into the upper six-foot by six-foot by eighteen-foot rock and cement soaking pool. From here it spills over into the lower slimy-bottom rock and mud pool where the temperature cools a degree or two. The pipe in the upper pool can be detached to stop the inflow and control water temperature. Remains of a volunteer-built wooden sunning deck and red wooden benches along the lower pool have collapsed due to erosion. The apparent local custom is clothing optional.

No services are available on the premises. It is one mile to a pack-in campground, six miles to a primitive National Forest campground, and twenty-seven miles to all other services.

Directions: See the directions to Big Caliente. At Juncal Campground, turn left on 5N15 for 3.2 miles where the road forks. Bear left for 4.8 miles where the road forks again. Bear right and drive another 0.9 miles to the parking area. At the upper end of the parking area, use the makeshift wooden steps to cross the creek and continue walking 100 yards to the spring. The brush becomes gradually greener as you get closer to the springs. Before heading to Little Caliente, it is advisable to check with the ranger station for information on road conditions and where to park. At times several of the gates are locked, (which may require more hiking), but generally the gates are open and you can drive to the spring.

Source map: *Los Padres National Forest.*
GPS: N 34 32.430 W 119 37.176

> Important Note: According to the sign at the springs all parked vehicles must display a Forest Adventure Pass which is available in town at places like Big 5 Sporting Goods, Mountain Air Sports, Far West Gun and Supply, and Dodge City Gun and Supplies. Be sure to get yours before you take the drive up there!

724 B   BIG CALIENTE HOT SPRINGS

(see map)

● **Near the city of Santa Barbara**

A concrete pool provides a soak at this hot spring located in a sparsely wooded canyon reached via ten miles of very windy, rocky gravel road. Elevation 1,500 feet. Open all year, subject to fire closure and road conditions during rainy season. Check with Los Padres National Forest Ranger Station, 805 967-3481.

Natural mineral water flows out of a bluff at 115°, then through a faucet-controlled pipe to a six-foot by ten-foot concrete pool. Water temperature in the pool can be controlled by diverting the inflow hose or shutting off the faucet. Please close the valve and divert the hose out of the pool when leaving, to prevent scalding others. When the valve is open, hot water showers into the pool. Continual flow-through keeps the water clean. A galvanized pipe ladder leads into the pool, and concrete decks and benches are on two sides. The apparent custom is clothing optional by mutual consent, although it is advisable to keep bathing suits handy in case the rangers check. Since you can drive right up to the pool, it is handicap accessible with assistance.

A second primitive soaking pool is at creek level below the source spring. From the far end of the parking area, a marked trail leads off toward Big Caliente Debris Dam. Across the creek, water seeps down the mountain from a source spring under a cotton-wood tree to the primitive 105° pool at creek level, which fills up with silt and mud and needs to be dredged periodically. This pool can be reached by rock-hopping where a pipe is visible underwater, approximately 100 yards from the trailhead.

Facilities include nearby changing rooms, clean pit toilets across the level parking area, and a picnic table under the trees. A trail from the changing rooms leads down to the cold creek, which has small waterfalls and several small sunning beaches. Several primitive Forest Service campgrounds are within three miles, and it is twenty-five miles to all other services in Santa Barbara.

Directions: Coming from the south on Hwy 101 in Santa Barbara, take Milpas St. exit (Rte. 144). Follow Rte. 144 east through city residential streets, and a five-point roundabout, for a total of 6.3 miles, to the end at Rte. 192. Turn left on Rte. 192 (Stanwood Dr.) for 1.2 miles to El Cielito Rd. At 0.3 miles, El Cielito crosses Mountain Dr. Continue straight uphill on El Cielito 0.5 miles to Gibraltar Rd. Turn right and follow Gibraltar for approximately 6.5 miles to the end at East Camino Cielo. Turn right on very windy East Camino Cielo which is paved for the first 6.8 miles, then unsurfaced for the next 5.5 miles. At Juncal Campground, turn left on 5N15 for 3.2 miles where the road forks. Take the right fork (5N16) 2.5 miles to the spring. (The left fork goes to Little Caliente.)

Coming from the north on Hwy 101, take Rte. 154 exit, heading east for 0.5 miles to Rte. 192 (called Foothill Rd.). At 4.7 miles is a reservoir (Foothill has changed to Mountain Dr. and again to Mission Ridge). At 0.4 miles past the reservoir, Rte. 192 makes a sharp left at a fire station and becomes Stanwood Dr. Follow Stanwood to El Cielito Rd. and continue as described above.

Source map: *Los Padres National Forest.*
GPS: N 34 32.352 W 119 33.876

Little Caliente (above) and *Big Caliente* (below) are the only natural hot springs accessible to the public in the Santa Barbara area.

Photos by Soakers Bible

725 LAS CRUCES HOT SPRINGS

(see map)

● **Near Gaviota State Park**

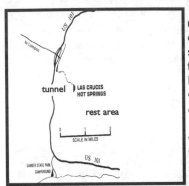

Two primitive, mud-bottom pools on a tree-shaded slope a few miles from the ocean. Elevation 500 feet. Open all year for day-use only.

Natural mineral water emerges at 96° directly into a shallow, knee-deep rock and mud soaking pool with relatively clear water, large enough for six to eight people. The overflow forms a waterfall over the earthen retaining wall into the larger lower pool, which averages 80° and has a slimy bottom. The water is murky. Clothing is optional with the mutual consent of those present.

There are no services available on the premises and overnight parking is prohibited in the parking area at the trailhead where a day-use self-parking fee is charged. Rangers check frequently and cite vehicles without valid parking receipts. It is three miles to a campground with RV hookups and six miles to all other services.

Directions: On Hwy101 approximately 35 miles north of Santa Barbara is Gaviota State Beach with its landmark railroad bridge. From here it is 3 miles to the turnoff for CA 1, west toward Lompoc. Directly across from this turnoff is the small road paralleling the highway and heading south to the parking area for Las Cruces. After Gaviota State Beach you will pass a rest area and go through a tunnel. It is 1 mile past the tunnel to the turnoff.

From the parking area, follow the steep dirt 4WD trail to where it forks at a white sign saying "no horses past this point." Bear right on a narrow trail approximately 0.75 miles from the parking area to the pools.

Oscar Voss

Phil Wilcox

Avila Valley Hot Springs has been in the hot water business since 1907, continually updating what is offered to the public to keep up with the times.

726 A   AVILA VALLEY HOT SPRINGS

250 Avila Beach Drive   805 595-2359
■ San Luis Obispo, CA 93405
www.avilahotsprings.com

A fun family destination, great for parties, with natural hot mineral water situated between oak-covered foothills that keep the morning fog away and make a natural year round air conditioner. Elevation 40 feet. Open all year; closed Tuesday and Wednesday from December to February.

Natural mineral water flows out of an artesian well at 130° and is piped to the outdoor twenty-foot square soaking pool (105°) which is drained and filled daily and requires no chemicals. The fifty- by one-hundred-foot outdoor swimming pool (86°) is filled with tap water and treated with chlorine and with two small water slides. Bathing suits required.

Massage, snack bar, pizza kitchen, arcade, twenty new cabins, RV hook-ups, lawn tent spaces, and a small store are located on the premises. All guests are invited to use the shaded picnic area with barbeque pits and tables. Major credit cards accepted. It is eight miles to all services in San Luis Obispo.

Directions: From either north bound or south bound U.S. 101, take the Avila Beach Drive exit (NOT the San Luis Bay Drive exit), and travel west towards the ocean. They are the first business on the right hand side of the road.

726 B   SYCAMORE MINERAL SPRINGS

■   1215 Avila Beach Dr.   805 595-7302
San Luis Obispo, CA 93401   800 234-5831
www.sycamoresprings.com

Delightful upscale resort, Integrative Retreat Center, spa and hot tub rental, offering secluded redwood hot tubs out under the oaks and a private natural mineral spa on the balcony of every room. Located on a wooded rural hillside two miles from the ocean. Elevation 40 feet. Open all year from 7AM to 2AM. Reservations required.

Natural mineral water is pumped from a well at 110° and piped to the tubs on the hillside. The large lookout tub on the hill has hot and cold faucets to regulate the temperature. The swimming pool is filled with tap water treated with chlorine. The "oasis," a natural-looking rock spa that will hold thirty people, is located next to the pool. Bathing suits are required except in the hillside hot tubs. Some pools and areas are handicap accessible.

Facilities include a restaurant, hotel rooms and suites with hot tubs on the balcony, luxury suites with spas and fireplaces, a one bedroom cottage with its own hot tub in a private enclosure, dressing rooms, meeting space and wellness center, and gift shop. Several varieties of massage and facials are available. A half-hour soak in one of the outdoor tubs is included in each appointment. In addition to the many retreat programs, guided local hiking tours are offered. On request, directions to a nearby clothing-optional state beach will be provided. Major credit cards accepted.

Directions: From US 101 8 miles south of San Luis Obispo, take the Avila Beach exit, then go 1 mile west on Avila Beach Dr. and watch for the resort sign on the south side of the road.

Marjorie Young

727 A   PASO ROBLES INN

■

1103 Spring St.   805 238-2660
Paso Robles, CA 93446   800 676-1713
www.pasoroblesinn.com

Originally built in 1864 and featuring a hot mineral springs bathhouse. The Inn, now a member of the National Trust Historic Hotels of America, has been completely refurbished. Located on the main street in Paso Robles. Open all year.

A newly redrilled geothermal well supplies the hot mineral water to the Inn's hot springs wing which features a mix of personal therapy spas and larger, family jet tubs. The pools themselves sit on the balconies which can be closed off with canvas curtains for a private soak. There are fireplaces in each room. There is also a large swimming pool and hot tub. Most of the rooms overlook the beautiful garden court. There is an indoor dining room, as well as one outdoors and a coffee shop.

Thirty new spa rooms, eighteen in the garden area and twelve above the historic ballroom have been completed, along with the total restoration of the hundred-year-old Grand Ballroom. A full-service health spa and salon with indoor/outdoor mineral water plunge bath, and a state-of-the-art conference center and meeting space are in the planning stage. Phone for status of construction.

The Inn was a fashionable favorite among sports heroes, millionaires, political bigwigs and Hollywood movie stars in its heyday. Today it is being restored to its former glory. The Inn is set in a tranquil setting of lush gardens and oak trees.

Phil Wilcox

Phil Wilcox

The runoff from this hot pool supports a fish farm where you can be prepared to catch and release Large Mouth Bass, Catfish, and Bluegill. As this is a private lake, a fishing license is not required. Bring your pole!

Directions: From 101 southbound at Paso Robles take the 16th St. exit and turn left on Riverside Dr. Go 0.8 miles to 13th St. and turn left. 13th St. becomes Creston Rd. Continue 4.5 miles on Creston Rd. to the hot springs.

Directions: From 101 northbound at Paso Robles take the Spring St. exit and go right on Niblick Ave. Go 1.8 miles to Creston Rd. and turn right. Continue 2.3 miles to the hot springs.

727 B   FRANKLIN LAKES HOT SPRINGS

■   3010 Creston Rd.   805 712-5373
         Paso Robles, CA 93446
         www.franklinhotsprings.com

Soaking tub, swimming area, and fishing hole in the rolling hills outside Paso Robles. Be prepared to see many species of waterfowl, muskrat, beaver and even huge turtles. Open all year, 8 AM to midnight, every day. Small fee.

A two thousand-foot-deep well produces 110° water at over 3300 gallons per minute. A large insulated pipe will bring the hot water to the surface to fill the large pool with a sand and gravel bottom that is forty-feet wide and eighty-feet long. It is three feet deep at the well head and slopes to eight feet at the spillway. Pipes coming out from the well head provide a nice shower. The water is high in sulfur and has some sodium bicarbonate, potassium, fluoride and calcium. Bathing suits required. A private soaking pool is now open and several others are under construction. A twenty-four inch deep wading pool with three small slides has been specially built for the children.

Picnic tables and toilets are provided and there are changing rooms. RVs are welcome. Massage is available by appointment, and a paintball field is also open for use. Alcohol and smoking are prohibited.

727 C RIVER OAKS HOT SPRINGS AND SPA
3725 Buena Vista Dr.   805 238-4600
■   **Paso Robles, CA 93446**
www.riveroakshotsprings.com

Nestled in the heart of Paso Robles Wine Country, with both indoor therapeutic mineral tubs and outdoor pools, River Oaks offers an intimate setting featuring a cozy fireside lobby, therapeutic mineral tubs, and lakeside gazebo for special events. Elevation 100 feet. Open all year.

An artesian well with a very mild mineral and sulphur content fills all of the tubs. The spa pavilion offers five patio spas which are cleaned and refilled daily, filtered every three minutes, and require only minimal chemical treatment. New outdoor tubs, filled with hot mineral water are located close to the main building. The indoor premises are handicap equipped, the tubs with assistance.

Innovative therapeutic massages, energy healing, and skin care are offered to help you reach greater levels of balance and awareness. Call for reservations. The lakeside setting offers a wonderful site for weddings and special events for up to 350 guests. Credit cards accepted.

Location: Conveniently situated off Hwy 46 East on Buena Vista Dr.

Courtesy of River Oaks

Courtesy of Esalen

728   ESALEN INSTITUTE
Workshop, Room Reservations
Hwy I   831 667-3000
Big Sur, CA 93920
www.esalen.org

Primarily an educational/experiential center rather than a hot spring resort. Located on CA 1, 45 miles south of Monterey. Elevation 100 feet. Open all year.

Esalen specializes in residential programs that focus on education, philosophy, and the physical and behavioral sciences. Access to the grounds is by reservation only for those wishing to take workshops or rent an available room. The hot springs are also open for up to thirty people each morning from 1 AM to 3:30 AM for a charge. To make a bath reservation, call 831 667-3047.

The bath house was constructed to both complement and highlight the natural setting. The hot mineral water flows out at 120° to gravity-fill the tubs and provide heating for both the shower water and the facility's radiant heat. The building has two main sections with a total of seven large tubs, three of which are partially covered and two that are outside, suspended above the rocks and ocean. Inside the bathhouse are several private claw foot tubs and four massage areas all facing the ocean. The bath facilities can accommodate sixty people comfortably. The upper level has an outdoor pool with a lift for handicap access, designed by the ADA.

Outside there are two areas: the "quiet side" and the "silent side." The "silent side" has two large tubs and two individual tubs. The "quiet side" has four single tubs and four larger tubs, two of which are perched on the edge of the cliff overlooking a rocky ocean beach. Some of the tubs are roofed over or partially roofed. The water temperature in all tubs can be individually controlled. No chemicals are necessary.

Facilities include housing and a dining room for registered guests. It is eleven miles to a restaurant, store, and service station. Massage is available on the premises. Credit cards are accepted for registered guests.

729   TASSAJARA ZEN MOUNTAIN CENTER
39171 Tassajara Rd.
Carmel Valley, CA 93924
Overnight Reservations   415 865-1899
Day Reservations   831 659-2229
Carmel Valley, CA 93924

Primarily a Buddhist Monastery with accommodations available to the public from late April to early September. Located in wooded mountains of the Ventana Wilderness southeast of Monterey. Elevation 1,500 feet.

Please, no drop-in visitors. Prior reservations are required. Guests are expected to respect the spirit of a monastic community.

Natural mineral water flows out of the ground at 140° into two large, enclosed soaking pools that average 110° and two outdoor pools at 106°. The water, which is not chemically treated, cools as it flows into nearby streambed soaking areas. The outdoor swimming pool is approximately 75°. There are also steambaths in the separate men's and women's bathhouses. Bathing suits are required in the swimming pool only and it is requested that robes be worn over bathing suits when walking around the grounds. Pools are handicap accessible with steps and handrails.

Rooms and meals are included as part of confirmed overnight reservation arrangements. The use of meditation facilities is also included. No credit cards accepted. It is ninety minutes to a store, cafe, and service station. The road is steep and dangerous, requiring good brakes and low gears.

Courtesy of Tassajara

730   SYKES HOT SPRING

(see map)

●   **Near the village of Big Sur**

Four hot pools located at the end of a beautiful, ten-mile hike up the Big Sur River in the Ventana Wilderness Area of the Los Padres National Forest. During times of high water, some pools can become submerged and the Big Sur River will be more difficult to cross. Elevation 1,000 feet.

Four small soaking pools offer rest and relaxation after a long hike up the Big Sur River. Four friends can share the largest pool, which averages about 100° and overflows into a riverside soaker below. The largest pool sits up on a bluff above the river so it shouldn't be affected by the weather. However, the three other pools are all right on the river and will undoubtedly be washed out or filled with sediment from above every winter. The hottest of the pools is the second soaker on the river, a small grotto is sandbagged to separate the hot water from the cold. Hot water is piped down the steep bluff and directly into the tub through a hose. The spring is near one of the most popular hiking routes, so the distance is no assurance of quiet or privacy during the summer months, particularly on weekends.

If you decide to camp near the springs you can choose from Sykes or Pine Ridge campgrounds. All services can be found in Big Sur including several options for lodging and dining. Be sure to fill up your tank in Carmel, the gas in Big Sur is very expensive.

Soakers Bible

Directions: From Monterey head south on Highway 1. Park at the Big Sur Ranger Station where you can get recent trail information, a hiking map and a permit for your campfire and cook stove. Follow the Pine Ridge Trail from the east side of the parking area, as it parallels between the highway above, and campground below. You'll cross a small creek before the trail heads moderately uphill for the first several miles. Five miles into the trail you'll pass through Terrace Creek Campground, a lush area with downed old growth, fern covered banks and a fantastic waterfall. This is a good place to have lunch. Continue on to mile 7 where there's a sign indicating Barlow Flat Campground down along the river. Barlow Flat is a sideshot, so don't bother going down another hill unless you want to camp there. Instead, keep going straight another 3 miles through old growth madrone and cedars to a series of downhill switchbacks which will lead you to the Big Sur River. Once you reach the river go downstream about 50 yards to find a good crossing. You will have to cross over and back again to pick up the trail leading about 0.25 miles down to the pools. They are on the left just after a huge down tree crosses the river.

Source maps for trails: USGS *Ventana Cones, Partington Ridge* (springs not shown).

GPS: N 36 14.916 W 121 41.112

Note: This location involves a ten-mile hike on the Pine Ridge Trail, and a Wilderness Permit must be obtained from the Big Sur Ranger Station. The Forest Service issues a trail map to those holding Wilderness Permits, and on request, will mark the hot-spring location on that map. Check your preparations, including water supply, with the ranger.

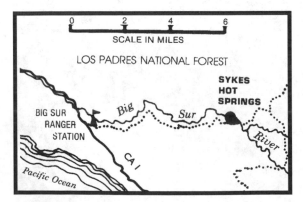

Warren Vidrine

731   MERCEY HOT SPRINGS
62964 Little Panoche Rd.   209 826-3388
Firebaugh, CA 93622
www.merceyhotsprings.com

One hundred sixty acres of rolling hills in California's central valley is home to the only hot spring resort in this area. Spring and Fall are choice times to visit when you can spend warm days in the swimming pool and cool evenings in one of the hot tubs. Altitude 1,200 feet. Open all year from 9 AM to 9 PM for day use. Reservations for camping and cabins highly recommended.

Natural hot mineral water comes out of a spring at temperatures of 119° allowing seven outdoor claw-foot style bath tubs located on a deck to be filled at whatever temperature the soaker wants. Bathing suits optional in this area. A new artesian well now provides 110° water to the swimming pool allowing it to be regulated for an optimum swimming experience year-round. Minimal chlorine is used in the pool. Swim suits are required.

A variety of cabins with and without kitchens and fire-places is available for rent. A newly renovated cabin will have its own private hot tub. There are also camping spaces with water and full RV hookups with water and sewer hookups. No electricity is provided. Day-use entitles you to the use of the picnic areas, swimming pool, and outdoor hot tub. Groups of ten or more get a ten percent discount. Gas and camping supplies can be bought thirty-five miles away in Los Banos. Ice and drinking water are available.

Directions: From the north—go south on I-5 for 24 miles past the I-5/Hwy 152 interchange. (Do not take the Mercey Hot Springs Rd. exit!) Continue 8 miles past the Mercey Hot Springs exit and get off at the Shields Ave./Little Panoche Rd. exit (J1), go right (west) for 13 miles.

From the south—go north on I-5 for 70 miles past Coalinga to the Shields Ave./Little Panoche Rd. exit (J1). Do not take the Panoche Road exit; go past the Panoche Rd. exit 11 miles to reach the Little Panoche Rd. exit. Take a left and drive west for 13 miles.

Courtesy of Kiva Retreat

732 A   KIVA RETREAT
702 Water St.   831 429-1142
Santa Cruz, CA 95060
www.kivaretreat.com

Meditative and social areas set among trees, grass, and flowers lend a peaceful ambiance to this unusual, clothing-optional, hot-pool rental establishment. Located near the city center. No alcohol, drugs, smoking or glass.

A single day rate gives entry to the communal grass area, two large hot tubs, a cold-tub plunge, and a large sauna. Adjoining indoor dressing and social rooms are also available. Pools use gas-heated tap water and are treated with chlorine and ozone. Two outdoor private enclosures, rented by the hour, have water maintained at 102°, and include a shower, massage table, and servings of herbal tea. Whispers only are allowed in the large sauna. Towels and locks can be rented, or bring your own. Bathing suits are optional everywhere except in the front entry.

Massage is currently on the premises and spa services will soon be available. Major credit cards accepted. Phone for rates, reservations, and directions.

Marjorie Young

Courtesy of Well Within

732 B   TEA HOUSE SPA
☐   112 Elm St.   831 426-9700
          Santa Cruz, CA 95060
          www.teahousespa.com

Beautiful tiled hot pool and sauna rooms overlooking a Japanese bamboo garden, located in the heart of downtown Santa Cruz and available for rent by the hour.

Four private-space suites, consisting of a shower, changing area, and tub use bromine-treated tap water. The fiberglass pools offer a view of the garden and sliding shoji doors can be opened. Three of the suites also offer saunas. Water temperatures are maintained at 104°. Many of the tubs are handicap accessible. Herbal tea and large towels are provided.

Massage is available on the premises. Credit cards accepted. Phone for rates and reservations.

732 C   WELL WITHIN
☐   417 Cedar St.   831 458-WELL
          Santa Cruz, CA 95060
          www.wellwithinspa.com

Beautifully appointed hot pool establishment with Japanese gardens, koi ponds, and waterfalls visible from the individual rooms. Located in downtown Santa Cruz and available for rent by the hour.

Four private indoor tubs and two outdoor tubs in private enclosures are maintained at approximately 102°. Two of the indoor tubs and both outdoor tubs have saunas which are cedar lined. The outdoor tubs can accommodate up to six people each and the gate between the two tubs can be opened to hold up to fourteen people. The tubs are treated with bromine. The entire facility is handicap accessible and one of the outdoor tubs is equipped with special railings.

A shower and changing area are found in each room. Towels and herbal tea are included. Massage and spa services are available by appointment. Credit cards accepted. Phone for rates, reservations, and directions.

---

733   GILROY YAMATO HOT SPRINGS

Sold to the Nature Conservancy of California.

734   GRAND CENTRAL SAUNA AND
HOT TUB CO.

376 Saratoga Ave.   408 247-8827

☐   San Jose, CA 95129

One of a chain of urban locations established by Grand Central, the pioneer in the room rent-a-tub business.

Twenty-one private indoor tubs are heated to 102-104° and treated with chlorine. The individual rooms each have a sauna and dressing room. Towels and soap are provided.

No credit cards or reservations are accepted. Phone for hours, rates, and directions.

735   WATERCOURSE WAY

165 Channing Ave.   650 462-2000

☐   Palo Alto, CA 94301

www.watercourseway.com

The beautiful oriental decor creates a comfortable and interesting environment, offering a variety of highly decorated rooms and experiences.

Pools for rent to the public use gas-heated tap water treated with chlorine. Nine individually decorated private rooms each have a different combination of hot pool, cold pool, sauna, and steambath. Water temperature in the pools is approximately 103°. To accommodate larger groups, two rooms can be joined.

Facials, spa treatments, massage (specializing in hot-stone massage) and gift store are available on the premises. Credit cards accepted. Phone for rates, reservations, and directions.

736 A   GRAND CENTRAL SAUNA AND
HOT TUB CO.

15 Fell St.   415 431-1370

☐   San Francisco, CA 94102

The first of a chain of urban locations established by Grand Central, a pioneer in the private room rent-a-tub business.

Pools in twenty-six private rooms, each with a sauna, are for rent to the public. The pools use gas-heated tap water treated with chlorine and are maintained between 102-104°. Towels and soap are provided.

Tanning booths are available on the premises. Credit cards are not accepted. Reservations are not accepted. Phone for rates and directions.

736 B   THE HOT TUBS

2200 Van Ness Ave.   415 441-TUBS

☐   San Francisco, CA 94109

One of the few stress-reduction establishments offering tile tubs and decks in a chrome and glass urban environment. Located on a main street just west of downtown.

Pools in twenty private rooms are for rent to the public. Gas-heated tap water treated with chlorine is maintained at 104°. A sauna, music, and rest area are included. Towels and soap are provided.

Massage and a juice bar are available on the premises. No credit cards are accepted. Phone for rates, reservations, and directions.

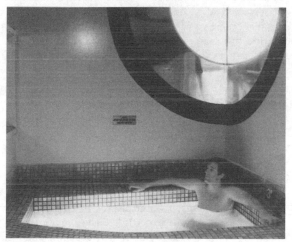

Hot Tubs of San Francisco welcomes you to "The Home of the 60-Minute Vacation," and "A Total Relaxation Experience." Sounds great.

737 F. JOSEPH SMITH'S MASSAGE THERAPY

158 Almonte   415 383-8260

☐ Mill Valley, CA 94941

www.josephsmithmassage.com

A Marin county healing center with two five-foot deep hot tubs nestled under redwood trees, located in a country setting.

Two private enclosures with chlorine-treated water and temperatures of approximately 104° are rented to the public. One of the tubs is available for communal use during the day. A cedar sauna is also for rent. Bathing suits are optional in the tub and sauna areas.

The prayer garden is open for relaxation and meditation. The crystal room also provides a space to meditate. Massage and advanced body therapy classes are available on the premises, as are chiropractic and acupuncture services. Massage classes and workshop space are available. Phone for rates, reservations, and directions.

738 SHIBUI GARDENS

19 Tamalpais Ave.   415 457-0283

☐ San Anselmo, CA 94960

An inviting blend of Marin County natural redwood hot tubs and lush landscaping. Located on a suburban side street.

Three privately enclosed hot tubs using bromine-treated, gas-heated tap water are for rent by the hour. Water temperatures are 101°. Enclosures are also equipped with cold showers. Bathing suits are optional inside the pool and sauna spaces.

A private indoor sauna is for rent on the premises. Massage is available. Phone for rates, reservations, and directions.

739 FROGS

10 School Street Plaza   415 453-7647

☐ Fairfax, CA 94930

May be the only nudist/naturist spa in the San Francisco Bay area. Located in a Marin County suburb and kept in pristine condition with clothing optional areas.

There are two outdoor hot tubs in private enclosures, plus a large communal hot tub and a cold plunge. There are two saunas, one completely redone in cedar, (and kept at the hottest temperatures in the Bay area) and a clothing-optional sundeck.

Voted "Best of Marin" for massage therapy, with therapists available until midnight. Walk-ins encouraged. Website offers links with naturist events and interests.

740 ALBANY SAUNA AND HOT TUBS

1002 Solano Ave.   510 525-6262

☐ Albany, CA 94706

www.albanysauna.com

Established in 1934 as one of the earliest rent-a-tub establishments in the Bay Area, it has since been extensively remodeled. Located two blocks west of San Pablo Ave.

Three outdoor, circular wooden tubs with jets enclosed pools for rent to the public use gas-heated tap water treated with chlorine and cleaned with a diatomaceous earth filtering system. Water temperature is maintained at approximately 105°. There are railings throughout the facility.

Four private, traditional Finnish-style rock-steam saunas, individually controlled for temperature with an outside air source for comfortable breathing, are available for rent. Eucalyptus scented towels are provided. Swedish-Esalen massage, and hair and skin care products are available on the premises. Major credit cards accepted. Phone for rates, reservations, and directions.

741 A THE HOT TUBS

1915 University Ave.   510 843-4343

☐ Berkeley, CA 94704

One of two urban locations in Berkeley and San Francisco.

Fourteen private rooms with pools use gas-heated tap water treated with chlorine. Water temperature varies between 102-104°. A sauna is included.

Towels and soap are provided. A juice bar is available on the premises. No credit cards or checks. Reservations are not accepted. Phone for rates and directions.

741 B   THE BERKELEY SAUNA

☐   1947 Milvia St.   510 845-2341
Berkeley, CA 94704

A stress-reduction establishment located a few yards north of University Ave.

Three private rooms with hot tubs, filled with gas-heated tap water. The bromine-treated water is maintained at temperatures from 104-106°.

Three private saunas are also for rent. Massage is available on the premises. Credit cards accepted. Phone for rates, reservations, and directions.

742 A   AMERICAN FAMILY SAUNA AND HOT TUB

☐   2367 Pleasant Hill Rd.   925 472-0852
Pleasant Hill, CA 94523
www.familyhottub.com

Outdoor establishment located near the intersection of Gregory and Pleasant Hill Rd. Closed Tuesday.

Ten private outdoor tubs in a garden setting, all with shower and dressing area. Some rooms are open to the sky. Gas-heated tap water treated with chlorine is maintained at 102-104°. Large, private Finnish-style sauna and therapeutic massage by our excellent staff available by appointment. Half price for half-hour tub before massage. Double and single massage rooms. Handicap accessible tubs available. Gift certificates. MasterCard and Visa accepted.

742 B   SUNSHINE SPA

☐   1948 Contra Costa Blvd.   925 685-7822
Pleasant Hill, CA 94523

Funky, fun-loving, rent-a-tub business that prides itself on its great massages. Located in the Pleasant Hill Plaza.

Pools using gas-heated tap water treated with bromine are for rent to the public. There are seven private rooms, each with an in-ground hot tub, shower, massage table, and mural. Pool temperatures range from 90-102°. Handicap accessible.

Massage is available on the premises. Major credit cards accepted. Phone for rates, reservations, and directions.

743   PIEDMONT SPRINGS

☐   3939 Piedmont Ave.   510 652-9191
Oakland, CA 94611
www.piedmontsprings.com

Urban rent-a-tub establishment situated in downtown Oakland.

Five private outdoor hot tubs, one in combination with a sauna, complete with redwood decks, changing areas, and showers. Water temperature is maintained at 102-104°. All tubs are ozone/chlorine treated. A dry Finnish sauna and a tiled private steam room are also available.

Massage, facials, body treatments, and other skin care services are offered. Phone for rates, reservations, directions, or a brochure. Credit cards accepted.

744   HOT TROPICS

☐   17389 Hesperian Blvd.   510 278-8827
San Lorenzo, CA 94580

Seniors, families, singles, and couples are welcome at Hot Tropics, just a couple of blocks off Hwy 880.

Fifteen private indoor rooms with tubs heated to 102-105° and treated with chlorine. Cool tubs are available in summer, or when requested. Seven rooms are also equipped with saunas, futons, showers, and radios. Saunas are large enough for two people to stretch out in and totally relax. Seven rooms do not have saunas but do have large skylights that roll open when the weather permits. Special minerals are added to the tubs. Handicap accessible.

No credit cards or reservations are accepted. Phone for hours, rates, and directions.

745   PARADISE SPAS

☐   5168 Mowry Ave.   510 793-7727
Fremont, CA 94538

Suburban rent-a-tub and tanning center located in a shopping center just off Highway 880.

Eight private rooms, including three with special black lighting, come complete with tubs and showers. The water is heated to 102-104° and is chlorine treated. Towels and radios are supplied.

Tanning booths are available. Credit cards accepted.

SOUTHERN CALIFORNIA

This map was designed to be used with a standard highway map.

MAP SYMBOLS

● Natural locations with minor improvements

■ Commercial mineral water establishments

□ Tap water resorts and rental locations

⌇ Paved highway

╍ Unpaved road

⋯ Hiking trail

Courtesy of Furnace Creek Resorts

Debbie Johnson

801 A FURNACE CREEK INN RESORT

PO Box 1   760 786-2345

■ Death Valley, CA 92328

www.furnacecreekresort.com

An historic resort built around a lush oasis on a barren hillside overlooking Death Valley. Elevation, sea level. Open mid-October to mid-May.

Natural mineral water flows out of a spring at 89°, into two outdoor pools, and through a large, palm-shaded arroyo. The swimming pool maintains a temperature of approximately 85°, and the flow-through rate is so great that no chemical treatment of the water is necessary. Bathing suits are required. Pools are for the use of registered guests only.

Facilities include two saunas, lighted tennis courts, rooms, two restaurants, live entertainment, dancing, and a bar. Major credit cards accepted.

801 B FURNACE CREEK RANCH RESORT

PO Box 1   760 786-2345

■ Death Valley, CA 92328

A family setting, the Furnace Creek Ranch was the home of the original "20-mule team." Located just down the hill from the Furnace Creek Inn in a green oasis setting surrounded by Death Valley National Park. Elevation 214 feet below sea level. Open all year.

Water from a natural warm spring is piped down from the 89° spring serving the Inn to a swimming pool at the ranch. The rate of flow-through is so great that a temperature of approximately 85° is maintained and no chemical treatment is necessary. The pool is for the enjoyment of registered guests only. Bathing suits are required. Most facilities are handicap accessible; handicap rooms are available.

Other amenities include 224 guest accommodations, three restaurants, a saloon, three retail shops, a service station, an eighteen-hole golf course, tennis courts, basketball courts, a children's playground, and horseback riding (October-May). Massage therapy is also offered. For those of you who want to fly in, there is a small airstrip located near by. All major credit cards accepted. Contact resort for further information.

Sally Jackson

Soakers Bible

802 A   WARM SPRINGS

● **North of Shoshone**
In Death Valley National Park

Fig trees, bamboo, mesquite, oleanders, cottonwood trees, tamarisk, and lots of grapevines line the trail to this warm spring located in a rocky canyon near several abandoned buildings and mines. Open all year, weather dependent.

Natural mineral water trickles out of the rocks at the top of a canyon creating a small pool about four-feet wide, six-feet long, and maybe a foot deep. The water temperature is 94°. The cooler water in this very hot climate would be great on one of those baking desert days.

No services on the premises but camping is not prohibited. All services are back in Shoshone.

Directions: One and one-half miles north of Shoshone, turn west on SR 178 heading toward Badwater. Continue 28 miles past Ashford Junction to West Side Rd. Turn west on this good gravel road for 3 miles, then turn left on Butte Valley Road and go 11 miles. It gets worse and worse the closer you get to the springs. You will travel through an abandoned talc mine as you head west through a canyon just before the turnoff to the springs. On the left at the base of the mountains are some large trees and the parking area.

GPS: N 35 57.995 W 116 55.918

802 B   SHOSHONE INN

■ Box 67   760 852-4335
Shoshone, CA 92384
www.shoshonevillage.com

Older resort located on CA 127 in desert foothills near the southern entrance to Death Valley. Elevation 1,600 feet. Open all year.

Natural mineral water flows out of a spring at 93° with such pressure that no pumps are needed to push it through the pipes to the outdoor swimming pool. The rate of flow-through is so great that a temperature of 92° is maintained and no chemical treatment of the water is necessary. A waterfall at the end of the pool cools the inflow for pool use in the summer. Pool use is available only to registered guests. Bathing suits are required.

Sixteen rooms, some with kitchenettes, include phones and cable TV, Crowbar Cafe and Saloon, general store and gift shop, and service station. RV hookups and overnight camping spaces are available at the ShoshoneRV Park (802 C). Major credit cards are accepted.

Location: Shoshone is 28 miles south of Death Valley Junction and 27 miles north of Pahrump on CA 127.

Note: Shoshone Airport, available for fly-in customers. Call Bishop Airport for details, 760 872-2971.

802 C   SHOSHONE RV PARK
■   Box 67   760 852-4569
     Shoshone, CA 92384

Lush, green, tree-shaded RV park one hundred yards north of the Shoshone Inn on the main street (CA 127) in Shoshone.

The natural mineral water outdoor swimming pool described at left is adjacent to the RV park and is for the use of registered guests of either facility and for local residents. Non-guests may use the pool by paying a day use fee (which is the same as the overnight RV park fee).

Half the hot geothermal well water supplies the RV park's showers, the Inn, and the pool; the other half is used for the town water supply. A reverse osmosis process is used to treat all the water

Major credit cards accepted.

Debbie Johnson

803 A   DELIGHT'S HOT SPRINGS RESORT
368 Tecopa Hot Springs Rd.

760 852-4343
■   Tecopa, CA 92389   800 928-8808

One of the original hot spring spas in the arid, alkali desert east of Death Valley, originally established in the early 1940s. Enjoy the two-acre lake. For adults only (ages 21-101). Elevation 1,400 feet. Open all year.

Hundreds of warm mineral springs supply water to the entire region. Delight's has four large, three-foot deep, private, coed indoor cement tubs that hold one to ten people. Water flows from a 438-foot artesian well into the tubs. Two pools are enclosed, two are roofless, and all have showers. Pools are open from 10 AM to 8 PM for those with a day pass and are drained and scrubbed nightly. If you are staying there pools are available to you all night. Chemical-free water and misters have been installed to help keep you cool. Pools have stairs and bars and are handicap accessible with assistance. No suits allowed in the pools.

Facilities include rustic housekeeping cottages, built of railroad ties, with refrigeration, microwaves, dishes, and everything else you need to cook a meal. There are no TVs, radios, or phones. Also available are full hookup RV spaces, tenting areas, showers, and rest rooms. The clubhouse has a stage, a fireplace and is large enough for banquets and weddings. Major services are thirty-five miles away in Pahrump or eighty miles east in Las Vegas. Be sure to bring water and food with you. Call first, as the owners are planning on building a restaurant.

Directions: From CA 127, 5 miles south of Shoshone or 55 miles north of Baker, drive east on Tecopa Hot Springs Rd. for 3 miles. A sign to the spa is on the east side of the street.

Shoshone photos by Justine Hill

Photos by Debbie Johnson

803 B   TECOPA HOT SPRINGS RESORT
PO Box 25   760 852-4420
Tecopa Hot Springs Rd. and Noonday Rd.
■ Tecopa, CA 92389
www.tecopahotsprings.org

Terraced hillsides overlook ancient Lake Tecopa and the southeast end of Death Valley National Park. Open seasonally. Elevation 1,400 feet. October through May. Day use available if resort is not full.

Recently restored two hot mineral water baths in private rooms off a common area outside the showers. After showering off with soap in the separate men's and women's bathhouses you can wrap up and go into one of the rooms to soak in water kept at 104°. As the tubs use a constant flow of water, chemicals are not needed. Private baths are coed and families are welcome.

Forty-three RV spaces with hookups, two rooms, two cabins with kitchenettes and bathrooms, and a trailer are for rent for overnighters, and dry camping spaces are available. There is also a gallery of local fine art in the office. The owners enjoy catering to groups and a restaurant is in the works. Facilities are rustic, no TVs, radios or phones in rooms. A circuit labyrinth with collected rocks representing two billion years of geologic time is available for your contemplation. Major services are fifty miles away in Baker or eighty miles east in Las Vegas.

Note: Every person who sent me information for Tecopa said that everyone should be sure to visit The China Ranch Date Farm while in the area.

803 C   TECOPA PALMS RV PARK
PO Box 35   760 852-4347
Tecopa Hot Springs Rd. and Elias Rd.
■ Tecopa, CA 92389

RV park providing lots of fun activities and places to soak. Elevation 1,400 feet. No day use.

There are two indoor, private cement tubs, large enough for two or three people. The water temperature is kept at 104°. There are showers and a changing area.

Thirty-five RV spaces with full hookups, four rentals for overnighters without an RV, a clubhouse, satellite TV, and coffee are offered. Many of the guests who come back year after year enjoy the constant activities of game nights, bonfires, holiday celebrations, and celebrations for any reason at all. Massages can be arranged for. Major services are thirty-five miles away in Pahrump or eighty miles east in Las Vegas.

803 D   POO-HAH-BAH
PO Box 299   760 852-4288
■ Tecopa, CA 92389

Traditional healing and prayer center located in the beautiful desert near the southeastern entrance to Death Valley. Offers traditional Native American healing and treatment from the mineral waters for no charge. Donations accepted.

Soaking pools available with the following restrictions: no mixed bathing in the hot tubs without prior approval; suits required; wear a bathrobe when outside; long hair must be tied up or wear a bathing cap; and no bare feet in the pool house, bring sandals or flip-flops.

Bring your own sleeping bags in order to bunk down in the dormitories (separate men's and women's), one family room for children, or there is room to pitch a tent.

Note: There are many other restrictions to be aware of before coming here. Please phone ahead to make sure you will feel comfortable in these surroundings.

Debbie Johnson

804 A TECOPA HOT SPRINGS (OPERATED BY CALIFORNIA LAND MANAGEMENT)

■ PO Box 158   760 852-4481
Tecopa, CA 92389
www.clm-services.com

A county-operated RV park, bathhouse and camp-ground, now run by a licensed operating company, located on the Tecopa loop off CA 127 in the Mojave Desert. Elevation 1,400 feet. Open all year; hours vary by the season (call for information). Fee charged per person. Children under five not admitted.

Natural mineral water flows out of a spring at 108° and is piped to separate men's and women's bathhouses. The women's side has one hot gravel-bottom, three-foot deep soaking pool maintained at around 104°, a cool pool, plus an enclosed outdoor sunbathing area. The men's tubs are cement. The indoor pool is twelve by twelve and the enclosed outdoor pool is eight-feet by twelve-feet; both pools have steps and grab bars for handicap access. There is also a clothing-optional private pool for rent that is also the only place where you can soak coed.

A fee is charged for the 250 RV hookups, 100 with electricity. Also there are flush toilets, and a dump station, a convenience store, playground and picnic areas on the premises. There is an air-conditioned community center with library, exercise classes, and social activities. Visa and MasterCard accepted. It is eight miles to a service station in Shoshone.

While suits are required in the separate men's and women's bathhouses and on the sunning decks, there is a private pool that can be rented and where suits are optional.

804 B TECOPA DESERT POND

Permanently closed. Posted, and people will be fined $200 if caught in the pond. In any case, waterflow into pond has become only a seep and the pond is mucky and not very attractive for soaking.

804 C TECOPA MUD BATHS

● **Near the town of Tecopa**

Warm, smooth, clay-mud lines the bottom and sides of this undeveloped, natural hot springs. The pool and nat-ural channel are surrounded by three foot high reeds in a starkly beautiful desert setting.

The water emerges from the ground at 118° in at least two points in the upper pool. The water channels through the reeds to an aluminum ladder which allows bathers to climb into 108° water. A few feet downstream temperatures are 104-106°.

Local wisdom says the thick, soft, greenish mud is ben-tonite which helps draw toxins from the body. The deep-er pool by the ladder is a good place to wash off before leaving. Although wading rapidly muddies the water, the clay settles back quickly. The pool near the source is rarely used as the shallow water is 118°. Local tradition seems to be clothing optional. Although water shoes or sandals may seem like a good idea, they stick in the clay and slip off. The depths are a few feet at most and the bottom is quite smooth and free of sharp objects. Walking down-stream is slippery. Some people prefer to do a combina-tion of dog paddle and propelling themselves on their hands instead of trying to walk. May be mud mites in summer.

Except for the ladder and a four-by-four support beam, there are no improvements. Restrooms, showers, baths, campground, community center, and pay phone are located a the Inyo County Baths, 0.9 miles away. A restau-rant and laundry are two miles beyond the bathhouses. Dry camping is available on BLM lands outside of town.

Location: The mud bath is 0.9 miles northeast of the Tecopa Hot Springs Bathhouses on Tecopa Hot Springs Rd. (shown as Furnace Creek Rd. on some maps) or 1.7 miles southeast of the intersection with Hwy 127. Park on the shoulder of the road. A clear but unmarked trail leads off to the right (if coming from the bathhouses; left from highway). On a small rise just to the left of the trail is a sign prohibiting off-road vehicles. It is about 100 yards to the ladder. A small tarp or mat is handy to stand on when drying off as the exit area may be muddy. Be sure to take cool drinking water.

GPS: N 35 53.415 W 116 14.193

805   DEEP CREEK HOT SPRINGS

● **Near the town of Hesperia**

Beautiful, remote, year-round springs on the south bank of Deep Creek in the San Bernardino National Forest. Elevation 3,000 feet. Open all year.

Natural mineral water flows out of several rock fissures at 108° and directly into volunteer-built, rock and sandbag pools on the edge of Deep Creek. Water temperature in any one pool will depend on the amount of creek water admitted. Clothing optional.

There are no services, and overnight camping is prohibited in the canyon near the springs. It is seven miles by a year-round trail to an overnight parking area. There is also a steep, two and one-half-mile, slippery trail of decomposed granite down the north side of the canyon from Bowen Ranch. A fee is charged for admission to the ranch and for overnight parking and camping. From either parking area it is ten miles to all services.

Directions: From I-15, take the Hesperia exit and drive for 8 miles along Main St. to a Y in the road, and bear left on Rock Spring Rd. This turns into Round Up at the intersection of Kiowa (stop light). Continue on Roundup for 4.3 miles (the last 1.3 miles are unpaved). Turn right (south) on Bowen Ranch Rd., a wide, unpaved, washboard road, and drive 5.5 miles to the ranch. Whenever you come to a fork, bear right to reach the ranch.

Directions to the year-round trail: Follow directions above to Deep Creek Rd. Turn right (south) for 5 miles to the pavement end. Bear left across the open space, heading toward the earthen dam. Park at the southeast end of the earthen dam near the overflow ramp. To reach the trailhead, go up the paved service road next to the overflow. From the top of the service road you can look down to the right and see a bathing beach at the creek and to the left, the trailhead marked with a rusty tin sign. There is a short, steep ascent to the trail, which hugs the side of the mountain for 6 miles to the springs.

Note: The trail from Bowen Ranch ends on the north bank of Deep Creek, which overflows during spring runoff so that it is not safe to ford.

Source maps: *San Bernardino National Forest*, USGS *Lake Arrowhead.*

GPS: N 117.1767 W 34.3402

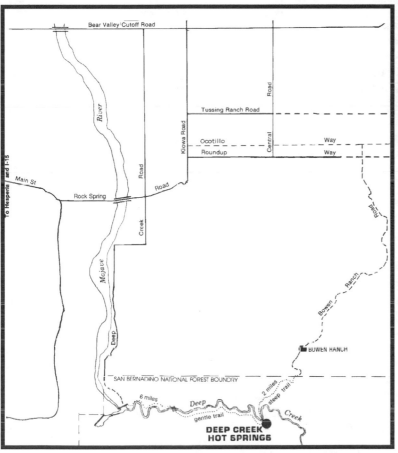

Photos by Dave Bybee and Chris Andrews

On the map:

Bear Valley Cutoff Road

River

To Hesperia and I-15

Main St

Rock Spring

Road

Road

Kiowa Road

Tussing Ranch Road

Ocotillo

Central

Way

Roundup

Way

Road

Creek

Mojave

Bowen

Ranch

Road

BOWEN RANCH

Deep

SAN BERNADINO NATIONAL FOREST BOUNDRY

6 miles

Deep

2 miles steep trail

Creek

gentle trail

DEEP CREEK HOT SPRINGS

197 SOUTHERN CALIFORNIA

Miracle Springs Hotel and Spa is one of the most luxurious locations to offer a full array of pampering, along with natural hot mineral water pools.

■ DESERT HOT SPRINGS
RESORTS, MOTELS, AND SPAS

Desert Hot Springs has been called "The Mineral Water Capital of the World," with natural crystal clear, tasteless, odorless, geothermal water, low in mineral content, throughout the entire town. Most facilities are open all year and require reservations.

All of the establishments listed below are in or near the city of Desert Hot Springs, ten miles north of Palm Springs. All of them pump natural mineral water from their own wells at temperatures ranging from 120-160 degrees and offer at least one chlorine-treated (except where noted) swimming pool and one hydropool. Some pools with enough flow-through do not require chlorine. Bathing suits are required at almost all locations. Those places that have indicated that they have handicap access are noted. You may wish to check with other places when you call.

Those sites marked with an * indicate that the facility welcomes day-use visitors.

The town of Desert Hot Springs provides all services. Most locations take credit cards, except where noted. For information contact the Chamber of Commerce, 11-711 West Drive, Desert Hot Springs, CA 92240. 760 329-6403. City and zip code for all locations is Desert Hot Springs, CA 92240.

806 A   ADOBE INN AND SPA
66365 7th St.   760 329-7292
www.adobespa.com

Outdoor therapy pool and swimming pool. Ten units with kitchens. Airport transportation. Extended day discount.

*806 B   AGUA CALIENTE HOTEL AND
MINERAL WATER SPA   760 329-4481
14500 Palm Dr.   800 423-8109
www.aguacalientehotel.com

Outdoor mineral water pool. Indoor therapy pool. In-room pools. Some rooms with kitchens. Handicap access. RV spaces. Day use.

*806 C   CJ GRAND HOTEL AND SPA
67585 Hacienda Ave.   760 329-4488
                         877 966-7367

Pool, two hydrojet spas, dry sauna, wet sauna. Some rooms with kitchens. Massage. Twenty two new rooms with in-room hot mineral tubs. Day use.

806 D   CRYSTAL HOTEL SPA AND RESORT
67585 Hacienda Ave.   760 439-4488
www.crystalhotelsparesort.com

Large hotel with resident naturopath, full service spa. Some rooms with private hot tubs. Japanese style bathhouse, indoor and outdoor pools. (See photo above.)

*806 E   DESERT HOT SPRINGS HOTEL AND SPA
10806 Palm Dr.   760 329-6000
www.dhsspa.com   800 808-7727

Olympic-sized swimming pool and eight soaking pools. Spa services. Massage. Restaurant. Day use.

806 F   DESERT OASIS INN
11330 Palm Dr.   760 251-4560

Outdoor therapy and swimming pool. Seven units with kitchens. Airport transportation. Extended day discount. Handicap access.

806 G   EMERALD SPRINGS RESORT
68055 Club Circle Dr.   760 288-0071
www.emeraldsprings.net

Seven mineral pools and swimming pool. Kitchens available. Restaurant on premises. Handicap access. Day use.

*806 H   FLAMINGO RESORT HOTEL
67221 Pierson Blvd.   760 251-1455

Therapy pool, sauna, and swimming pool. Kitchens available. Handicap access.

806 I   HACIENDA HOT SPRINGS INN
12885 Eliseo Rd.   760 251-2885

Six cozy rooms, aromatic gardens, lagoon, mineral water pools and stunning views. Rock sauna. Spa treatments based on native plants and herbs from the garden.

806 J   HIGHLANDER LODGE
68187 Club Circle Dr.   760 251-0189

Indoor Roman spa, outdoor pool. Eighteen unit boutique style resort and spa. Pets okay.

806 K   HOPE SPRINGS BED AND BREAKFAST
68075 Club Circle Dr.   760 329-4003
www.hopespringsresort.com

Artfully restored motel. Lovely garden with lap pool and two pools with jets. Four of the ten rooms have kitchens.

*806 L   LAS PRIMAVERAS RESORT AND SPA
66659 Sixth St.   760 251-1677

104° indoor hot tub, 92° outdoor swimming pool, sauna. State-of-the-art outdoor cooling system cools outdoor temperature fifteen to twenty degrees. Luxury units with jet tubs, kitchens. Handicap access. Day use.

806 M   LA TOSCANA
11000 Palm Dr.   760 329-6484
www.latoscana resorts.com 800 635-8660

Large hotel in town. Kids and pets welcome. Full service spa. Bar, resaurant. rooms and suites. Reasonable rates.

806 N   LIDO PALMS SPA MOTEL
12801 Tamar Dr.   760 329-6033

Two outdoor pools, large indoor spa, dry sauna. Kitchenettes. Massage.

806 O   LIVING WATERS SPA
13340 Mountain View Rd.   760 329-6666
www.livingwatersspa.com   866 329-9988

Clothing optional mini-resort. Two outdoor pools. Massage. A full layout on this wonderful resort is found on page 201.

806 P   MIRACLE MANOR RETREAT
12589 Reposo Way   760 329-6641
                           877 329-6641

Enclosed hot pool, outdoor pool. Therapeutic massage, facials.

**806 Q   MIRACLE SPRINGS RESORT
AND CONFERENCE CENTER**
10625 Palm Dr.   760 251-6000

Eight outdoor hot spas at different temperatures, including an eighteen-inch deep "champagne" bubbling spa and two dry saunas. Whirlpool bathtubs in separate men's and women's areas. Massage. Restaurant, banquet facilities, approved gaming. Handicap access.

*806 R NURTURING NEST
11149 Sunset Ave.   760 251-2583

Holistic retreat. Therapy and swimming pools. Seven units, six with kitchens. Minimalist zen style. Extended day discount.

*806 S SAGEWATER SPA
12689 Eliseo Rd.   760 251-1688

Swimming pool, and therapy pool. All rooms with kitchens. Day use. Full spa services. No children or pets.

*806 T SAHARA SPA MOTEL
66700 E. Fifth St.   760 329-6666
www. saharaspamotel.com

Indoor spa, indoor swimming pool, sauna, hot waterfall. Handicap access. Day use.

*806 U SAM'S FAMILY SPA HOT WATER RESORT
70875 Dillon Rd.   760 329-6457
www.samsfamilyspa.com

Well-managed family spa with nice park setting. One of largest, multi-service resorts with all facilities open to the public for day use as well as to registered guests. Large outdoor swimming pool (80°) uses chlorinated mineral water. Gazebo-enclosed wading pool and four covered hydropools use flow-through mineral water, requiring no chemical treatment and are drained and cleaned every night. Day use.

Coed sauna, motel rooms, RV hookups, camping spaces, store, laundromat, playground, exercise room. Barbeque area. Handicap accessible with assistance. No pets. No smoking. (See photo below.)

*806 V THE SPRING RESORT & SPA
12699 Reposo Way   760 251-6700
www.thespringsresort and spa.com

Upscale, small resort with heated mineral pools and sauna. Nine guest rooms, six with custom kitchens and full conveniences, and one suite. Large mineral water pool and private courtyards. Luxurious spa packages offered. (See photo above.)

*806 W SWISS HEALTH RESORT
66729 Eigth St.   760 329-6912

Start the day with an invigorating nature walk followed by a special Swiss Water Massage. Indoor mineral pool, hydropool, outdoor mineral pool, all flow-through requiring no chlorine. No small childer or pets. Handicap aceess. Day use. (See photo below.)

806 X "THE LAST RESORT"
67780 Arena Blanca   760 322-8759

Smaller motel with heated mineral pools and sauna.

*806 Y TWO BUNCH PALMS RESORT AND SPA
A full layout on this resort is found on page 202.

Photos courtesy of Living Waters Spa

"Enjoy Hot Natural Mineral Water, Naturally"
A mini-resort offering couples both a natural hot mineral water soak and a clothing optional experience. The very nice owners will be happy to answer any of your questions if this is new for you.

---

806 O   LIVING WATERS SPA
13340 Mountain View Rd.   760 329-9988
866-329-9988
■   **Desert Hot Springs, CA 92240**
www.livingwatersspa.com

The only clothing optional hotel or spa in Southern California that has natural mineral water from it's own well. This small resort offers beautiful views of Mt. San Jacinto, and the surrounding desert while guaranteeing complete privacy. Offers day use of pools and spa. Open all year.

Crystal clear hot mineral water from the well fills two pools. One, a large swimming pool, is open to the sky, and the second, a therapy/soaking pool with jets under a covered awning, can seat twenty people. The water "flows" through the pools so there is no chlorine content in the therapy pool and minimal amounts in the large pool.

Nine guest rooms and six condos are beautifully furnished in a Euro/Retro style with seven of the rooms complete with kitchens. Breakfast is served in the large lounge, complete with a romantic fireplace for those cold desert mornings (also good for romantic evenings). Workshops and seminars designed to enhance personal growth are planned, and massage is also offered.

Be sure to visit their web site and call and talk to the very friendly owners if you have any questions.

DESERT HOT SPRINGS

806 Y TWO BUNCH PALMS RESORT AND SPA
67245 Two Bunch Palms Trail

760 472-4334
800 472-4334

■ Desert Hot Springs, CA 92240
www.twobunchpalms.com

A fifty-six acre adult-only desert oasis. Walkways with trails amid the abundant wildlife that thrive in preserved wilderness areas are an added bonus to the world renowned spa and natural mineral water hot springs. An aquifer provides the resort with both hot (148-152°) and cold mineral water; this was a natural spot for a healing, restful destination resort.

The Grotto, using one of the country's largest free-flowing bodies of natural hot mineral water, is regarded by many as the resort's heart and soul. It features two adjoining bodies of hot natural mineral water maintained at slightly different temperatures—each being continuously replenished by free-flowing streams of fresh water requiring only a gentle cleaning with a bromide wash early each morning. The hotpool side of the Grotto is kept at a toasty 104°, while the larger soaking pool side is maintained at a soothing 98° . After passing through the Grotto, the water cascades down through a series of rock-lined brooks and several lakes, nourishing flora and fauna, and ultimately settling into a small marsh thicket where it soaks back down into the earth. The water is virtually odorless and has a wonderful taste. The hot water is used in all of the showers, two watsu treatment pools and the swimming pool, where it is chlorinated. The water from the cooler artesian wells is used for drinking.

Guestrooms, suites, and villas are located in either the spectacular natural hot springs Grotto area offering rustically elegant vintage architecture, or in the dramatically panoramic lake and tennis area where contemporary architecture is surrounded by naturally landscaped gardens and preserved wilderness areas. A full Continental breakfast is included. For the rest of your meals prepare to dine in style. Purchased individually or as a package, you can choose from a large selection of close to forty-five spa treatments and massage modalities.

807 TURTLEBACK MESA B&B
PO Box 8038   760 347-5358

■ Palm Springs, CA 92263
email: trtlbkmesa@aol.com

Modern spacious adobe located approximately twenty miles east of Palm Springs in the Indio Hills, surrounded by rocky Nature Conservancy land in desert tortoise country. Elevation 1,200 feet. Open all year.

Natural 130° mineral water pumped up from 425 feet underground heats the building through radiant floor coils and flows into a large outdoor swimming pool where it mixes with cold city water. The large outdoor hot tub, which can hold twenty-eight to thirty people, is maintained at 105-110°. No chemicals are added to this mineral water which has the same mineral content as the Ouray Caves in Colorado.

Facilities include two rooms with private toilets and a shared shower. Rooms open directly onto the patio and pool area. Sculptures of turtles from cultures around the world turn this bed-and-breakfast into an ethnic art gallery. All other services, including restaurants, shopping centers and casinos are fifteen to twenty-five minutes away.

Management prefers guests who are comfortable in a clothing optional environment. Facilities are only available to non-smoking registered guests. Call for reservations.

Courtesy of Turtleback Mesa

Courtesy of Palm Springs Resort

808 PALM SPRINGS SPA HOTEL AND CASINO RESORT

100 N. Indian Canyon Dr.   760 325-1461
■ **Palm Springs, CA 92262**
www.spa resortcasino.com

A major destination resort with an elaborate mineral water spa where you can sample the ancient tradition of the "taking of the water." Located in downtown Palm Springs. Elevation 500 feet. Open all year.

Natural mineral water flows out of historic Indian wells on the property at temperatures of 106°. The spa has separate men's and women's sections, each containing fourteen marble tubs separately controllable with mineral water temperature up to 104°. These tubs are drained and refilled after each use so that no chemical treatment of the water is necessary. Each spa also has vapor-inhalation rooms, a steambath, and a dry sauna. Bathing suits are required in the outdoor pool area, optional in the bathhouse and solarium. Fees to use the spa are discounted for hotel guests.

Services and facilities on the premises include massage, hot stone therapy, beauty shop, rooms (handicap accessible rooms are on the ground floor), restaurant and lounge, pool bar, snacks, airport pickup, and group conference rooms. Also available is an Indian-owned gaming casino, open twenty-four hours. All major credit cards accepted. Pool and spa facilities are available to the public as well as to registered guests.

Directions: Take the Indian Canyon Dr. exit from I-10 and drive south 6.5 miles to the resort.

809 A BASHFORD'S HOT MINERAL SPA

10590 Hot Mineral Spa Rd.   760 354-1315
■ **Niland, CA 92257**
www.bashfords.com

Primarily a winter RV resort for adults (eighteen and up), located on a desert slope overlooking the Salton Sea. Elevation 50 feet below sea level. Open October 15 to May 30.

Natural hot mineral water flows out of an artesian well at 160° and flows through a cooling tower from which it is piped to the six mineral baths after it is cooled down to between 101-104°. These four-by-six tubs are drained and refilled after each us so that no chemical treatment is required. The swimming pool is maintained at 84-86° and the therapy pool at 101-102°. The water in both pools is heated through the hot well by heat exchange and is chlorine treated. Bathing suits required.

RV hookups, overnight spaces, and a laundry room and many activities are offered on the premises. A barbeque and a picnic area can be used for cookouts. Credit cards accepted. It is seven miles to a local motel, with restaurants at Bombay Beach. There is a snack shop one-half mile away and gas can be found two-and-one-half miles south.

Courtesy of Bashford's Spa

809 C IMPERIAL HOT MINERAL SPA, INC.
10595 Hot Mineral Spa Rd. 760 354-4100
■ Niland, CA 92257

Imperial Spa is backed up to the Chocolate Mountains overlooking the Salton Sea. Elevation is 87 feet below sea level. Open year around. Facilities are available to registered guests only.

Natural mineral water flows out of an artesian well at 174 degrees into a large cooling tank from which it is piped into seven outdoor pools. Five spas are maintained at 98–104°. The two three-foot deep wading pools are maintained at 98-100°. The wading pools and spas are all treated with chlorine (due to regulations). There are also five Roman tubs that you fill yourself with hot mineral water and do not need to be chemically treated as they are drained after each use. There is also a fresh water pool. Bathing suits required.

Restrooms, showers and designated full hook-ups sites are handicap accessible. RV hookups, overnight camping spaces, café and store are on premises. Credit cards accepted. It is sixteen miles to a service station in Niland.

809 B FOUNTAIN OF YOUTH SPA
10249 Coachella Canal Rd.
760 354-1340   888 800-0772
■ Niland, CA 92257
www.foyspa.com

The largest of the RV parks in this area, located on a desert slope overlooking the Salton Sea. Elevation sea level. Open all year.

Natural mineral water flows out of an artesian well on the property at 137°, is cooled by heat exchangers, and is piped to two pool areas, one of which is reserved for adults. The two outdoor swimming pools range in temperature from 85-90°. The five outdoor hydropools range in temperature from 100-107°. The water in all pools is chlorine treated. Pools are available to registered campers only. No day use. Bathing suits required.

The facilities include rental units, a laundromat, store, cafe, RV hookups, overnight camping spaces, recreation rooms, library, exercise and fitness room, tennis courts, horse shoe and bocce courts, and car wash. Winter services include massage, beauty and barber shops. Church services and activity programs are also offered. If no hookup spaces are available, it is possible to dry camp and get on a waiting list. It is two and one-half miles south to a service station across from the border patrol on CA 111 and four and one-half miles north to a motel and restaurant at Bombay Beach.

Directions: From CA 111, 3 miles south of Bombay Beach, drive east on Hot Mineral Spa Rd. for 1.5 miles, then right onto Spa Rd. for 1.1 miles.

809 D LARK SPA
10016 Frink Rd.   760 354-1384
■ Niland, CA 92257

Mobile home and RV winter resort located on a desert slope overlooking the Salton Sea. Elevation fifty feet below sea level. Open all year.

Well water, gas-heated and chlorine-treated, is used in an outdoor hydropool maintained at 102°. Bathing suits required.

Overnight spaces and RV hookups are available on the premises. No credit cards are accepted. It is one mile to a store and service station and four miles to a motel and restaurant.

Directions: From Niland, drive 10.5 miles north to Frink Rd. and turn right (east) for 1 mile. Frink Rd. is 3 miles south of the border patrol station on CA 111.

Phil Wilcox

810 FIVE PALMS WARM WELL OASIS (HIGHLINE NORTH)

● Near the city of Brawley

An exotic, true desert oasis surrounded by palm trees and tall bullrushes in the otherwise arid, sparsely vegetated Imperial Valley desert south of the Salton Sea. Elevation 27 feet above sea level. Open all year.

Natural 92° mineral water bubbles up from an artesian well through a three-inch pipe in the middle of a large, clean, sandy-bottom soaking pond that is eighteen inches deep and large enough for a dozen people. Bullrushes and palms help shade the pool. The custom is clothing optional.

There are no services available except plenty of open BLM desert where overnight parking is permitted with a fourteen-day limit. Caution: choose your parking space carefully; vehicles have been known to get stuck in the soft sand underneath a deceptively firm crust. Parking is not permitted within a 150-foot radius of the springs, and overnight camping is not permitted within approximately a one-half mile radius of the well so that animals will feel safe to come to the water. Please help by cleaning up any party trash. All services are available in Brawley, approximately sixteen and one-half miles away.

Directions: From Brawley, drive 15 miles east on CA 78, crossing the canal. Take the second dirt road right (0.5 miles past the canal). Follow the one-lane road for 1.6 miles to five tall palms, the only greenery in the area. The one-lane, graded, unsurfaced road has some soft, sandy spots that can usually be negotiated by normal passenger vehicles.

Five Palms, (now twenty) pictured below, is a true natural desert oasis for animals and humans. In order to provide a place to soak, the BLM has built concrete pools at Highline.

Oscar Voss

811 HIGHLINE SOUTH HOT WELL

● Near the town of Holtville

Two cement soaking pools and a large pond, fed by an artesian well, located just off the I-8 right-of-way on the east side of Holtville. Elevation sea level. Open all year; closed midnight to 5 AM.

Natural mineral water flows out of an artesian well at 125° and splashes on the edge of a six-foot by six-foot by five-foot deep cement cistern. Hot water showers in through holes in an overhead swing-arm horizontal pipe, which can be diverted when the desired pool temperature is reached. A smaller, cement, bathtub-size pool is next to the larger tub. There is little self-cleaning action, and algae growth is rapid. Volunteers regularly scrub the pools with bleach, which also removes the algae smell. Because the pools are visible from I-8, bathing suits are recommended. A four-step ladder makes the tub handicap accessible with assistance. A sign reminds campers that "soap is prohibited in spa/pond." The area is posted for day-use only and the sheriff patrols regularly.

Overflow from the tub goes into a large, shallow, sandy-bottom "olde swimming hole" that used to be stocked with fish. Water temperature measures 90° in the summer, and fan palms offer a spot of shade.

Facilities include wooden benches, a cement walkway, trash cans, nearby BLM pit toilets, and a fenced-off parking area where overnight parking is prohibited. A primitive BLM campground with a fourteen-day limit is located twenty yards north of the well, across the road. Camping permits are required September to April and a fee is charged. Free overnight camping is available one mile outside the long-term camping area. All services are in Holtville.

Directions: At the east end of Holtville, take the Van Der Linden exit (CA 115) from I-8. Go north and immediately take the first right turn onto a frontage road paralleling I-8. At approximately 0.3 mile you will cross over the Highline Canal. Just past the canal on the right (south) is a flat, fenced parking area with pit toilets. The pools are just ahead toward I-8.

GPS: N 32 45.352 W 115 16.181

Courtesy of Jacumba Hot Springs Spa

Courtesy of Agua Caliente

812 JACUMBA HOT SPRINGS SPA AND LODGE

44500 Old Hwy 80

PO Box 466   619 766-4525

■ Jacumba, CA 91934

jacumbaspa@sbcglobal.net

An older motel spa located just off I-8, 80 miles east of San Diego. Elevation 2,800 feet. Open all year.

Natural mineral water with a slight sulfur odor flows out of a spring at 140-150 gallons per minute at a temperature of 101° and is then piped to an indoor hydropool and an outdoor swimming pool.Continuous flow-through maintains a temperature of 97-98° in the hydropool and 85° in the swimming pool, with no chemical treatment of the water required. Hot mineral water showers are in the spa room. The pools are available to the general public for a use fee. Pools are handicap accessible, with assistance. Bathing suites are required.

Facilities include twenty-four poolside newly furnished rooms, a rustic Alpine restaurant, bar, sauna, tennis and shuffleboard courts, a beer garden patio with Mexican sculpture and pottery, and a lawn area with shade trees. Massage is available on the premises. Major credit cards accepted. It is one block to a store and service station and one-half mile to RV hookups.

Directions: Take the Jacumba exit off I-8 and go 2.5 miles to the tiny town of Jacumba. The spa is located on the north side of Historic Old Highway 80, and the main street through town.

813 AGUA CALIENTE COUNTY PARK

For reservations   858 565-3600

39555 County Route S-2

■ Located in the Anza Borrego Desert

www.sdcounty.ca.gov/parks

A county-operated, desert campground located in a wildlife refuge area in the Anza Borrego Desert. A wide variety of animals and beautiful spring wildflowers and succulents are native to this area. No pets are permitted at any time! Elevation 1,300 feet. Open September through May. Day use, also.

Natural mineral water flows out of several springs at 96° and is then piped to two pools where it is filtered and chlorinated. The outdoor swimming pool with a water temperature at a natural 90° is available for families. The large indoor hydropool is located in a recently built glass pool enclosure. The chlorine-treated mineral water is solar and gas heated to 104°. The hydropool, showers, restrooms, and dressing area are all handicap accessible. Bathing suits are required. Pool facilities are available to the public for day use, as well as to registered campers.

Facilities include 140 RV hookups and overnight camping spaces, hiking trails, picnic and barbeque area, horseshoe pits, shuffleboard, and a children's play area. Credit cards accepted. It is one-half mile to a small general store, cafe and phone; twenty-five miles to a gas station; and thirty-five miles to a motel. There is a nearby airstrip for small planes.

Directions: Take the Ocotillo exit off I-8, 27 miles east of El Centro and 95 miles east of San Diego. Follow Imperial County Rd. S-2 for 25 miles into the Anza Borego Desert to the sign for Agua Caliente Springs. Bear left 0.1 mile to the general store and left again for 0.5 miles to the campground.

Courtesy of Warner Springs

Courtesy of Carlsbad Spa

814   WARNER SPRINGS RANCH

31652 Hwy. 79   760 782-4200
■   Warner Springs, CA 92086
www.warnersprings.com

Private upscale destination resort in rural northeastern San Diego County. Elevation 3,100 feet. Open all year.

Natural mineral water flows out at 130-140° into an Olympic-size swimming pool where it is cooled to 102° and a hot soaking pool. A cool freshwater pool is adjacent to the hot pool. Bathing suits are required. Handicap accessible.

Facilities include 234 early California style casitas, sauna, spa, equestrian center, golf, tennis, restaurants, and an airport. Spa services can be booked ahead. There are no phones or TVs in the rooms. Major credit cards accepted. Conference facilities. Phone for rates, reservations, and directions.

815   THE TUBS

7220 El Cajon Blvd.   619 698-7727
❑   San Diego, CA 92115

San Diego's original rent-a-tub establishment, located on a main suburban street near San Diego State University.

Eleven spa suites for rent to the public use gas-heated tap water that is treated with chlorine and maintained at 102°. Saunas are included in all rooms as are showers, towels, and body shampoo. Each suite is equipped with an AM/FM stereo cassette player. The VIP Suite, large enough for twelve people, has a bathroom, a steambath, a sauna, and includes a VCR and TV.

A juice bar is available on the premises. Credit cards accepted. Phone for rates, reservations, and directions.

816   CARLSBAD MINERAL WATER SPA

2802 Carlsbad Blvd.   760 434-1887
■   Carlsbad, CA 92008
www.carlsbadmineralspa.com

Historic mineral water spa and therapeutic baths located on the site of an 1880s health spa and hotel. The original spa (and entire town) was named for the famous Karlsbad health resort in Bohemia which has a similar mineral water content. Open all year.

Carbonated mineral water from an aquifer 1,700 feet deep is recharged from the Cleveland National Forest, sixty miles east of Carlsbad. No chemicals are necessary as a fresh bath is drawn for each customer.

Each room is lavishly decorated using an Egyptian-Roman or Oriental theme. They also bottle and sell their mineral water.

Services include carbonated mineral water baths, mud or clay facials, total-body clay, aromatherapy, massage, body wraps, and special spa packages. Credit cards accepted. Phone for rates and reservations.

817   NEPTUNE'S LAGOONS

2784 W. Ball Rd.   714 761-8325
❑   Anaheim, CA 92804

Modern, suburban pool-rental facility near Disneyland and Knott's Berry Farm. Open Monday to Saturday.

Private-space hot pools using gas-heated tap water are treated with chlorine. There are four indoor fiberglass pools with water temperatures maintained at 101-104°. Three of the rooms have saunas.

Each room has a hydrojet tub with bubble controls, a dimmer for lights, air conditioning, relaxation bed, shower, towels, hair dryer, tape player, and sky light. Each room as an AM/FM cassette player. TV and VCR are available. Handicap accessible.

All major credit and ATM cards are accepted. Phone for rates, reservations, and directions.

Courtesy of Beverly Hot Springs

Courtesy of Puddingstone Resort

The deluxe pool is a memorable choice for that special occasion. Other pools, all with magnificent views, are just perfect whether you bring along the kids or it is only you and a friend.

819   PUDDINGSTONE HOT TUBS RESORT
1777 Camper View Rd.   909 592-2222
❏   San Dimas, CA 91773
www.hottubsresort.com

A one-of-a-kind hot tub rental facility that offers both privacy and spectacular views, located in Bonelli County Regional Park twenty-five miles east of Los Angeles. All tubs are built on a hillside overlooking Puddingstone Lake and the valley towards Los Angeles..

Twelve regular and eight deluxe hot tubs are available for hourly rental. The regular tubs hold up to six people while deluxe tubs can accommodate ten people. All tubs have an excellent view of the sunset and are enclosed on three sides for privacy. Each tub has its own changing room and water temperature controls. They provide candlelight, a CD player, and all tubs have air jets. This picturesque location provides a romantic atmosphere for couples. Bistro-style table and chairs are alongside all the tubs. The resort offer a variety of desserts along with "special occasion" packages including roses, balloons, and cider, perfect for an intimate picnic. All facilities are handicap accessible.

You are also welcome to bring your own picnic basket and enjoy a unique and unforgettable outing with family and friends. An RV park, golf course, horse stables, boat rentals, and Raging Waters recreation area are available in the adjoining regional park.

View our website or call for rates, reservations, and directions.

818   BEVERLY HOT SPRINGS
308 N. Oxford Ave.   213 734-7000
■   Los Angeles, CA 90004
www.beverlyhotsprings.com

A modern, Korean-style, indoor spa built over a hot water artesian well a few miles west of downtown Los Angeles. Elevation 300 feet. Open all year.

From a well drilled in the early 1900s, the only 100% pure alkaline mineral water in Los Angeles, flows out at a temperature of 105° and is piped to large, tiled, soaking pools equipped with hydrojets in the women's section (first floor) and the men's section (second floor). Each section also has a pool of cooled mineral water. All pools operate on a continuous flow-through basis so that no chemical treatment of the water is necessary and temperatures range from 96-105°. Bathing suits are not required in pool rooms.

Facilities include a dry sauna and a steam sauna in each section, plus a restaurant and beauty salon. Shiatsu massage, cream massage, and body scrubs are available on the premises. Visa and MasterCard accepted. Phone for rates, reservations, and directions.

820 GLEN IVY HOT SPRINGS SPA

■ 25000 Glen Ivy Road 951 277-1202
Corona, CA 92883 888 CLUB-MUD
www.glenivy.com

Continually expanding, beautifully landscaped day-use resort and spa located on the dry east side of the Santa Ana mountains seventy miles from Los Angeles. Elevation 1,300 feet. Open all year, except Thanksgiving, Christmas, and Easter Sunday. (You must be over sixteen years of age to be admitted.)

Natural mineral water from two wells at 90° and 110° is mixed and piped to a wide variety of pools. There are seven sunken hydrojet tubs with temperatures of 104-106°, using continuous flow-through, unchlorinated mineral water. Individual whirlpool baths are are now available. The other pools have automatic filters and chlorinators. An outdoor swimming pool is maintained at 85°, a covered soaking pool at 103°, two outdoor hydropools at 101° and 104°, two outdoor shallow bubble pools at 103° and 100°, a large outdoor floating pool at 90°, and a California red clay-bath pool at 100°. (Guests should bring an old bathing suit to wear in the mud bath as the clay does stain some fabrics.) Bathing suits required.

Facilities include a shop, men's and women's locker rooms equipped with hair blowers, a coed dry sauna, and cafe. An expanded spa facility offers treatments including Swedish, shiatsu, and aromatherapy massage, eucalyptus wraps, apricot body scrubs, European facials, manicures, pedicures and waxings for persons over eighteen. Advance reservations for these services are highly recommended. A new underground Grotto area offers aloevera and sea kelp body treatments with no reservations necessary. Entrance to the spa facilities and restroom are handicap accessible, but no attendants or lifts for the pools are provided. All major credit cards, ATMs, and personal checks accepted.

Directions: Eight miles south of Corona on I-15, exit right onto the Temescal Canyon Rd., pass Tom's Farms, then turn right onto Trilogy Parkway, left on Warm Springs Road. Continue right one Glen Ivy Road and follow the signs to the end.

BAJA CALIFORNIA

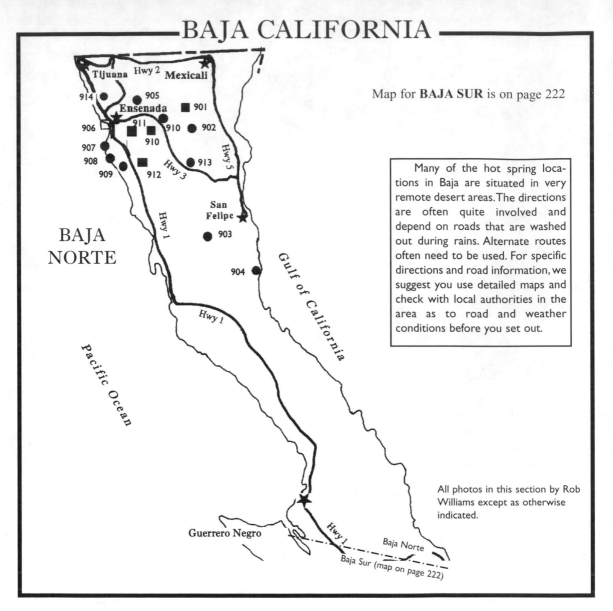

Tijuana
Hwy 2
Mexicali

914
905
Ensenada
901

906
911
910
902

907
910

908
913

909
912
Hwy 3
Hwy 5

Hwy 1

San Felipe
903

904

BAJA NORTE

Pacific Ocean

Gulf of California

Hwy 1

Guerrero Negro

Hwy 1
Baja Norte
Baja Sur (map on page 222)

Map for **BAJA SUR** is on page 222

Many of the hot spring locations in Baja are situated in very remote desert areas. The directions are often quite involved and depend on roads that are washed out during rains. Alternate routes often need to be used. For specific directions and road information, we suggest you use detailed maps and check with local authorities in the area as to road and weather conditions before you set out.

All photos in this section by Rob Williams except as otherwise indicated.

This map was designed to be used with a standard highway map.

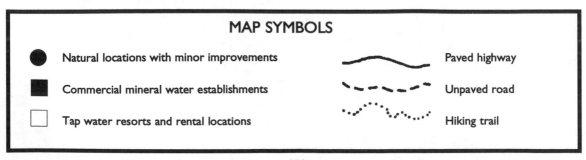

MAP SYMBOLS

● Natural locations with minor improvements

■ Commercial mineral water establishments

□ Tap water resorts and rental locations

∿ Paved highway

- - - Unpaved road

⋯ Hiking trail

901 GUADALUPE CANYON HOT SPRINGS

■ **Southwest of Mexicali**
www.guadalupe-canyon.com

Beautiful mineral water soaking pools, waterfalls, and campsites in a remote palm canyon on the east slope of the Sierra Juarez Mountains. Elevation 1,300 feet. Open all year. Best time to visit is from October to June. Reservations required for all weekends and holidays. Bookings begin three months in advance. For campground reservations email Rob williams at CanyonmanRob @earthlink.net.

Natural mineral water emerges from several springs at 125° and flows through man-made aqueducts to pools and flush toilets. More than twenty drainable soaking pools, built of rocks and cement, are scattered through palm forests and piles of boulders. Bathing suits are required except at night.

Arturo's Campo 1 has ten deluxe camps with private hot tubs, palapas, some with fireplaces, sinks and tile counter tops. Small store in campground. No electricity and no telephones. No ice or gas for sale in the camp. All services are sixty miles away in Mexicali. Ancient Indian caves, cascading waterfalls, and thick palm forests are within hiking distance. Other palm canyons may be explored for primitive hot springs, but the use of an experienced guide is recommended.

Directions (via Tecate): From San Diego go East on Hwy 94 approximately 40 miles. Turn south on Tecate Rd. (188) and go 1.3 miles to the border crossing (open 6 AM to midnight). Four blocks past the border, turn left on Mexico Hwy 2. Travel east 41 miles to La Rumorosa (last chance for gas). Just east of La Rumorosa you will begin the winding descent to the desert. At approximately 65 miles from Tecate you will see a large highway sign for Guadalupe Canyon. Turn right onto partially paved/dirt road. Road is mostly "wash board" with some bad dips. Drive past the Olive Plantation and turn right at mile 27. Last part is slower and last two miles is very bad. A high clearance vehicle is recommended and a 4 WD is a good idea. Take the right fork at the information sign. The office for Campo 1 is one-half mile.

GPS: N 32 09.504 W 115 46.224

Half the fun when you get to Guadalupe Canyon is trying to decide which camping area and which pools you like best.

Top photo: Rob Williams
Bottom Photo: Camilla Van Sickle and Bill Pennington

The water in the source pool is over 140 degrees. It is a good idea to go over 300 feet downstream and make a pool where the temperature is closer to 105 degrees.

902   PALOMAR CANYON HOT SPRINGS

● **Southwest of Mexicali**

Small wilderness hot springs in a remote palm canyon on the east slope of the Sierra Juarez Mountains, 45 miles from the nearest paved road. Elevation 1,725 feet. Open all year, but summer temperatures often reach 110°.

Natural mineral water bubbles out of three small source pools at 98° and then sinks into the sand as it flows down the canyon. A small cement pool at 96° is good for bathing but is only eighteen inches deep. A large rock and cement pool at 85° degrees has just been built. At this remote location, the apparent local clothing custom is the mutual consent of those present.

There are no facilities or services, but there is an all-year cold water stream in the canyon and excellent camping locations for backpackers. Four-wheel drive is required on the last few miles of the access road, and the springs are a two-hour hike up the canyon beyond the end of the road.

GPS: N 31 56.25 W 115 45.06

903   VALLE CHICO HOT SPRINGS

● **Southwest of San Felipe**

A remote, primitive hot spring in a barren canyon in the eastern escarpment of the Sierra San Pedro Martir. Elevation 2,041 feet. Open all year, but summer temperatures often exceed 110°.

Natural mineral water bubbles out of a large source pool at 144° and flows across the canyon into a year-round cold water stream. Volunteers could build a soaking pool at that confluence but have not yet done so. At this remote location, the apparent clothing custom is the mutual consent of those present.

There are no services at this location.
GPS: N 30 38.85 W 115 12.41

The tiny pueblo of Puertocitos does provide such necessary services as gas, vehicle repair, a small store, campsites, a restaurant, fishing, and boat ramps.

904   PUERTOCITOS HOT SPRINGS
On the Gulf of California

● **South of San Felipe**

Geothermal water bubbles up from under volcanic rock along the edge of the Sea of Cortez and collects in waist-deep soaking pools that are under water during high tide and useable only several hours each day during low tide. Elevation sea level. Open all year, although summer air temperature can soar above 110°.

Natural mineral water flows up through the gravel bottom of the soaking pools that have been blasted out of the volcanic rock. Two rectangular pools are large enough for a dozen people each; while a third round pool can accommodate six people. Pool temperatures vary widely, depending on the mix of geothermal water and sea water. There is only a brief time each low tide when the mixture makes it possible to soak. Bathing suits are recommended.

There are no services at this location. It is 0.25 miles to all services in the tiny pueblo of Puertocitos. Services include gas (honk your horn 8 AM to 8 PM for service), vehicle repair, a four-room hotel, small store for provisions, and campgrounds all along the Sea of Cortez south from San Felipe.

Directions: From the roundabout at the Pemex Station just past the arches in San Felipe, follow Hwy 5, which is the road toward the airport. At 6.4 miles take the turnoff toward Laguna Chapal, Percebu, and El Faro. Pay careful attention to signs along this road warning of "vados" (dips), which are deep, steep, and imperceptible until you are upon them. It is 53 miles from the roundabout in San Felipe to the town of Puertocitos, where the paved road ends.

In Puertocitos, just before the Pemex station, turn left toward the pink entranceway marked "Private Property: Puertocitos Hot Springs, boat ramp..." The owners collect a fee per person to go to the springs. At 0.2 miles past the gate, on the left is "Taller Panama," a large tin building where the dirt road veers to the right up a hill past the boat ramp. Follow this road for 0.6 miles to a cul-de-sac and turn around. The hot springs are in the tide pools on the right below a green building. There are parking turnouts on both sides of the road. There is a cement walkway through the volcanic rock down to the pools.

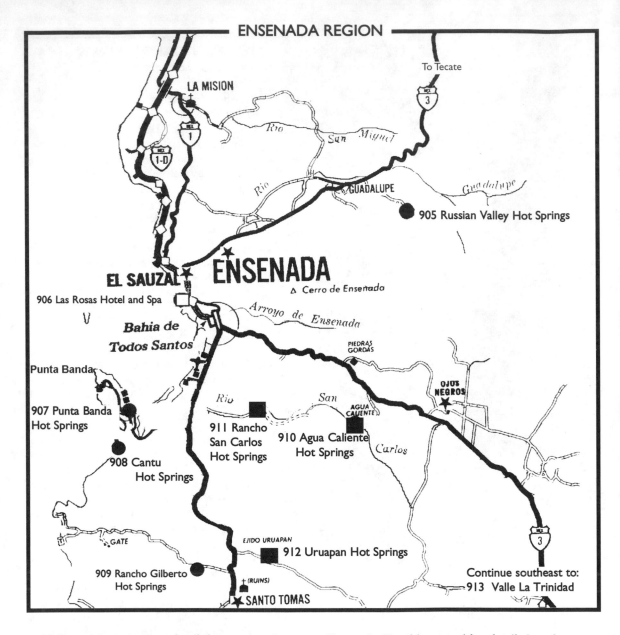

This map shows in more detail those springs in or near Ensenada. Use this map with a detailed road map.

As arid as this land appears, less than a quarter of a mile away is a lovely cold stream and waterfall.

905   RUSSIAN VALLEY HOT SPRINGS

(see map on page 214)

● **South of Tecate**

Several undeveloped wilderness hot springs near a beautiful waterfall in a remote valley that was named for an historic Russian settlement. Elevation 1,500 feet. Open all year. You are likely to be charged a small fee by the owners of the Rancho.

Natural mineral water flows from two main source springs at 125°. In one sandy-bottom pool, the geothermal water bubbles up from below and is cooled by evaporation to maintain the pool temperature at approximately 110°. The other source spring flows out of a sandy bank into a rock-lined pool where it is mixed with creek water and the temperature is controlled by moving rocks to admit cold water. In this remote location, the apparent local clothing custom is the mutual consent of those present.

There are no services on the premises, but there is a delightful cold pool and waterfall beside the access trail a quarter mile from the springs. All services are twenty five miles away in Ensenada.

The hot springs area is located fifty miles south of Tecate and ten miles east of Hwy 3. See map at right for detailed directions. A high clearance vehicle is needed past the rancho, but it's an easily walk in if your vehicle won't make it.

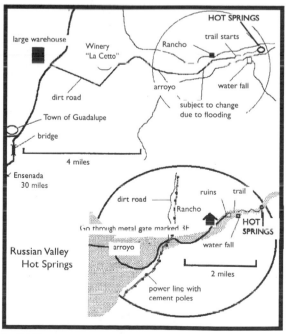

906 LAS ROSAS HOTEL & SPA

(see map on page 214)

Post Office Box 316 011-52-61-74-43-10

❑ Ensenada, Baja California, Mexico

A charming, upscale, small hotel/resort on the magnificent shoreline north of Ensenada. Elevation sea level. Open all year.

Tap water, heated with propane, is used in a seaside pool maintained at 80° and in a hydrojet spa maintained at 104°. Bathing suits are required. Pools are available for day use except during the busiest summer months. Inquire by telephone to determine current status.

Rooms, restaurant, fitness center, and racquetball court are available on the premises. It is two miles to all other services in Ensenada. Visa and MasterCard are accepted.

Directions: From Tijuana, take the Hwy 1 toll road south for 60 miles to Las Rosas, which is 2 miles north of Ensenada.

907 PUNTA BANDA HOT SPRINGS

Estero Beach (see map on page 214)

● **On the Punta Banda Peninsula**

A unique opportunity to literally dig your own hot spring pool at low tide on an easily accessible beach south of Ensenada. Elevation sea level. Open all year.

Natural mineral water (up to 170°) bubbles up through many yards of beach sand. During high tide swimmers can feel the extra warmth in the surf. During low tide it is possible to dig pools in the beach sand. These fill with a soakable combination of hot mineral water and cold sea water. Bathing suits are required.

Parking is available in the adjoining trailer camp, which offers its tenants hot mineral water piped from geothermal wells on the premises. It is eight miles to all other services in Ensenada.

Directions: From Ensenada, drive south on Hwy 1 to Hwy 23 Maneadero. Turn right on the paved road for approximately 8 miles to the Agua Caliente Trailer Camp. This beach is also known as La Jolla and is near the Baja Beach and Tennis Club.

Soakers travel thirteen miles of very scenic, improved, dirt road, climbing to 2,000 feet before crossing the Punta Banda ridge and dropping to a remote beach on the Pacific Coast.

908   CANTU HOT SPRINGS
(see map on page 214)
● **South of the Punta Banda Peninsula**

A small pool at the edge of the ocean on a remote rocky beach just past Rancho Cantu. Elevation 20 feet. Open all year.

Natural mineral water flows from a small, 90° stream down an arroyo to a shallow, hand-made pool about 100 yards from the beach. You may need to do some further digging to enlarge the pool to your specifications. Due to the remote location, clothing is optional.

There is free camping on the windswept bluffs, fifty feet above the beach. There are no services on the premises, and it is thirty miles (one hour driving time) back to Ensenada. This is a good area for fishing, diving, and surfing.

Directions: Take Hwy 23 0.5 miles past La Jolla Beach and turn left onto graded dirt road. There is a sign for Ej. Cantu. The dirt road winds up the mountain and crosses over the top, then drops down to the Pacific Coast. Note the kilometer markers (small cement posts on the side of road).

909   RANCHO GILBERTO/
ST. TOMAS HOT SPRINGS
(see map on page 214)
● **South of Ensenada**

Hot water comes up in several locations in a small stream which flows down into a valley near Santo Tomas and is surrounded by farming areas and tree-covered hillsides. Elevation 500 feet. Open all year.

Natural mineral water flows up from the streambed at 100° in several places. You will need to dig your own pool and place rocks and sand around the edge to hold the water. Temperatures are regulated by mixing hot water with cold stream water. Bathing suits are required.

There are no services on the premises, but overnight parking is available at the farmhouse 100 yards away. It is fifteen miles to a campground at La Bocana Beach and four miles to a store and restaurant.

Directions: From Ensenada, travel 20 miles south on Highway 1. Turn right on the dirt road with a sign for La Bocana. Drive 4.1 miles on graded dirt road toward the ocean. Rancho is on the left side, no sign.

The only way to find out where the hot water comes up in this stream is to feel for it. Then, build yourself a pool to soak in.

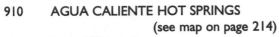

910   AGUA CALIENTE HOT SPRINGS
(see map on page 214)

■   **East of Ensenada**

An older commercial hot springs "resort" located in an arid valley five miles south of Hwy 3. Elevation 1,500 feet. Open all year, but the bar and restaurant are open only during April through August.

Natural mineral water flows out of several springs at temperatures ranging from 80 to 108°. The warmest source spring supplies 108° water to the bathhouse tubs, which are drained and filled after each use. It also flows directly into a large concrete outdoor soaking pool which maintains a temperature of 97°. Water from the coolest spring is piped to a large swimming pool at a temperature of 75° which is drained and filled every week. No chemical treatment is added. Water from a third spring at 97° is piped to the motel rooms, bar, and restaurant as tap water. Bathing suits are required except in individual tubs.

Motel rooms (somewhat run down) with bar and restaurant service operating during spring and summer months only. It is sixteen miles to all other services in Ensenada.

Directions: (Do not attempt in wet weather.) From Ensenada, drive east on Hwy 3 to marker KM 26. Watch for "AGUA CALIENTE" sign and turn right on a 5-mile dirt road that ends at the resort. Not recommended for trailers or low clearance vehicles.

As there is no telephone or mailing address, it is not possible to secure reservations. It is very crowded during Easter vacation.

911 RANCHO SAN CARLOS HOT SPRINGS
(see map on page 214)

■ **South of Ensenada**

Very popular weekend and vacation spot, especially during the summer, set in a nicely wooded canyon. Open all year; road may be impassable during wet weather.

Natural hot mineral water at 110° comes out of the source pool which is built into the side of a cliff. The water is piped to a large cement pool about forty feet in diameter and three to four feet deep. In the summer the pool is around 102°. A year-around cold stream has been damned up to create a cool pool adjacent to the large pool. There is also a mud bath and one small soaking pool beside the stream. Bathing suits required.

A campground in a narrow and pretty part of the canyon is open although there is no electricity or phones and it is not possible to make reservations. Bath, tubs, and showers are also available. A small store sells soda and wood and small fires are permitted. It is best to come during the week or weekends in the winter as it is can be very crowded.

Directions: Drive south of Ensenada approximately 5 miles. Turn left after crossing La Puente San Carlos (San Carlos Bridge). There is a traffic light and it is the entrance for the Baja Country Club golf course. Drive 1.5 miles on this 2 lane paved road, then turn left onto a dirt road where there is a sign for Rancho San Carlos hot springs. Make the first right and continue up the wash which becomes a wooded canyon. There will be a total of 10 water crossings. It is 9.3 miles before the dirt road ends at the hot springs.

912   URUAPAN (AQUA TERMALES) HOT SPRINGS

(see map on page 214)

■   **South of Ensenada**

A well-worn combination bathhouse and laundry in a green fertile valley at the base of coastal scrub foothills two miles from Hwy 1. About thirty miles before Ensenada. Elevation 678 feet. Open all year. Heavily used by the locals, particularly on Sundays.

Natural mineral water flows out of many pastureland springs at temperatures ranging from 108 to 138° and is piped to a fifty-year-old building with five individual bath-tub rooms and five outdoor washing machines. Larger size tubs, three, four, can accommodate two persons, and room five is big enough for five or six. Clearly, the tubs at about 104° are for cleanliness bathing, not recreational soaking, and clothing is optional only in private spaces.

There is also a very nice picnic area near Highway 1.

Directions: From Mexico Hwy 1, turn off in Ejido Uruapan, 23 miles south of Ensenada and 12.7 miles south of Maneadero onto paved road. Turn left at school (1.09 miles), right in 0.01 miles and follow good signs to spring.

GPS: N 31 37.75 W 115 43.68

Uruapan is a great place to stop when returning from a long trip in Baja to enjoy a good bath in good, clean, sulfur-free water. You can also wash your clothes—all for $1.00.

The photo below is one of the three pools at *Valle de Trinidad*.

913   VALLE DE TRINIDAD/RANCHO LOS POZITOS

(see map on facing page)

●   **Southeast of Ensenada**

Three sandy bottomed, semi-developed pools, at the headwaters of a stream in an open valley. Surrounded by small hills, low mountains, and agricultural lands in the midst of old ranchos. Elevation 2,800 feet. Open all year.

Natural mineral water flows up from the bottom of the first pool at 105°. This eight-foot square pool has a sandy bottom, brick walls, and tin roof. The second pool is lined with rocks and located in the middle of the stream. In the third, water flows into a six-foot square brick pool. Bathing suits are required even though there is a metal wall around each tub for privacy.

Overnight parking is permitted at the farm house about 100 yards away. It is five miles to a store, restaurant and other services.

Directions: Go east from Ensenada on Highway 3 about 60 miles. Turn right toward Valle De Trinidad on paved road. After 1 mile turn right onto dirt road at church. Continue 2 miles toward west end of valley and follow dirt road about 5 miles with some signs for San Isidoro. Look for Rancho Los Pozitos, Family Arballo.

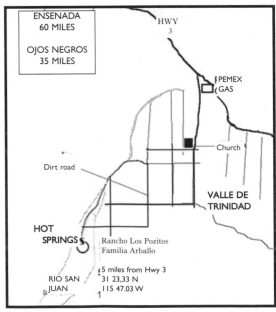

Families, and specially the children, enjoy a cooling soak in one of the three tubs at *Valle de Trinidad*, located in a hot, arid valley.

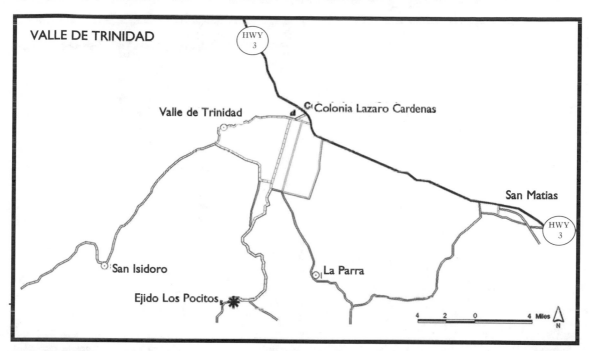

VALLE DE TRINIDAD

914   MISSION SAN BORJA HOT SPRINGS

● **East of the town of Rosarito**

A small, historic source pool on the grounds of a well-preserved mission in a remote and enchanting part of the Sierra La Libertad. Elevation 2,200 feet. Open all year.

Natural mineral water at 96° flows out of a rock-lined source pool built by the missionaries in the early 1800s. It is located at the edge of the mission cornfields, a five-minute walk southeast from the main building. The runoff from the spring was commingled with a nearby cold stream to water the mission's fields. Bathing suits are required.

There are no facilities or services, but camping is permitted anywhere among the ruins of the old mission buildings.

Directions: At Rosarito, from Hwy 1, turn east on a dirt road for 21 miles. There will be no sign for the mission, but there are two ranchos on the way, and the road ends in a remote valley where the mission is located.

BAJA SUR

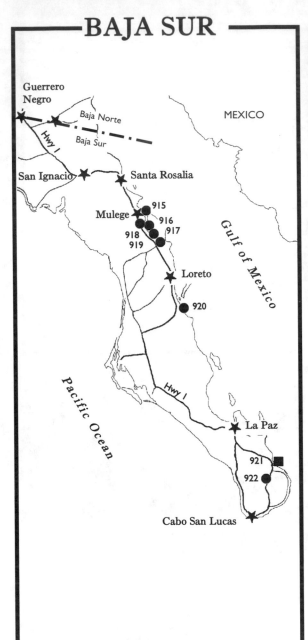

Guerrero Negro

Baja Norte

Baja Sur

MEXICO

Hwy 1

San Ignacio
Santa Rosalia

Mulege
915
916
918 917
919

Gulf of Mexico

Loreto

920

Pacific Ocean

Hwy 1

La Paz

921
922

Cabo San Lucas

915   MULEGE MISSION WARM SPRINGS

● **Near the town of Mulege**

Warm water springs found in the middle of a stream creating a jungle-like oasis complete with fan palms and ponds surrounded by desert and a view of the mountains. Elevation 50 feet. Open all year.

Natural mineral water bubbles up through the sand into the cool streambed at 90°, creating an interesting effect as you sit in the stream. Bathing suits are required.

There are no services on the premises. It is two miles to a campground and one mile to all other services in Mulege.

Directions: Park at the mission and walk downhill. Cross stream in front of the dam. Continue 100 yards downstream; gas bubbles can be seen rising in the stream. Suggestion: On Hwy 1 at Mulege, ask for Arcadio Valle Somora at the ABC Bus Station and hire him to guide you.

This squishy-bottom pool at Santispac Beach is located above the tide line, so it is available for soaking all day.

916   SANTISPAC BEACH

●   **South of Mulege, on Concepcion Bay**

Two squishy-bottom soaking pools built by volunteers near a mangrove swamp on the edge of the bay. Elevation sea level. Open all year.

Natural mineral water oozes up through the rock-encircled mud bottom of one source spring, maintaining a temperature of 106° except when flooded by high tide. A second source spring, on slightly higher ground, has been excavated by volunteers to create a squishy-bottom pool that maintains a temperature of 102°. Bathing suits are required.

Santispac Beach is a popular RV and camping destination on the Sea of Cortez. Camping is $5 per car per night, and there is a small restaurant on the beach. All other services are ten miles north in Mulege.

Directions: From Mulege, drive 10 miles south on Hwy 1 and turn left into the commercial parking and camping ground. Drive to the far right side of the cove, to a small area for parking, and walk approximately 100 yards on a dirt trail around the mangrove swamp to the two pools.

917   CONCEPCION BEACH

●   **South of Mulege, on Concepcion Bay**

On the edge of a beautiful bay, very hot water flows from rock fissures into rock and sand pools which are usable only when the high tide brings cold water for mixing. Elevation sea level. Open all year.

Natural mineral water flows out of cracks above the high tide line at more than 135° into volunteer-built soaking pools on the beach below. Twice a day the high tide supplies enough cold water to bring the pool temperatures down to tolerable soaking levels. Bathing suits are required.

Directions: There are no direct routes down the steep cliffs that border this beach. Therefore, it is necessary to hike south along the tide pools from Santispac Beach (see 916) or north from Los Cocos Beach.

Since these pools require cold ocean water to cool them down to a soakable temperature, it would be a good idea to bring along a tide table to figure out when to expect a high tide.

918   EL COYOTE WARM SPRING

● **South of Mulege, on Concepcion Bay**

A small permanent soaking pool in a fantastic setting on the edge of Concepcion Bay. Elevation sea level. Open all year.

Natural mineral water seeps into a tide pool at the base of a cliff. Volunteers have built a rock-and concrete wall around the tide pool, which maintains a temperature of 86° at low tide. Small shrimp have been observed in the warm, partly salty water. Bathing suits are required.

The camping fee at El Coyote Beach is $10 per night, but there is no additional fee for using the hot spring. There are no other facilities at the beach, but there is a restaurant at Rancho El Coyote across the highway. All other services are seventeen miles away in Mulege.

Directions: From Mulege, drive 17 miles south on Hwy 1 to the El Coyote Beach commercial campground. Park and follow a rocky trail 100 yards to the pool.

Waiting for the tide to go out so that you can build a pool where the hot water seeps up through the sand.

919   BUENA VENTURA HOT SPRINGS

● **South of Mulege, on Concepcion Bay**

Build your own pool in Concepcion Bay as hot water flows up through the sand at low tide on this beach twenty-five miles south of Mulege. Elevation sea level. Open year round.

Natural mineral water at 100° pushes up through various spots in the sand at low tide, just waiting for someone to build a small soaking pool with the available rocks. The apparent local custom is clothing optional.

The Playa Buenaventura Hotel and Restaurant is nearby. It is twenty-five miles to all other services in Mulege.

Suggestion: See Mike at the Playa Buenaventura Hotel and Restaurant for boat rentals and for progress on future plans to build a hot pool.

920   AGUA VERDE HOT SPRINGS

● **Near Agua Verde, south of Loreto**

Two pools in the Sea of Cortez, surrounded by a very rocky coastline and panoramic ocean views. Elevation sea level. Open all year.

Natural mineral water percolates up through the sand into two large eight-foot and ten-foot rock pools. The temperature at low tide in the upper pool is 110° and 105° in the lower pool. High tide covers the pools. The apparent local custom is clothing optional.

There are no services available on the premises, but overnight parking is permitted (watch the tides). It is 200 yards to the nearest campground and thirty miles to all other services. This is a very good area for snorkeling.

Directions: Go 29 miles south of Loreto and turn at sign for Agua Verde. Go another 12 miles and take the first turn onto the beach. Go north on beach 1 mile. You must wait for low tide to drive to the site.

Along with some of the best diving, spectacular views, and an oceanside campground, there are two large soaking pools available at low tide.

921   HOTEL BUENA VISTA RESORT
PO Box 574   800 731-4914
■   La Paz, Baja California Sur, Mexico

This full destination resort is located on the coast between the Baja desert and the Sea of Cortez, southeast of La Paz. Elevation sea level. Open all year.

Natural mineral water flows up from several wells at 180° into pools that are drained and refilled once a week. The large swimming pool, with a swim-up bar, is maintained at 80°, and a smaller swimming pool is 80-100°. There is also a hydropool. All three use an ion filtration system. Hot water also seeps up on the beach next to the hotel at low tide. The pools are open to the public for day use for a charge. Bathing suits are required.

Luxurious rooms, tennis courts, gift shop, a restaurant, and entertainment on Saturday nights are available on the premises. The hotel also has its own fishing fleet. Deep sea fishing is legendary in this area. Major credit cards are accepted. Phone for rates, reservations, and directions.

922   AGUA CALIENTE (SANTIAGO) HOT SPRINGS

●   **Near the town of Santiago**

Mountains and trees surround two small hot pools located in a canyon with fresh water streams and cold pools. Elevation 900 feet. Open all year.

Natural mineral water at 115° flows into a two-foot by three-foot source pool and then through a ditch to a three-foot by four-foot pool big enough for one or two people, where the water has cooled to 108°. The only way to further cool this tub is to block up or divert the water flow. The apparent local custom is clothing optional.

There are no services on the premises, but there is room for three or four cars to park overnight. It is seven miles to all other services.

Directions: From the town of Santiago, go east 5 miles to the town of Agua Caliente. Continue east 1.5 miles to Rancho El Chorro. Pass the nature preserve (El Santuario) 0.5 miles, then go 0.3 miles further to the end of the road and the springs.

HAWAII
The Big Island

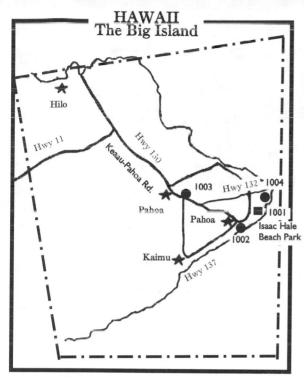

This map was designed to be used with a standard highway map.

MAP SYMBOLS

● Natural location with minor improvements

■ Commercial mineral water establishments

□ Tap water resorts and rental locations

Paved highway

Unpaved road

Hiking trail

You would think that with all the volcanic activity that created the chain of islands known as Hawaii hot springs would be prevalent over all the islands. Actually the only island that has any soakable pools is the Big Island which supports numerous springs—most of them warm, hardly qualifying as hot. (At this point, steam vents and caves, which are very hot, are being counted as hot springs.) Many of the springs are on private land or inaccessible; many appear and disappear with the tides, and even the steam vents are not always able to be accessed due to excessive heat and location. This section is based on the reports of Skip Hill, publisher of the *Hot Springs Gazette*; Oscar Voss, a dedicated hot springs soaker who wrote that Hawaii ought to be in the book, and then provided the information; Philip Maise, who owns the guesthouse near the steam vent; my friends Shea and Jerry Moss; and the super friendly people who once owned the Hale Kia O Kiana guest-house. Thanks to all of you.

The "Red Road" referred to in the directions is the meandering coastal road from Kaimu to Kapoho that winds along one of the most beautiful coast lines in the world. Pack a lunch, take a good book, your fishing rod, and enjoy the day.

While you may come across some warm shallow ponds off the beaten path, you should use a great deal of discretion when taking off your clothes. The native Hawaiians are very offended by nudity. It is illegal in most areas and you can be heavily fined. I understand that there is an explicit anti-nudity regulation covering the entire state park system, but no similar regulation for Hawaii county parks, which might lower the legal hazards. The steam vents are customarily clothing optional. Kehena is a clothing optional beach, pictured below.

Courtesy of Hale Kipa O Kiana

Just another beautiful beach with blue skies and white surf. Only at Kehena is clothing optional okay.

1001   AHALANUI WARM SPRING AND PARK

■   **East of the town of Pahoa   808 961-8311**
(Phone number for Hawaii County Parks and
Recreation in Hilo, no phone on site)

Ahalanui, sometimes called the "Hot Pond", a large saltwater pool next to the ocean, in Ahalanui County Park, about a mile northeast of Pohoiki Hot Spring on the Puna Coast southeast of Hilo. (This is part of the Isaac Hale Beach Park and managed by the Department of Parks and Recreation for the County of Hawaii.) Elevation sea level. Open all year.

Ground water, heated by the Kilauea volcano, flows toward the sea where it comes in through cracks in the lava bed up through the sandy bottom of the large rock and concrete pool that covers about one-half acre. The pool has an outlet to the ocean which allows sea water to mix with the spring water. A concrete and lava sea wall and canal protect the pool from the ocean waves and provides fresh saltwater during high tide. Pool depths vary from two to eight feet, depending on tide levels and whether you are in the shallow or deep end, but are usually around five feet. The water temperature ranges greatly all the way from 80° up into the nineties. The area is wheelchair accessible with paved walkways. Bathing suits required.

The pool is open 7 AM to 7 PM and has a full-time lifeguard on duty. Alcoholic beverages, dogs, and unattended children are not allowed. There are group kiosks for family barbeques, more picnic tables, toilets and showers. Other services are in Pahoa, about eight miles inland.

Lava rocks and boulders can be encountered underwater in the center of the pond, and the only wildlife tends to be around the rocks.

Directions: From Hilo, take route 11 south 7 miles toward Keaau. Just north of Keaau turn left (east) onto route 130 (known as the Keaau-Pahoa Rd.) toward Pahoa. Travel about 10 miles to the junction with route 132 (the Pahoa-Kapoho Rd.) on the east side of Pahoa. Turn left (east) onto route 132. After 2.5 miles, there is a sign for the turnoff to Pohoiki. Go straight ahead and take the turnoff to the right (instead of left to stay on route 132). The road is paved but narrow, sometimes one lane. Continue straight ahead for 4.7 miles from the junction with route 130, and where the pavement ends, passing an unmarked turnoff for route 137 (the "Red Road") at mile 4.5, you will come to the entrance to Isaac Hale Beach Park. Turn left (northeast) after mile marker 9, away from Isaac Hale. Continue about 0.8 miles. The park entrance will be on the right (toward the ocean).

From points along the coast, take route 137 (the "Red Road") to the park entrance at mile 10.6. To the east of the pool are several warm springs that vary in temperature. They are more private and secluded but most are very shallow.

Note: If the parking lot is full, park off the road along the fence, but be careful where you park, as route 137 in front of the park entrance is very narrow. As with any tourist destination in Hawaii, to reduce the risk of vehicle break-in, do not leave valuables in your car. Also, do not park under a coconut tree—they can drop any time and cause severe dents in the top of your car.

1002   POHOIKI HOT SPRING (POHOIKI WARM POND)

● **East of the town of Pahoa 808-961-8311**
(Phone for Hawaii County Parks and
Recreation in Hilo, no phone on site)

Soaking pool about twenty yards from the ocean and
an easy walk from the highway, in Isaac Hale Beach Park
(county), off Pohoiki Bay on the Puna coast of Hawaii's Big
Island southeast of Hilo. Elevation sea level. Open all year.

Ground water heated by the Kilauea volcano flows
toward the sea, where it mixes with ocean water seeping
inshore, and rises to fill a natural pool. The source comes
in and around the lava boulders on the uphill end of the
pool. The pool is approximately twenty-feet long by ten-
feet wide by four-feet deep (depth fluctuates by a foot or
so with the tides), with a temperature of about 98°. The
pool is next to a rocky beach popular with surfers, and is
near houses, so bathing suits are advisable.

The spring is within 400 feet of the boat ramp in Isaac
Hale Beach Park, where there are portable toilets and an
emergency phone. Other services are available in Pahoa,
about eight miles inland.

Directions: From Hilo, take route 11 south about 7
miles toward Keaau. Just north of Keaau, turn left (east)
onto route 130 toward Pahoa. Travel about 10 miles, to
the junction with route 132 on the east side of Pahoa,
Turn left (east) onto route 132. After 2.5 miles, there is a
sign for the turnoff to Pohoiki. Go straight ahead onto
the turnoff (instead of left to stay on route 132). The road
is paved but narrow, sometimes one lane.   Continue
straight ahead for 4.7 miles from the junction with route
130), passing an unmarked turnoff for route 137 at mile
4.5, to a "T" intersection at the entrance to Isaac Hale
Beach Park. Turn right into one of the parking areas on
either side of the boat ramp. From the boat ramp, follow
the path to the right, heading southwest along the shore.
The spring will be about 400 feet from the boat ramp, on
the right.

From points along the coast, take route 137 (the "Red
Road") to the Isaac Hale boat ramp at mile 11.4, then follow the directions above from the boat ramp.

As with any tourist destination in Hawaii, to reduce
the risk of vehicle break-in, do not leave valuables in your
car.

GPS: N 19 27.492 W 154 50.602

Skip Hill, above in the white cap, made three new
friends from Sweden at *Pohoiki* and deemed it "a paradise." Thanks to Oscar Voss, pictured below, for all of
his photos and information.

Top photo by Skip Hill
Bottom photo by Oscar Voss

1003   PAHOA STEAM CAVES
(PAHOA STEAM VENTS)

● **Southeast of the town of Pahoa**

Natural steam caves and open-air steam vents, within an easy hike from the road, in the Keauohana Forest Reserve (state) on Hawaii's Big Island southeast of Hilo. Elevation about 800 feet. Open all year.

Several open-air steam vents, and two steam caves, are scattered in the forest within 500 feet of a parking area on a state highway. They reportedly were created less than fifty years ago, by volcanic activity along the east rift zone of the Kilauea volcano, and emit steam from super-heated groundwater. The most popular steam cave is the most distant (about 500 feet) from the highway, in the bottom of a volcanic "splatter cone," with a volunteer-provided ladder down into the cave and also a changing bench at the top. It is the hottest and most humid cave, with temperatures fluctuating from day-to-day but feeling like it's above the 150° range. It is about five-feet square inside by four-feet tall, with a small bench inside that holds three to four people. A second cave is cooler and less humid, and somewhat roomier, but with a smaller entrance. It has wood planks inside for people to sit on. The open-air vents also usually have wooden benches, with room for one person each. The apparent local custom is clothing optional.

The trails up into the basalt cones where the caves and vents are located can be steep and/or slippery, over volcanic rock that can cause nasty cuts if you fall. Also, stay close to the cave entrances so you can get out if the heat becomes unbearable. The area is open twenty-four hours a day, but there is no artificial lighting, so bring a flashlight and use caution if visiting at night. There reportedly is a significant risk of vehicle break-ins at night (even in the day, do not leave valuables in your car). There are no services on site. The nearest services are in Pahoa, about five miles away.

Photos by Oscar Voss

Directions: From Hilo, take route 11 south about 7 miles toward Keaau. Just north of Keaau, turn left (east) onto route 130 toward Pahoa. Travel past Pahoa, about 10 miles, and start looking for the mile markers along the right side of the road. Across the road from mile marker 15, there is a posted "scenic overlook," with room for several cars to park along the westbound side of the road. Park there, and look for steam from mounds of small basalt cones rising out of the foliage. A web of trails from the parking area connects the vents and caves. The most distant cave from the road is in the last and largest of the splatter cones (once there, you'll see a guesthouse on adjacent property, and a steamy black field marked "no trespassing"). The other vents and caves are between the last splatter cone and the road.

GPS: N 19 26.431, W 154 56.527 (hot and humid steam cave, the one most distant from the road); GPS: N 19 26.418, W 154 56.555 (the cooler and less humid cave, closer to the road).

The steam caves are open to the public and anybody can just park their car along Hwy 130 at mile marker 15 at the turnout and go to them.

Entrances to the caves include one where you climb down a ladder. One of the caves has benches to sit on.

1004   THE CHAMPAGNE POND

● **Near the town of Kapoho**

A thermally heated pool located in Beach Lots, a private, residential area off the coast of Kapoho. The pond and some beach area is open to the public. The remote and uncrowded area promotes turtles and other sea life to come here to relax and they will often swim alongside.

Three interconnected pools of seawater and fresh water are fed by volcanic hot spots. They are called The Champagne Pond because the heat rises as a gas and emits tiny bubbles during active periods. Temperatures range from 80-100° depending on ambient temperature. The pond is approximately 100 feet in length and is protected from the open ocean by a reef. During low tide the pond may be five- to eight-feet deep, and during high tide it is eight- to twelve-feet deep. Fins or water shoes are recommended as the pond bed and all the surrounding beaches are lava. Bathing suits required.

Directions: From Hwy 11 exit at Keaau. Go through town and turn onto Hwy 130 towards Kapoho and Pahoa. Drive several miles (about 20 minutes) to Pahoa and turn left onto Hwy 132, the Pahoa-Kaphoho Rd. Follow the signs to Kapoho. At the first fork, stay right. At the second fork (after Lava Trees Park) veer left. When you get to 137, (the left veer) the road becomes dirt and heads out towards the lighthouse. Keep your eyes peeled to the right for an unmarked, well-used track. Drive slowly and carefully as unmarked hazards such as potholes may exist. It is a good idea for one person to walk ahead of the vehicle and scout the track to eliminate dead ends. To the left is open ocean. Some less-used tracks lead to unmarked swimming holes that are accessible during low tide and protected by small reefs. The main track will end at the pond. Be careful and don't park on private property.

If you don't want to subject yourself and your vehicle to this heavily rutted, lava road, you can turn right onto Hwy 137 and drive about one-half mile to Kaphoho Beach Rd. and turn left. Drive to the locked gate and park off the road where you can do so safely. It is permissible to walk through the gate. Everything is private property except where the lava road comes into the pond. It is not a long walk to the pond. Walk to the right of the tennis court and stay on this road. Many small roads intersect. In about one-quarter of a mile you will come to a small pond on the right ringed about Palm and Ohio trees and signs saying that it is unlawful to harm turtles. You are almost there.

To the left of the second driveway is a poorly marked path that says "residents only". Most people will not bother you if you use this path respectfully. It squeezes past two bungalows. The ponds immediately in front and back of these bungalows are private. At the end of the short path is the entrance to the Champagne Pond, bordered by the crude rock sea wall. You can leave your towels along the seawall. Just across is a small heavily vegetated island. You can walk around this island and you will be on the beach where the road from the lighthouse ends. This is public beach. From the sea wall you can walk or float out the Champagne Pond. You will come out in the middle pool. To the right is the quiet pool where turtles sleep. To the left is a larger pool and the reef. Good swimmers can walk over the reef and swim to the right into Kapoho Bay. About 50 feet from shore is an old sea wall that is just under the surface. At low tide a tall person can walk along this wall and be waist deep in water.

Note: Before you come here be aware that this pool is surrounded by private property. Do not drive in the gate to the community and stay on the path when walking in. Be respectful of your surroundings.

GOING NATURAL IN PALM SPRINGS

❑ The following listings cover a growing industry in Palm Springs—going uncovered in lush, upscale surroundings. These clothing optional resorts have varying amenities, but all of them will arrange for airport pickup, are open all year, and accept credit cards. The pools use tap water and are gas heated and chlorine treated. Phone for rates, reservations, and directions.

Courtesy of Villa Escondida

MORNINGSIDE INN

888 N. Indian Canyon   760 325-2668
                            800 916-2668

Palm Springs, CA 92262
www.morningsideinn.com

Exclusive, secluded, clothing optional bed and breakfast for couples in the heart of Palm Springs.

Suites and cabana rooms are available. Suites contain fully equipped kitchens, and some have patios. The pool and spa, a covered workout area, and a massage table are available for your use along with a barbeque area. A misting system operates to keep customers comfortable all year around.

Snacks, afternoon sweet tray and beverages, and lunch on the weekends are available for your enjoyment.

VILLA ESCONDIDA

280 Mel Ave.   760 323-2676
Palm Springs, CA 92262   877-RELAX-US
www.villaescondida.com

Distinctive romantic hideaway rests on lush private grounds where the mission is to provide guests with a natural environment that enhances relaxation. Majestic mountain views and clear starry skies add to the ambiance.

A beautiful, large swimming pool and a spa, along with a misting system for those hot summer days encourage guests to relax and enjoy the gardens.

Eleven cabanas have been completely refurbished to meet the standards of a quality hotel. Nine rooms have well-stocked kitchenettes. All visitors are invited to use the communal barbecue and cooking area. Continental breakfast served daily. One room is fully handicap accessible. Massage available. Adult only policy.

Call for reservations.

Courtesy of Terra Cotta

Courtesy of Ballentines Hotel

"Palm Springs' Best Hideaway," according to *The Arizona Republic. Los Angeles Magazine* names it, "one of our four favorite resorts for couples in Palm Springs."

THE TERRA COTTA INN

2388 E. Racquet Club Rd.   760 322-6059
Palm Springs, CA 92262
www.sunnyfun.com

A premier clothing optional resort for couples surrounding a secluded, romantic garden. Situated on a private, colorful acre with magnificent mountain vistas.

A large, pristine pool is heated year-round, and the fifteen-person hydropool spa has fantastic mountain views. Both pool and spa are open twenty-four hours a day and are situated in a very spacious, private garden. The pool patio is micro-mist cooled for relaxing sunbathing in all temperatures.

The seventeen luxurious rooms are lavishly appointed. The charming grounds feature a private shade fountain retreat and several sun patios. A special suite is available with a private patio, sunken tub, and terrarium bathroom garden. Amenities include a sumptuous poolside breakfast, hot hors d'oeuvres in the afternoon, and pampering services such as massage and spa treatments.

Call or email (info@sunnyfun.com) for a free brochure, or check out the website for more information.

BALLENTINES

1420 N. Indian Canyon   760 320-1178
Palm Springs, CA 92262
www.ballentineshotels.com

The 50s retro look with an empahsis on vintage 50's kitsch lends a special ambiance to this small boutique hotel. Ideal place for romance or just to relax.

All fourteen rooms are differently themed with private patios. A poolside bar, lounge for reading, games, and private parties, and a private massage room (poolside) are there for your enjoyment.

If you want your very own party, or a party for a group of your friends, the entire facility can be rented.

Nudity is "topless only."

Photos courtesy of Desert Shadows

DESERT SHADOWS INN
RESORT AND VILLAS
1533 Chaparral   760 325-6410
Palm Springs, CA 92262

A secluded retreat for the discerning naturist with a magnificent view of the San Jacinto Mountains. Only minutes away from downtown Palm Springs.

Three grand pools are heated to 86°. The main pool has a waterfall created by jets of water flowing from three stone lions. The "quiet" pool has classical music playing softly in the background from behind flowering bougainvillea and citrus trees. The "villa" pool has three distinct entrances and steps for sitting comfortably in the crystal clear water. Two magnificent outdoor spas are heated to 102°. The original spa rests under a canopy complete with skylights for stargazing and is surrounded by a unique misting system. The second spa is 250 square feet in a free-form clover pattern making pockets for relaxing or socializing au naturel.

Choose from the private courtyard rooms, the main chaparral rooms or the two-story deluxe villas complete with private whirlpool baths. A full service restaurant on the property means you never have to leave the acres of lushly landscaped grounds. Steam room, massage, facials, hair salon, manicures and pedicures, and herbal body wraps are offered at the spa at Desert Shadows. A handicap accessible room is available.

GOING NATURAL—PLACES TO STAY

To help those of you who like to stay in places that cater to the naturist lifestyle, included is a list of clubs offering varying types of accommodations. Always call first to check on available amenities.

ARIZONA

Casa Blanca Hot Spring   casablancahotspring@mindspring.com
Tonopah, AZ

El Dorado Hot Springs   602 386-5412 (See listing in Arizona for full description)   PO Box 39, Tonopah, AZ 85354

Mira Vista Resort   521 744-2355
7501 N. Wade Road, Tucson, AZ 85743

Shangri La   623 465-5959, 800 465 8760
www.shangrilaranch.com
46834 N. Shangri La Rd., New River, AZ 85027

CALIFORNIA

De Anza Springs Resort   619 766-4301
www.deanzasprings.com
1951 Carrizo Gorge Rd. Jacumba, CA 91934

Deer Park Nudist Resort   909 880-0803 www.dpnr.com
1924 Glen Helen, San Bernardino, CA 92407

Glen Eden Sun Club   800 843-6833 www.gleneden.com
25999 Glen Eden Rd., Corona, CA 92883-5223

Laguna Del Sol   916 687-6550 www.lagunadelsol.com
8683 Rawhide Lane, Wilton, CA 95693

Lupin Lodge   408 353-9200 www.lupinlodge.org/tns
20600 Aldercroft Heights Rd., Los Gatos, CA 95033

Olive Dell Ranch   909 825-6619 www.olivedell.com
26520 Keissel Rd., Colton, CA 92324-9526

Sequoians Family Nudist Park   510 582-0194
10200 Cull Canyon Rd., Castro Valley, CA 94546

Silver Valley Sun Club   760 257-4239
www.silvervalleysunclub.com
48382 Silver Valley Rd., Newberry Springs, CA 92365

Sun Island Resort   619 445-3754
1631 Harbison Canyon Rd., El Cajon, CA 92019

COLORADO

Mountain Air Ranch   303 697-4083, 877 TRY-NUDE
PO Box 855, Indian Hills, CO 80455

HAWAII

The Banana Patch   808 322-888, 800 988-2246
PO Box1107, Kealakekua, HI 96750
www.bananabanana.com

NEVADA

Nevada Sun Rancho   702 723-5463   www.sunrancho.com
PO Box 19205, Jean, NV 89019

TEXAS

Acorn Acres Resort   409 657-3061
10220 F.M. 442, Boling, TX 77420

Bluebonnet   940 627-2313   www.bluebonnetnudistpark.com
699 CR 1180, Alvord, TX 76225

Emerald Lake Nudist Resort   281 354-0497
www.emeraldlakeresort.com
PO Box 1865, Porter, TX 77365

Live Oak Nudist Resort   409 878-2216
R#1 Box 916, Washington, TX 77880

Riverside Ranch   830 393-2387   www.riversideranch.com
1238 County Road 125, Elmendorf, TX 78112

Lone Star Resort   936 825-0225   www.lonestarresort.com
18198 FM 362, Navasota, TX 77868

Sahnoans at Star Ranch   512 273-2257
PO Box 845, McDade, TX 78650

Sandpipers Holiday Park   956 383-7589
www.sandpipersresort.com
9504 N. Seminary Rd., Edinburg, TX 78541

Sunny Pines   903 873-3311
PO Box 133 Wills Point, TX 75169

Vista Grande Ranch   817 598-1312
1149 FM 1885 Road, Weatherford, TX 76088

Wildwood Naturist's Resort   940 627-2280
241 Private Road 1179, Decatur, TX 76234
www.wildwoodnaturist.com

BAJA (Mexico)

Eden Ranch (near Loreto, Baja Sur)
01152 (113) 30700

INDEX

This index is designed to help you locate a listing when you start with the location name. The description of the location will be found on the page number given for that name.

Within the index the abbreviations listed below are used to identify the specific state or geographical area of the location. The number shown after each state listed below is the page number where the KEY MAP of that state will be found.

AZ = Arizona / 108
BJ = Baja (Mexico) / 210
CCA = Central California / 144
CO = Colorado / 50
HI = Hawaii / 227
NV = Nevada / 14
NM = New Mexico / 82
NCA = Northern California / 122
SCA = Southern California / 190
TX = Texas / 78
UT = Utah / 40

NUBP = Not Usable By the Public
Some springs that have recently become NUBP are still included in the directory for your information.

A

AGUA CALIENTE COUNTY PARK   SCA   206
AGUA CALIENTE HOT SPRINGS   BJ   218
AGUA CALIENTE (SANTIAGO) HOT SPRINGS   BJ   226
AGUA VERDE HOT SPRINGS   BJ   225
AHALANUI WARM SPRING AND PARK   HI   228
ALKALI (SILVER PEAK) HOT SPRINGS   NV   34
ALBANY SAUNA AND HOT TUBS   CCA   188
AMERICAN FAMILY HOT TUB   CCA   189
ANTERO HOT SPRINGS CABINS   CO   60
ARIZONA (RINGBOLT) HOT SPRINGS   AZ   110
ARTESIAN BATH HOUSE   NM   92
ASH SPRINGS   NV   32
AVILA HOT SPRINGS   CCA   178

B

BAILEY'S HOT SPRINGS   NV   34
BAKER HOT SPRINGS   UT   46
BALLENTINES   Palm Springs   233
BARTINE HOT SPRINGS   NV   28
BASHFORD'S HOT MINERAL SPA   SCA   203
BENTON HOT SPRINGS   see
   OLD HOUSE AT BENTON HOT SPRINGS   CCA   158
BERKELEY SAUNA, THE   CCA   189
BEST WESTERN TWIN PEAKS MOTEL   CO   73

BEVERLY HOT SPRINGS   SCA 208
BIG BEND HOT SPRINGS   NCA 127
BIG CALIENTE HOT SPRINGS   CCA 177
"BIG HOT" WARM SPRINGS   CCA (NUBP)
BLACK ROCK HOT SPRINGS   NM 84
BLANEY HOT SPRINGS   CCA 164
BODHI MANDA ZEN CENTER   NM 90
BOG HOT SPRINGS   NV 16
BOQUILLAS HOT SPRING   TX   see
  LANGFORD HOT SPRINGS 79
BOWERS MANSION   NV 38
BOX CANYON LODGE AND HOT SPRINGS   CO 73
BOY SCOUT HOT SPRINGS   AZ 111
BROCK CANYON   NM 104
BUBBLES HOT SPRINGS   see   SAN
  FRANCISCO HOT SPRINGS—UPPER   NM 105
BUCKEYE HOT SPRING   CCA 149
BUENA VENTURA HOT SPRINGS   BJ 224
BUENA VISTA HOT WELLS   AZ (NUBP)

C

CALIFORNIA HOT SPRINGS   CCA 169
CALISTOGA OASIS SPA   NCA 134
CALISTOGA SPA HOT SPRINGS   NCA 134
CALISTOGA VILLAGE INN AND SPA   NCA 134
CANTU HOT SPRINGS   BJ 217
CARLIN COUNTRY COTTAGES   NCA 135
CARLSBAD MINERAL WATER SPA   SCA 207
CARSON HOT SPRINGS   NV 38
CHAMPAGNE POND   HI 231
CHARLES MOTEL AND BATH HOUSE   NM 92
CHINATI HOT SPRINGS   TX 80
CHUKAR GULCH   NV 19
COMFORT INN   NCA 135
CONUNDRUM HOT SPRINGS   CO 58
CONCEPCION BEACH   BJ 223
COTTONWOOD HOT SPRINGS INN   CO 59
CRAB COOKER   CCA 155
CRESCENT VIEW HOT SPRING   NV 29
CROWLEY (WILD WILLIE'S)   CCA 156
CRYSTAL HOT SPRINGS   UT 41
CRYSTAL SPRINGS   NV 32

D

DAKOTA HOT SPRINGS   CO 63
DEEP CREEK HOT SPRINGS   SCA 196-197
DELIGHT'S HOT SPA   SCA 193
DELONEGHA HOT SPRINGS   CCA (NUBP)
DESERT HOT SPRINGS MOTELS, RESORTS,
  AND SPAS   SCA 198-202
  Within this section, Motels, Resorts, and Spas are
  listed in alphabetical order.
DESERT REEF HOT SPRING   CO 64
DESERT SHADOWS INN   Palm Springs 234
DIAMOND FORK HOT SPRINGS   see
  FIFTH WATER CANYON HOT SPRINGS   UT 45
DIANA'S PUNCH BOWL   NV 27
DIRTY SOCK HOT SPRING   CCA 168

DR. WILKINSON'S HOT SPRINGS   NCA 135
DRAKESBAD GUEST RANCH   NCA 129
DRY SUZIE (HOT SULPHUR) HOT SPRINGS   NV 29
DUCKWATER POND   NV 31
DUNTON HOT SPRINGS   CO 76
DYKE HOT SPRING   NV 17

E

EAGLE CREEK HOT SPRING   AZ 121
EAGLEVILLE HOT SPRING   NCA 124
EL COYOTE WARM SPRING   BJ 224
EL DORADO HOT SPRINGS   AZ 114
ESALEN INSTITUTE   CCA 183
ESSENCE OF TRANQUILITY   AZ 116
EUROSPA AND INN   NCA 135

F

FAIRMONT SONOMA MISSION INN   NC 131
FALES HOT DITCH   CCA 148
FAYWOOD HOT SPRINGS   NM 96
FINNISH COUNTRY SAUNA & TUBS   NCA 143
FIFTH WATER CANYON HOT SPRINGS   UT 45
FIREWATER LODGE   NM 93
FISH LAKE HOT WELL   NV 35
FIVE PALMS WARM WELL OASIS   SCA 205
F. JOSEPH SMITH'S MASSAGE THERAPY   CCA 188
FOUNTAIN OF YOUTH SPA   SCA 204
FRANKLIN LAKES HOT SPRINGS   CCA 181
FRISCO BOX HOT SPRINGS   NM 107
FROGS   CCA 188
FURNACE CREEK INN   SCA 191
FURNACE CREEK RANCH   SCA 191

G

GANDY WARM SPRINGS   UT 47
GAVIOTA HOT SPRINGS   see
  LAS CRUCES HOT SPRINGS   CCA 178
GEYSER WARM SPRING   CO 77
GIGGLING SPRINGS   NM 89
GILA HOT SPRINGS VACATION CENTER NM 100,
  RIVER CAMPGROUND 100
GILLARD HOT SPRINGS   AZ 118-119
GLEN AND CHICKEN HOT SPRINGS   NCA 123
GLEN IVY HOT SPRINGS   SCA 209
GLENWOOD HOT SPRINGS   CO 55
GOLD STRIKE HOT SPRINGS   AZ 111
GOLDEN HAVEN HOT SPRINGS   NCA 135
GRAND CENTRAL SAUNA & HOT TUB   CCA
  San Jose 734   San Francisco 734
GROVER HOT SPRINGS   CCA 145
GUADALUPE CANYON HOT SPRINGS   BJ 211

H

HANNAH HOT SPRINGS   AZ 120
HARBIN HOT SPRINGS   NCA 138
HAY-YO-KAY HOT SPRINGS   NM 93
HIDEAWAY COTTAGES   NCA 136
HIGHLINE SOUTH HOT WELL   SCA 205
HILLSIDE HOT SPRINGS   CCA 146
HOBO POOL   CO 56
HOMESTEAD, THE   UT 43
HOT CREEK   CCA 153
HOT CREEK SPRINGS AND MARSH AREA   NV 33
HOTEL BUENA VISTA   BJ 226
HOT SHOWERBATH   CCA 147
HOT SULPHUR SPRINGS   CO 53
HOT TROPICS   CCA 189
HOT TUB   CCA 157
HOT TUBS, THE   CCA
   Berkeley 188   San Francisco 204
HOT WELL DUNES   AZ 117
HOURGLASS, THE   CCA 176
HOUSE LOG CANYON   NM 102
HUNT AND KOSH HOT SPRINGS   NCA 128
HYDER HOT SPRINGS   NV 25

I

IMPERIAL SEA VIEW HOT SPRINGS   SCA 204
INDIAN SPRINGS   NCA 136
INDIAN (STINKY) SPRINGS   UT 41
INDIAN SPRINGS NATURAL...   NM 93
INDIAN SPRINGS RESORT   CO 53
IVA BELL   CCA 159

J

JACUMBA HOT SPRINGS SPA...   SCA 206
JEMEZ SPRINGS BATH HOUSE   NM 90
JERSEY VALLEY HOT SPRINGS   NV 24
JORDAN HOT SPRING   CCA 169
JORDAN see
   HOUSE LOG CANYON HOT SPRINGS   NM 102
JOYFUL JOURNEY   CO 66

K

KACHINA MINERAL SPRING SPA   AZ 116
KAISER WARM SPRINGS   AZ 112
KEOUGH HOT DITCH   CCA 165
KEOUGH HOT SPRINGS   CCA 165
KERN HOT SPRING   CCA 168
KERNVILLE WARM SPRINGS   CCA 170
KIVA RETREAT   CCA 185
KOSH CREEK HOT SPRINGS   see
   HUNT HOT SPRINGS   NCA 128

L

LANGFORD HOT SPRINGS   TX 79
LA PALOMA HOT SPRINGS   NM 94
LARK SPA   SCA 204
LAVENDER HILL SPA   NCA 136
LAS CRUCES (GAVIOTA) HOT SPRINGS   CCA 178
LAS ROSAS HOTEL & SPA   BJ 216
LEMON HOT TSPRINGS   CO 75
LEONARD'S HOT SPRING   NCA 123
LEWIS CREEK WARM SPRINGS   CCA 160
LIL' HOT CREEEK   CCA 154
LINCOLN AVENUE SPA   NCA 136
LITTLE CALIENTE HOT SPRINGS   CCA 176
LITTLE EDEN AND ROSE GARDEN   CCA 162
LIVING WATERS SPA   SCA 201

M

MACFARLANE HOT SPRINGS   NV 21
MANBY HOT SPRINGS   see
   STAGECOACH HOT SRPINGS   NM 85
MCCAULEY HOT SPRING   NM 87
MEADOW HOT SPRINGS   UT 47
MEADOWLARK COUTNRY HOUSE   NCA 133
MEADOW WARM SPRINGS   NM 102
MELANIE HOT SPRINGS   NM 97
MERCY HOT SPRINGS   CCA 185
MIDDLE FORK (LIGHTFEATHER) HOT SPRING   NM 90
MIRACLE HOT SPRINGS   CCA (NUBP)
MISSION SAN BORJA   BJ 221
MOLLIE'S HOT SPRINGS   CCA 151
MONO HOT SPRINGS   CCA 161
MONTEZUMA HOT SPRINGS   NM 91
MORNINGSIDE INN   Palm Springs 232
MORTON WARM SPRINGS RESORT   NCA 131
MOUNT PRINCETON HOT SPRINGS   CO 62
MOUNTAIN SPAA RESORT   UT 42
MOUNT VIEW SPA   NCA 136
MUIR TRAIL RANCH   CCA 163
MULEGE MISSION WARM SPRINGS   BJ 222
MULESHOE RANCH   AZ 121
MYSTIC HOT SPRINGS OF MONROE   UT 48

N

NANCE'S HOT SPRINGS   NCA 137
NATURIST LANDED CLUB LISTINGS   234
NEPTUNES LAGOONS   SCA 207
NEW WAGNER WARM SPRING   NV 20

O

OGDEN HOT SPRINGS   UT 42
OJO CALIENTE...RESORT   NM 83
OLD HOUSE AT BENTON HOT SPRINGS, THE   CCA 158
ORR HOT SPRINGS   NCA 142
ORVIS HOT SPRINGS   CO 74
OURAY HOT SPRINGS POOL   CO 72

P

PAGOSA SPRINGS POOL (THE SPA MOTEL)   CO 69
PAHOA STEAM CAVES   HI 230
PAH TEMPE HOT SPRINGS RESORT   UT 49
PALMPOOL WATERFALL HOT SPRINGS   AZ 110
PALM SPRINGS SPA HOTEL...   SCA 203
PALOMAR CANYON HOT SPRINGS   BJ 212
PANACA WARM SPRINGS   NV 31
PARADISE SPAS   CCA 189
PARADISE VALLEY HOT SPRINGS   NV 21
PARAISO HOT SPRINGS   CCA (NUBP)
PASO ROBLES INN   CCA 180
PELICAN SPA   NM 94
PENNY HOT SPRINGS   CO 58
PIEDMONT SPRINGS   CCA 189
PIEDRA RIVER HOT SPRING   CO 71
PINTO HOT SPRINGS...NV 17
POHOIKI HOT SPRINGS   HI 229
POKEY HOT SPRING   UT 44
POO-HAH-BAH   SCA 194
POTTER'S AZTEC BATHS   AZ
POTT'S RANCH HOT SPRINGS   NV 27
PUDDINGSTONE HOT TUBS   SCA 208
PUERTOCITOS HOT SPRINGS   BJ 213
PULKY'S POOL   CCA 156
PUNTA BANDA HOT SPRING   BJ 216
PYRAMID HOT SPRING   CCA 172

R

RADIUM HOT SPRINGS   CO 54
RAINBOW (WOLF CREEK PASS) HOT SPRINGS   CO 68
RAINBOW HOT SPRINGS   see
  SMITH CREEK HOT SPRINGS   NV 25
RANCHO GILBERTO   BJ 217
RANCHO SAN CARLOS   BJ 219
RED'S MEADOW HOT SPRINGS   CCA 159
REESE RIVER HOT SPRINGS   NV 23
REMINGTON HOT SPRINGS   CCA 171
RICO HOT SPRINGS   CO 77
RINGBOLT HOT SPRINGS see
  ARIZONA HOT SPRINGS   AZ 110
RIVERBEND HOT SPRINGS   NM 95
RIVER OAKS HOT SPRINGS AND SPA   CCA 182
RIVER RUN HOT SPRINGS   CCA 147
RIVERSIDE HOT SPRINGS   CCA 146
ROGERS WARM SPRING   NV 33
ROMAN SPA   NCA 137
ROPER LAKE STATE PARK   AZ 117
RUBY VALLEY HOT SPRINGS   NV 30
RUSSIAN VALLEY HOT SPRINGS   BJ 215

S

SALIDA HOT SPRINGS   CO 63
SALINE VALLEY HOT SPRINGS   CCA 166-167
SAN ANTONIO HOT SPRINGS   NM 86
SAN CARLOS WARM SPRINGS   AZ 115
SAND DUNES SWIMMING POOL   CO 67

SAN FRANCISCO (BUBBLES) HOT
  SPRINGS—UPPER   NM 105
SANTISPAC BEACH   BJ 223
SARATOGA SPRINGS RETREAT   NCA 141
SESPE HOT SPRINGS   CCA 172-173
SHEEP BRIDGE HOT SPRING   AZ 114
SHEPHERD HOT SPRING   CCA 155
SHIBUI GARDENS   CCA 188
SHOSHONE INN   SCA 192
SHOSHONE RV PARK...   SCA 193
SIERRA GRANDE LODGE AND HOT SPRINGS   NM 95
SIERRA HOT SPRINGS   NCA 130
SILVER ROSE INN ...   NCA 137
SMITH CREEK (RAINBOW) HOT SPRINGS   NV 25
SOLDIER MEADOWS (GROUP)   NV 18-19
SOUTH CANYON HOT SPRINGS   CO 57
SPENCE HOT SPRING   NM 88
SPENCER HOT SPRINGS   NV 26
SPLASHLAND HOT SPRINGS   CO 67
SPRINGS RESORT, THE   CO 70
STAGECOACH (MANBY) HOT SPRINGS   NM 85
STEAMBOAT SPRINGS   CO 52
STEAMBOAT VILLA HOT SPRINGS & SPA   NV 39
STEWART MINERAL SPRINGS   NCA 127
STINKY SPRINGS see INDIAN SPRINGS   UT 41
STRAWBERRY PARK HOT SPRINGS   CO 51
SUNDIAL HOT SPRINGS   NM 106
SUNSHINE SPA   CCA 189
SUPRISE VALLEY HOT SPRINGS   NCA 124
SWEETWATER SPA AND INN   NCA 143
SYCAMORE HOT SPRINGS   CCA 179
SYKES HOT SPRING   CCA 184

T

TASSAJARA ZEN MOUNTAIN CENTER   CCA 183
TEA HOUSE SPA   CCA 186
TECOPA DESERT POND   SCA (NUBP)
TECOPA HOT SPRINGS   SCA 195
TECOPA HOT SPRINGS RESORT   SCA 194
TECOPA MUD BATHS   SCA 195
TECOPA PALMS RV PARK   SCA 194
TEN THOUSAND WAVES   NM 91
TERMINAL GEYSER HOT SPRINGS   NCA (NUBP)
TERRA COTTA INN, THE   Palm Springs 233
THATCHER HOT WELL   AZ (NUBP)
"THREE DISH" WARM SPRINGS   CCA 166
TRAVERTINE HOT SPRINGS   CCA 150
TREGO HOT DITCH   NV 20
TRIMBLE HOT SPRINGS   CO 71
TRUTH OR CONSEQUENCES AREA   NM 92-95
TUBS, THE   SCA 207
TURKEY CREEK HOT SPRINGS   NM 103
TURTLEBACK MESA B&B   SCA 202
TWELVE MILE HOT SPRINGS   NV 30
TWO BUNCH PALMS RESORT AND SPA   SCA 202

U

URUAPAN HOT SPRINGS   BJ 220

V

VALLE CHICO HOT SPRINGS   BJ 212
VALLE DE TRINIDAD   BJ 220
VALLEY VIEW HOT SPRINGS   CO 65
VERDE HOT SPRINGS   AZ 113
VEYO RESORT   UT 49
VICHY SPRINGS   NCA 140
VILLA ESCONDIDA   Palm Springs 232
VIRGIN VALLEY WARM SPRING   NV 16

W

WALKER WARM SPRINGS   NV 36
WALLEY'S HOT SPRINGS RESORT   NV 37
WALTI HOT SPRINGS   NV 28
WARM SPRINGS   SCA 192
WARNER SPRINGS RANCH   SCA 207
WASATCH SPA   UT 42
WATERCOURSE WAY   CCA 187

WATSON WASH HOT WELL   AZ (NUBP)
WAUNITA HOT SPRINGS RANCH   CO 62
WELL WITHIN   CCA 186
WEST VALLEY RESERVOIR   NC 126
WHITE SULPHUR SPRINGS RESORT   NCA 132
WHITMORE HOT SPRINGS   CCA 157
WIESBADEN HOT SPRINGS SPA AND
   LODGINGS   CO 72
WILBUR HOT SPRINGS   NCA 139
WILDERNESS LODGE AND HOT SPRINGS   NM 99
WILD MINT HOT SPRING   NCA 125
WILDWOOD RETREAT   NM 98
WILLETT's HOT SPRINGS   CCA 174-175
WILSON HEALTH SPRINGS   UT 46
WOLF CREEK PASS see
   RAINBOW HOT SPRINGS   CO 68
WOODY'S FEATHER RIVER HOT SPRINGS   NCA 129

Y

YAMPAH SPA   CO 57

CALIFORNIA	UTAH	ALASKA	CANADA
ARIZONA	COLORADO	IDAHO	WYOMING
NEW MEXICO	NEVADA	OREGON	MONTANA
TEXAS	HAWAII	WASHINGTON	

BAJA (MEXICO)

$21.95 ISBN 1-890880-07-8

CENTRAL, EASTERN, SOUTHERN STATES
PUERTO RICO
$19.95 ISBN 1-890880-04-3
(21.95 after Jan. 2008)

Order form can be found on our web page
www.hotpools.com
To pay by credit card go to the web site and
click on the link to Pay Pal

Name			
Street			
City		State	Zip
		Order Quan.	Amount
Hot Springs and Hot Pools of the Northwest $19.95 (21.95 after Jan. 2008)			
Hot Springs and Hot Pools of the Southwest $21.95			
Postage: $5.00 first book, $2 each additional book			
Canadians: Please send in US dollars			
BOOK Make check to: AQUA THERMAL ACCESS 831 426-2956			
MAIL ORDER Mail to: 55 Azalea Lane, Santa Cruz, CA 95060		TOTAL	